Collins

Cambridge IGCSE®

Economics

TEACHER'S GUIDE

Also for Cambridge O Level

Neil Buchanan,
Clive Riches, Ian Rowbory

Collins

William Collins' dream of knowledge for all began with the publication of his first book in 1819.

A self-educated mill worker, he not only enriched millions of lives, but also founded a flourishing publishing house. Today, staying true to this spirit, Collins books are packed with inspiration, innovation and practical expertise. They place you at the centre of a world of possibility and give you exactly what you need to explore it.

Collins. Freedom to teach.

Published by Collins
An imprint of HarperCollins*Publishers*
The News Building
1 London Bridge Street
London
SE1 9GF

10 9 8 7 6 5 4 3 2 1

ISBN 978-0-00-825410-0

British Library Cataloguing in Publication Data

A catalogue record for this publication is available from the British Library.

Author: Neil Buchanan, Clive Riches, Ian Rowbory
Additional contributor: James Beere
Development editor: Hetty Marx
Commissioning editor: Lucy Cooper
In-house editors: Alexander Rutherford, Letitia Luff
Project manager: Amanda Harman
Copyeditor: Andrew Lowe
Proofreaders: Andrew Lowe, Life Lines Editorial Services
Cover designer: Kevin Robbins and Gordon MacGilp
Cover illustrator: Maria Herbert-Liew
Internal designer / Typesetter: Jouve India
Production controller: Tina Paul
Printed and bound by: CPI Group (UK) Ltd, Croydon, CR0 4YY

All exam-style questions and sample answers in this title were written by the authors. In examinations, the way marks are awarded may be different.

Contents

Introduction

The *Collins Cambridge IGCSE Economics Teacher's Guide* has been written to support the teaching and learning of the IGCSE® Economics syllabus 0455 and O level syllabus 2281. It is intended to be used alongside the Student's Book as a tool for enhancing the learning experience. The Teacher's Guide has been matched unit by unit to the Student's Book to allow easy cross-referencing between the books. The material within each unit also follows the order of the material within the Student's Book. Photocopiable materials supporting delivery of the course and Answers to the Knowledge check questions and Chapter review questions are collated at the end of the book for easy reference and printing.

The suggestions for teaching and the additional activities are provided to help you prepare your lessons. However it is assumed that you will use and adapt the material in whatever way would work best for your class.

Getting the most from this book

This Teacher's Guide is divided into six chapters and each chapter is divided into units in the same way as the Student's Book. Each of the units is organised in the same way and has the following features:

The **Learning objectives** and **key terms** from the Student's Book are included at the start of each unit in the Teacher's Guide. The definitions of the key terms are shown in margin boxes in the Student's Book in the unit where the term is first introduced and can also be found in the glossary at the back of the Student's Book.

Language support

It is important that students are able to communicate their ideas clearly and accurately both verbally and in writing. This can be particularly challenging for students who do not have English as their native language.

Strategies to support students with verbal communication:

- Allow students sufficient thinking time when asking them to respond to questions in class. As non-native English speaking students are having to think about what to say as well as how to say it, it can take them more than a few seconds to formulate a response to a question.
- Give students an opportunity to discuss their ideas in the safety of pairs or small groups before reporting back or presenting to the whole class.
- Set up activities which encourage students to discuss key concepts in small groups within a meaningful context – many of the supplementary activities in the Teacher's Guide are designed with this purpose in mind.

Strategies to support students with written communication:

- Use exemplar written responses and analyse them with students in terms of language used. For example, ask students to highlight the words used to link cause and effect when developing chains of analysis, such as '*this leads to*', '*as a result*' and '*consequently*'.
- Provide students with writing templates which scaffold them in terms of the structure and the organisation of their written work.
- Model written responses for students by writing them on the whiteboard or large sheets of poster paper with input from students.

Starting point: The questions in this section encourage students to reflect on prior knowledge and perhaps make links to their own experience or relate to a familiar context. They can be used to refresh or reinforce material from previous units. Allow students a few minutes to discuss the content of the questions in pairs. Brief notes could be made. After this, nominate students from different groups to share their answers with the whole class. Take this opportunity to identify and correct any misconceptions.

Exploring: The questions in this section are open questions designed to stimulate interest in and thought about the content of the unit ahead, building on what they already know. Encourage students to discuss the content of the questions in pairs. Again, brief notes could be made. Then bring students together to discuss the questions as a class. Bear in mind that these questions are designed to prepare students for the concepts they will be encountering in the unit so they are not expected to know all of the answers. Encourage students to make predictions about what they will be learning but resist the urge to provide them with all of the relevant information at this point. Allow them to discover this for themselves as they work through the developing section of the unit. You can use their answers to gauge the areas of the unit that students may find more difficult or that may need additional explanation. Students could use the Exploring questions as revision before their final examinations once they have completed all of the taught content.

The two sets of questions can be used together as the starter activity for the first lesson on the unit. The Teacher's Guide provides guidance on how to develop the discussion if necessary and **suggested answers**.

Discussions

Discussions allow students to engage both with the content and with their peers. It is an important aspect of any taught session. Students need to feel comfortable to interact with the class and participate in the discussion. It is important that you manage the discussion to ensure all students have the opportunity to speak and engage in the session. By ensuring the views of every student are heard, you are also able to gauge student progress, understanding and achievement.

Developing: This section starts with teaching notes for each unit. These might highlight common misconceptions and errors or provide suggestions for how to teach specific points.

The Student's Book includes **questions** within the text of each unit. They are intended to allow students to check their understanding of key concepts or to encourage them to come up with an answer before it is explained in the text. The Teacher's Guide provides guidance on using these questions and **suggested answers**.

Eliciting responses from students

Eliciting responses from students is a common feature of most classrooms. Try out some of the following techniques to encourage quality responses from all students in a group or class:

- When eliciting words, rather than providing the word and asking students to supply the definition, try providing the definition and asking students to supply the word.
- When asking questions of the class during lessons, rather than students putting their hands up to answer, try using some kind of random name generator to nominate students. For example, write the names of all the students on lollypop sticks and draw one at random from a cup or a bag.
- Closed questions can be useful when checking students' understanding of key concepts. However, try to also use open questions to stretch students in their thinking and to encourage them to speak at length. Follow up with prompting questions, if necessary, to help them develop their ideas more fully or guide them in their reasoning.

Some units include **Application tasks** encouraging students to apply what they have learned and **worked examples** demonstrating how a problem or question can be addressed and what constitutes a good response. **Suggested answers** or approaches for questions are included in the Teacher's Guide.

Case studies are provided in the Student's Book, which focus on different areas of the world and help to provide a real life context. They include questions to help students develop their understanding of the impact of economic concepts around the world. Tips for using the case studies and **suggested answers** are included in the Teacher's Guide.

A range of **diagrams** are included in the Student's Book to develop their core skills in analysis and manipulating data.

Using the diagrams in the Student's Book

In Economics, it is important that students are able to use diagrams effectively to support their written responses and to be able to produce them quickly and accurately.

When using diagrams to support their written explanations, students should be encouraged to produce diagrams which are:

- at least one-third of an A4 page in size
- accurately drawn using a ruler
- fully labelled.

Two activities which can be used to give students practice at drawing diagrams:

- You call out a diagram and the students draw it on mini whiteboards. For example, 'the effect on a market of an increase in costs of production'. Each student then draws their diagram on their mini whiteboard before holding it up for you to check.
- A good starter or revision activity is for students to take a card out of a bag with the name of a diagram on it. For example, 'a production possibility curve showing unemployment of resources in an economy'. Students must then sit down and accurately produce the diagram on a scrap piece of paper or mini whiteboard before checking it against their notes or with you.

Extension questions have been included to challenge students. **Extension topics** are designed to enhance students' understanding. It is not necessary for students to learn the content of these boxes as they do not form part of the syllabus.

The Teacher's Guide also includes **Support and Extension questions and activities**. These are additional questions or activities (along with suggested answers) to **support** students who need more help or to **extend** and challenge those students who find the activities easy or finish quickly.

Teaching mixed ability classes

It is important to differentiate lessons so that individual students of all abilities are sufficiently challenged to achieve to their full potential. Some strategies which can be used to differentiate learning include the following.

- Group students so that higher ability students are able to model and scaffold concepts and processes for those of lower ability. Alternatively, grouping students of similar ability together may help to stretch and challenge them when completing a small group task or activity.
- Grade tasks so that they are appropriate to the abilities of the individual students. For example, the knowledge check questions at the end of each chapter get progressively harder. Higher ability students could be asked to complete the later questions while those of lower ability could focus on completing the earlier questions.
- During small group work, move between the groups monitoring student progress. Help to scaffold the learning of lower ability students and stretch higher ability students through the use of questioning and dialogue with students.

The Teacher's Guide also includes suggestions for **additional activities** to use during lessons to give you choice in how to develop students' knowledge and skills. Where appropriate, **photocopiable resource sheets** are provided at the end of the book. These can be photocopied and distributed among students.

Each unit in the Student's Book ends with an **Applying** section which provides an opportunity for students to bring together their learning through discussion with their peers. It starts with **Project work**. Projects are very valuable in increasing motivation and collaboration between students. They also integrate various skills and allow for more independent learning. Projects are suitable for students of every level, as those with different abilities and interests can do different tasks as part of the whole project. If internet access is not available, students should use reference books or you could provide handouts with the relevant information. The Teacher's Guide includes **teaching notes and expected outcomes** for project work.

Quality feedback

When providing feedback to students on their performances, particularly on their written responses, try to improve the effectiveness of the feedback you provide by:

- telling students *how* to improve their written responses as well as *what* to improve. For example, if the feedback is to develop chains of analysis in their writing, provide the student with an example showing them how this can be achieved
- encouraging students to respond to your written feedback in some way, rather than simply looking at their mark. This could be done by asking students to summarise the comments you have provided by writing one thing they did well and one thing they need to improve for next time
- encouraging students to identify the areas they need to improve for themselves when providing them with verbal feedback on their written work. This can be achieved through questioning or by giving individual students feedback and then asking them to summarise for you their main areas for improvement.

The **Knowledge check** questions could be completed as an unseen test at the end of the unit. They could be self-marked or marked by you. Weaker students might be allowed the use of the textbook but should be encouraged to paraphrase the textbook where appropriate. Alternatively, use the Knowledge check questions at relevant points during the unit.

Check your progress encourages students to reflect on each of the learning objectives. Students should self-assess their knowledge of the unit and consider which of the following statements best reflects their level of knowledge: *'I struggle with this and need more practice'*; *'I can do this reasonably well'* or *'I can do this with confidence'*.

For some of the units, students could also verbally test each other on their knowledge of the unit in pairs using the learning objectives as question prompts.

The **Chapter reviews** provide exam-style questions drawing on material from across the chapter. These can be used when a chapter has been completed, either in class, for assessment or for homework, or could be reserved for revision.

The Teacher's Guide also includes two additional sections. There is a bank of photocopiable **Activity sheets** for use with the additional activities suggested in this book. In addition, **Answers** to the Knowledge check questions and Chapter reviews are found at the end of the Teacher's Guide along with guidance about how to allocate marks to the students' answers. The questions, example answers, marks awarded and/or comments that appear in this book were written by the authors. In examinations, the way marks would be awarded to answers like these may be different. In some cases the marks sum to more than the total available for the question. This is because there are sometimes different possible routes to achieving maximum marks. The additional marked points have been included to illustrate different points that might be made. Of course, no student could ever be awarded more than the maximum mark available. All 8 mark 'discuss' questions would be given a maximum mark of 5 if the answer were to be one-sided, for example considering only the benefits of a course of action. Some answers include the / notation, which indicates that there are two (or more) ways of answering the question, but a maximum of 1 mark may be awarded.

We hope that you enjoy teaching the course and find these resources useful.

1.1 The nature of the economic problem

Learning objectives

By the end of this unit, students should be able to:

- define what is meant by finite resources
- explain what is meant by unlimited wants
- give examples of the economic problem in different contexts
- explain the difference between an economic good and a free good.

Key terms

The economic problem; needs; wants; basic needs; unlimited wants; scarcity; finite resources; renewable resources; economic goods; free goods

STARTING POINT

The starting point questions place the context of the economic problem at an individual level. Ensure that students know the difference between goods and services before they start these tasks. One approach could be to get the pairs to write their lists on A3 sheets of paper and attach these to the wall so that both you and the students can see the goods and services needed for survival and the goods and services that people would like. It could be useful to run a plenary session to go through the responses to the third question. These responses are likely to centre on limited budgets and having so many things they would like to buy and consume. You can then extend this to business and government. It might be useful to introduce the notion of having to choose and how individuals might come to their buying decisions.

EXPLORING

Working in pairs, give students a few minutes to come up with a list of materials needed to make a car. Ensure that the students know what is meant by materials. Nominate pairs to share their lists with the class. Note these down on a whiteboard. The lists are likely to include steel, stainless steel, aluminium, glass, rubber, plastics (polyester, polyurethane, polycarbonate, poly-propylene) leather and cotton. You could ask what the different materials might be used for:

- aluminium for radiators
- leather for interiors
- steel for the car body
- stainless steel for exhausts.

It is useful to have the list on the whiteboard as this will help the pairs with the rest of the questions.

Working in the same pairs, give students a few minutes to come up with their responses for questions two, three and four. Nominate pairs to share their responses.

- Question 2: the pairs could say that items such as steel made from iron ore, coal and limestone are likely to run out.
- Question 3: they are likely to say that natural rubber will not.
- Question 4: the responses will focus on discussing that the more we consume as a society, the more we hear about how vital ores and minerals are dwindling, so it seems logical to assume that a few may be about to disappear. They are non-renewable resources. This includes things like coal, oil, copper, aluminium and iron. Students could mention that a renewable resource can be used repeatedly and replaced naturally, such as solar energy and timber.

- Working in their pairs, the students will consider question 5 (you might consider a whole class discussion or extending the task to a research task on recycling of cars; a visit from a manager of a car breakers yard could also be organised). Possible responses include recycling and seeking alternatives. Some might suggest improving public transport so that people do not need cars. In fact, the typical car consists of about 65% steel and iron and car bodies currently use 25% recycled steel. Recycling steel conserves iron ore, coal and limestone. Each year nearly 100% of cars leaving the road are recycled for their iron and steel content. Many car materials can be recycled, such as engine oil which can be cleaned and reused, oil filters, auto glass, remanufactured engines, scrap metal and tyres. Remanufactured items such as water pumps, starters and alternators. The growing popularity of electric cars is one way of moving away from fossil fuels and some European governments intend to ban cars powered by fossil fuels in the future.

DEVELOPING

Teaching tips

- The economic problem is a concept that underpins much of economic theory and practice. It is not a difficult concept to grasp, however at this early stage it is useful to spend time on the application of the economic problem to individuals, households, the world of business and government.
- It is useful to explore the ideas around unlimited wants and scarce resources and that difficult choices have to be made. This can be easily shown from the basis of individuals.
- From these early concepts, it is important to encourage a questioning mind. Is it inevitable that resources will run out? Should essential goods be rationed? Are there any free goods?
- Some economists argue that finite resources will never 'run out' because their eventual relative scarcity will drive up their price – motivating the search for cheaper alternatives.

Suggested answer to in-text question 1:

Consumers have to make choice decisions every day. They might have to decide on how to go to work. Should they go by car, cycle, walk or use public transport? These decisions will be based on their resources available as well as time factors. Other decisions could involve housing and whether to buy or rent their home. A choice that workers might have to make is whether to work full time or part time. Is it worthwhile delaying work by studying for a university degree? Producers must choose how best to use their workers and machinery. Should they use technology and less labour? Can they invest in machinery that would make them more efficient? Government has to decide what their priorities are. If they decide to build a hospital, what are the consequences of that decision.

Suggested answer to in-text question 2:

A free good is a good with zero opportunity cost. This means it can be produced by society in as much quantity as needed with little or zero effort. Rain water is a free good, in the sense that if you took a few buckets of rain water, there would be no opportunity cost to other people in society. However, there are costs of getting the water supply to homes and businesses. Some countries, such as Ireland, provided water free to their citizens but this had a cost to society. Water has to be collected and treated and a distribution network established. By privately paying for water, households help the environment and add to government revenue. When water costs more, we use less. A perfect example of the law of demand, Ireland used two or three times more water than their EU neighbours when Irish water was free. In addition, a revenue stream for water allows money for use elsewhere.

Additional activity

My economic problem

Use Activity sheet 1.1.

- This activity is suitable for students of all abilities. Students should keep a diary of their spending and income for two weeks. As this information can be sensitive, inform the students that you are the only person who will see the information. Hand out and go through the diary sheet (Activity sheet 1.1). Encourage the other students in the class to list and make notes on each of the aims discussed.
- There are two questions linked to this activity. The first is a scenario where the students' income falls by 20%. Students have to indicate how their spending decisions would change and give an explanation as to how they have made their decisions. The second scenario is where the students' income rises by 20%. Students have to indicate how they might choose to use their increased income.
- It might be useful to hold a plenary session afterwards asking students to share the reasons for their spending decisions for the two scenarios.

Case study

Famine declared In South Sudan

It would be helpful to students to provide some background to the situation in South Sudan. The civil war has damaged the infrastructure of the country. Over 300,000 have died, 3.5 million people have been displaced and it is estimated that 6 million people face starvation.

Suggested answers:

1. Students should be able to identify the reasons that have been provided in the case study. South Sudan has suffered from years of civil war which has a serious detrimental effect on the economy. The low rainfall and drought conditions have disrupted farming. Many farmers have left their land because of the Civil War and the farmers who remained could not afford to irrigate their land, buy fertilisers and seeds, resulting in food shortages.
2. For many people living in South Sudan there are limited choices. If they have money do they spend it on food or do they buy seed to plant as crops? However, some students might point out that many in South Sudan have few choices, living in poverty and dependent on aid.
3. South Sudan has the third highest military spending as a percentage of GDP in the world, so a choice could mean that the government spends less money on the military and more on infrastructure such as investing more in the oil industry.

APPLYING

Project work

It is important with this project to provide clear instructions and parameters. Discuss in advance with the students where they can find the information about finite resources. If using the internet is a problem, you might have to provide hard copies of relevant information including relevant news and magazine articles. This would help less able students in particular. Explain to the students that it is more than saying yes or no to the questions about renewable resources usage. There needs to be evidence that backs up their assertions. The OECD provides useful statistics on renewable energy for most countries in the world.

Expected outcomes

- Students use data to identify the finite resources that are being used up. They could reflect on historical data to work out the rate of depletion.
- Students will identify renewable resources. Renewable resources can be replaced as they are used to produce goods and services. Examples are: oxygen, fresh water, solar energy, timber and biomass.
- Students could refer to a range of examples of renewable energy and produce evidence that it is being used. Renewables include the use of hydro, geothermal, solar, wind, tide and wave sources.

- The extension questions linked to this project allow the students to use examples from other countries. The first extension question asks for examples of governments trying to stop resources being used up more quickly than they are being replaced. Students could refer to recycling programmes as well as use of taxation to reduce consumption. Others might point out policies to switch away from fossil fuels.
- The second extension question asks if there is anything being done by governments to encourage the use of renewable energy. You could suggest that in their research the students research Germany and its renewable energy policy. Germany is often called the world's first renewable energy economy.

Knowledge check questions

Ask students to complete the knowledge check questions at the end of Unit 1.1 in the Student's Book.

Checking progress

Ask students to complete the Check your progress section in the Student's Book.

1.2 The factors of production

Learning objectives

By the end of this unit, students should be able to:

- define the four factors of production
- give examples of each of the factors of production
- identify the rewards that go to the factors of production
- explain what affects the mobility of factors and whether the factors can be moved to other industries
- explain what causes changes in the quantity and quality of the factors.

Key terms

Factors of production; land; labour; capital; enterprise; mobility of factors of production

STARTING POINT

The starting point question places the context of factors at an individual level. The pairs should be asked to answer this question by producing a list. Advise that this list should be as comprehensive as possible and should include everything that is needed to build a wooden playhouse. After allowing the pairs sufficient time for discussion, invite selected pairs to go through their resources. Students are likely to come up with a list of materials such as wood, screws and equipment they need to use to build the playhouse. Some students could mention the design process in establishing the design of the playhouse as well as the creative input in terms of colours, getting advice from others about safety requirements, negotiating with family as to the best position of the playhouse, organising others to help build the playhouse. All of these help to draw out the concept of factors of production beyond a list of resources. It would be useful to discuss the role of the organiser (enterprise).

EXPLORING

Working in pairs, give students a few minutes to come up with the resources needed to establish an ice cream business. Ensure that the students know that you are looking for more than the ingredients of ice cream and that the starting point question indicates the approach that they should take. Nominate pairs to share their lists with the class. Note these down on a whiteboard. Students might point out that ice cream is a popular product and one of the first decisions is deciding on the distribution method to the market. Will it be via a mobile van, or an ice cream parlour shop or distributing ice cream to retailers? These all have implications for resources. Students might refer to the equipment needed to make ice cream. The ice cream business needs all the proper equipment and supplies. Depending on the location or type of store, this may range from one or two sinks, coolers, ice cream cabinet, and dry storage to several soft-serve machines and ice-cream cabinets, computer and cooling systems and backup generators. In addition, the business will need day-to-day supplies if they are selling direct to the consumer such as cones, plastic spoons, bowls etc. They need to consider the labour required and the skills from those involved in making the ice cream as well as the organisational skills. People (labour) who would also be involved could include an accountant and other administrative staff. The pairs should use the headings of the factors of production to structure their response.

After the plenary session on the ice cream business, set the scene for establishing a textiles factory to manufacture clothes. The principles and processes that they used in the ice cream business can be used for this larger-scale textile factory. This time, get the pairs to write their responses on A3 paper under the factors of production heading and use these during the plenary session.

The focus of the plenary session could focus on comparing the resources for the ice cream business and the textiles factory. Draw a table with two columns on the whiteboard. Column headings are 'Similarities' and 'Differences'. Through question and answer, fill in the two columns as the students compare the resources and the reasons for the differences between the resources needed for each project.

DEVELOPING

Teaching tips

- It is important to emphasise that labour (human resources, human capital) refers to the productive abilities of people. It is not only the work that they do but the skills, knowledge and talents of people. Ensure that students understand that labour can be improved through education or training.
- Make sure that they understand that land includes all natural physical resources such as fertile farm land and oil fields as well as harnessing wind power, solar power and other forms of renewable energy. This can build on Unit 1.1 where this was examined. A useful way of understanding land is, for example, if an additional barrel of petroleum is used for production, the amount of this resource available for future use is reduced. They need to understand that scarce land affects price. The price of land in a city is much higher than land in the countryside.
- Understanding the factor of enterprise is an important part of understanding the dynamics of the market economy. It is vital that students know that it is the entrepreneur who sees new opportunities to satisfy demand, who finds new, better or more efficient ways to use resources. They explore new ways to satisfy consumer demand. It is the role of enterprise that keeps markets competitive. Without an organiser there would be no goods and services.

Additional activity

Qualities for the enterprise function

- This activity examines the factor of production enterprise by looking at the qualities of an entrepreneur.
- Students can work either individually or in pairs and should produce a list of qualities of the entrepreneur and why these qualities might be important for the enterprise function. After students have written their responses, discuss together as a class. It would be useful to discuss well known entrepreneurs in your country to identify their qualities compared to the qualities that the students have listed.
- Task: Enterprise is vital in bringing together the factors of production to produce goods and services. An entrepreneur is the individual who risks their own money by setting up a business. There are so many qualities that are important to be a successful entrepreneur. Write a list of the qualities you think are needed by an entrepreneur and why these qualities are important if the business is to be successful.

Suggested answers to in-text question 1:

Labour would be out of work, capital equipment would lie idle.

Suggested answers to in-text question 2:

The answer appears immediately underneath the question.

Application task

The task asks the students to fill in a table on how easily factors of production could be changed to an alternative industry. Suggested answers are provided in page 8.

Factor of production	Is it mobile? Yes/No?	Reason for your answer of Yes or No
Power station	No	Has no alternative use. If a nuclear power station, land has long decommissioning times.
Lorry	Yes	Lorries could be used by other firms easily so could be sold easily.
Field used for growing rice	Yes and No	Yes, in the short term the land could be used for a different crop. No, for other uses it would take time to change the use of the land from agricultural to factory use or housing.
Manager of a factory	Yes	Has transferable skills.
Computer	Yes	Can be sold and used again easily.
Shop	Yes and No	Yes, in the short term to another retailer. No, for other uses, such as converting space to a restaurant as this takes time.
Electrician	Yes	Has transferable skills.

Case study

Introduction of the steel mini-mill

- You will need to provide some background as the steel industry will be unfamiliar to students.
- An integrated steel mill has all the functions for primary steel production such as iron making (conversion of ore to liquid iron), steel making (conversion of pig iron to liquid steel), casting (solidification of the liquid steel), roughing rolling/billet rolling (reducing the size of blocks), product rolling (finished shapes).
- The principal raw materials for an integrated mill are iron ore, limestone, and coal (or coke). These materials are charged in batches into a blast furnace where the iron compounds in the ore give up excess oxygen and become liquid iron. At intervals of a few hours, the accumulated liquid iron is tapped from the blast furnace and either cast into pig iron or directed to other vessels for further steel making operations.
- A mini-mill is smaller, cheaper, less complex and more efficient. Mini-mills cannot produce such products as sheet steel and heavy construction items. A steel mini-mill makes metal from scrap mixed with directly reduced iron (DRI), not from the ore.

Suggested answers

1. Students will identify that it is capital that has improved in quality.
2. The introduction of the mini-mill has led to increased output as it is far more efficient than traditional steel plants. Improved capital goods increase labour productivity and switching to mini-mills means that productive capacity has increased.
3. The price of steel will depend on demand factors as well as supply factors. If steel production increases without an increase in demand, then the price of steel would fall.
4. If the price of steel falls, this would benefit the firms buying the steel. For steel users, it is likely that steel will be a significant element of their costs and a fall in the price of steel would lead to a fall in their costs of production. Firms might decide to benefit from their costs falling by enjoying greater profits or they could pass on some of falling costs to their customers to make them more competitive.

APPLYING

Project work

It is important with this project to provide clear instructions and parameters. Discuss in advance where they can find the information about training courses provided by the local college or university. You could organise a visit from someone from the institution who could talk about the training courses they provide and who funds them. They could provide information on government sponsored training.

The students need to outline the benefits to firms in the area that might arise from these training schemes and the impact of training. Students in their research need to examine what the purposes of these courses are.

The extension questions ask the student to analyse why some training courses are more effective than others at increasing output in the economy. Talk this through with the student and agree a structure to this task. They could consider what courses might have an impact on increasing output. These could be courses that equip people with the skills that firms need. Students will then consider the courses they identified earlier and show whether there is a good match. This could be in the form of a short report.

Expected outcomes

- Students identify the range of courses provided by the local college or university.
- Students identify government sponsored training.
- Students will go through some of the courses which they have researched and what the aims and objectives of those courses are. In general, any training will improve human capital which will make workers more efficient and productive. This makes the firms they work for more competitive which could lead to increasing the production of goods and services.
- Students will discuss the impact on the country. If the skills of the workforce increase productivity, then this will make domestic firms more competitive. It could lead to an increase in economic growth and see standards of living rise.
- Extension students produce a short report mapping courses to skills that firms need.

Knowledge check questions

Ask students to complete the knowledge check questions at the end of Unit 1.2 in the Student's Book.

Checking progress

Ask students to complete the Check your progress section in the Student's Book.

1.3 Opportunity cost

Learning objectives

By the end of this unit, students should be able to:

- define opportunity cost
- give examples of opportunity cost in different contexts
- explain how opportunity cost influences decision making by consumers, workers, producers and governments when allocating resources.

Key term

Opportunity cost

STARTING POINT

The starting point questions are an opportunity to look back at Unit 1.1. Expect, at this stage of the course, developed responses which show a good understanding of the economic problem from a variety of perspectives and that, because of scarcity, choices have to be made. An alternative to working in pairs is for you to ask these questions. This would enable you to articulate questions, for example, as follows.

- Show the relevance of the economic problem to individuals.
- Show the relevance of the economic problem to business.
- Show the relevance of the economic problem to government.

EXPLORING

The exploring questions ask students to decide which goods or services they buy and what goods they do not buy. Reference could be made to the My Economic Problem activity in Unit 1.1 where a diary of spending was suggested. One suggestion is to get each member of the pair to offer their opinion of the ranked preferences. In a plenary, invite pairs to talk about their preferences. Use these questions to show how the economic problem forces individuals, business and governments to choose.

DEVELOPING

Teaching tips

- Opportunity cost is an underpinning concept in economics and needs to be understood to enable successful progression.
- Students sometimes get confused by the word 'cost'. They often find it more difficult to understand the concept in a personal context than a business or government context. This is primarily because the sorts of decisions young people make are often not crucial ones. They think that having to choose between a pizza and a cinema visit is not that important. They understand that if a new road is built, that means there is less money to spend on other things like a nursery school or that building a road might mean that there is a loss of countryside and so the pleasure of the view is forfeited. A good approach is to think of the future decisions that a young person might soon have to make such as whether to go to college or go into employment, or whether to choose a course at university that interests them or one that makes them more employable.

Suggested answer to in-text question 1:

Students will give examples of opportunity cost. Encourage students to give examples of important decisions where it was difficult to make the decision.

Suggested answer to in-text question 2:

This question uses a choice table which has a first choice decision that has been made. The question asks what might cause the decisions to be reversed. The consumer might decide that a watch is more important if they need to ensure that they are not late for important work appointments. A worker might choose to spend more time with their children because they have had an increase in pay so they no longer need to work so much overtime. A producer faces a lot of competition locally so it becomes vital to have a marketing campaign and increase advertising expenditure. A government might need to encourage people to work for a government department by offering higher wages, especially in areas where they have shortages.

Additional activity

Making choices

Use Activity sheet 1.3

Present the scenario in Activity sheet 1.3 to the class. Divide the class into three. Each team are to present a case to the rest of the class. Team 1 will argue for the resource to be spent on a Youth Centre, Team 2 will argue that resource should be spent on a Day Centre for the elderly and Team 3 will argue that the money should be spent on a nursery. Each group should prepare their arguments. Provide feedback to each group. At the end of the presentations there could be an individual vote to see which project the class as a whole thinks should get the go-ahead.

Case study

Aldi business expansion through training and development

You should:

- discuss some of the concepts in the case study such as 'value for money' and 'value for customers'
- discuss what links there might be between investing in training and development and offering value for money
- provide further background information on Aldi.

Suggested answers

1. Aldi could have invested more resources in marketing.
2. The opportunity cost of Aldi choosing to invest in its employees is what they have sacrificed in terms of marketing. Increased marketing would bring more customers into their shops. Aldi has lost the revenues that these extra customers would have provided.
3. Aldi probably recognises the importance of having a skilled and knowledgeable workforce. Training means that their staff can be more efficient or provide better customer service which makes the staff more productive and therefore Aldi stays competitive. Providing training for staff allows for employees to see career opportunities within Aldi's business and so employees are less likely to want to leave. A grater retention rate means that in the future they need to spend less on training new employees.

APPLYING

Project work

This project examines the decisions made by individuals, business and government. It is important to brief students thoroughly to ensure they know what the expected outcomes should be. Use your knowledge of the students to decide how to approach this opportunity cost project.

- Firstly, students need to ask someone at home about a decision. Talk through with the students how to explain what is meant by choices. It would be useful for each student to have a script in order to prevent any misunderstanding. It might be useful to prepare this in advance along with a worksheet to record the choices and the explanation. Stress that this does not mean that sensitive information has to be shared. If it is a problem to ask someone at home then an alternative would be to ask a neighbour or an adult you have chosen. Ensure that all child safety procedures are followed.

- The second and third part of this project is for the student to ask someone who works in business and someone who owns a business. Again you need to provide a briefing sheet to be used to ensure the business knows what is expected of them. For any students who feel nervous or do not have access to this setting, you could arrange for a small group of students to meet a business representative. You could brief the representative first.
- Discuss with the students approaches to researching the choices your government has made. Ensure that students have suitable and accessible sources. You might need to collate together articles from newspapers if this is going to be an in-class activity.
- Discuss with the students what is required for the presentation and write a presentation brief. If appropriate, students could prepare slides for their presentation. You could decide to pair up students or put them into small groups. The emphasis of the presentation should be on explaining in the variety of contexts that choice is a result of the economic problem. Provide feedback for each presentation.

Expected outcomes

- Evidence of the 'home' decision with an explanation
- Evidence of the business decision with an explanation
- Evidence of research into government choices with an explanation
- Notes and/or slides for the presentation
- Taking part in a presentation

Knowledge check questions

Ask students to complete the knowledge check questions at the end of Unit 1.3 in the Student's Book.

Checking progress

Ask students to complete the Check your progress section in the Student's Book.

1.4 Production possibility curve diagram

Learning objectives

By the end of this unit, students should be able to:

- define what is meant by a production possibility curve (PPC)
- draw a production possibility curve
- interpret a PPC diagram
- explain the significance of the location of production points on the diagram
- explain opportunity cost and movements along the PPC
- explain the causes and consequences of shifts in a PPC in terms of an economy's growth.

Key term

Production possibility curve

STARTING POINT

You will only need to allow a few minutes for these two open-ended questions. After this, invite responses from the pairs going through a variety of possibilities. The yield of each crop could be a factor in choosing which crop to grow as well as the price in the market.

EXPLORING

Use the same approach as in the starting point questions. Students are more likely to come up with reasons for the choice. It depends on the cost of manufacture as well as the demand of the models. One model might be a high price but low sales model while another might be a high sales but low price model. Students could comment that it would be more efficient to concentrate on one model. Other students could suggest that by producing both models this might bring about the most profit and also the most efficient use of resources.

DEVELOPING

Teaching tips

- Revision work might be needed regarding drawing curves and accurate labelling of diagrams. Curves and diagrams are often used in economics.
- For many students, a rectangular hyperbola will be a new experience as straight-line diagrams are more common. It is important that they understand why the PPC is the shape it is; this unit explains the reasons in detail. The bow-out shape occurs because economic resources are not perfectly adaptable to the production of different goods, so the opportunity cost of producing a good will increase as more and more resources are allocated to the production of that good. This is a difficult concept to understand quickly.
- For weaker students, there is value in drawing a straight-line PPC as it still illustrates scarcity, choice and opportunity cost.

Additional activity

Difficult choices

It is advised that this activity should be undertaken when all other work on the unit has been completed. This activity uses three quotes from historical figures. You might need to explain some of the background. The point of the activity is not the individuals who are quoted but what they indicate about the choices that society faces. Divide the class into groups of four and go through the statements and the discussion points. After allowing sufficient time for discussion, run a plenary session inviting comments from the groups. Discuss the choices that societies have to make and how these choices can be captured in a PPC.

Minister of Propaganda in Nazi Germany, Joseph Goebbels, stated: "We can do without butter… , One cannot shoot with butter, but with guns." Hermann Göring announced in a speech a few weeks later "Guns will make us powerful; butter will only make us fat."

Another use of the term was UK Prime Minister Margaret Thatcher's reference in a speech that, "The Russians put guns over butter, but we put almost everything over guns."

Discussion points

What do you think is meant by the choice between guns and butter?

How would you reflect these choices on a PPC?

Support question

This support question is for students who might have struggled with the concept of Production Possibilities. It allows you to assess how much students have understood before moving on to the next unit.

John Smith owns and runs a juice stall by himself where he makes a variety of healthy drinks. Some drinks take less time to produce, such as fresh juices, which are his most popular product. The other product he sells is smoothies, which take longer and need more ingredients but which he can sell at a higher price.

- If he concentrates on just making fruit juice, what might he be losing out on?
- Do you think he should concentrate on just making smoothies?
- If he just makes smoothies, what would happen to the availability of fruit juices?

If students have understood, they should be able to answer without prompting that concentrating on making fruit juices means he is missing out on the income of the smoothies. They might suggest that he should make both and work out the best combination. If he just makes smoothies, fruit juices would not be available.

Suggested answers to in-text questions 1–7:

1. This question is based on the example in the Student's Book on the straight-line diagram showing combinations of wheat and rice. The PPC is likely to be a curve because some fields will be more suitable for growing wheat and some will be more suitable for growing rice. This may be because the soil is more suited for growing either wheat or rice.
2. This question is based on the example in the Student's Book of using fields for wheat and/or rice. Students need to find the information from the table. The opportunity cost of wheat when one field is changed over to growing rice is the loss of ten units of wheat.
3. The answer is given immediately below the question.
4. This question follows a discussion about choices in the economy. It would not be wise for an economy to only produce consumer goods. An economy will not be able to grow if an insufficient amount of resources is allocated to capital goods. There would be less consumer goods in the future if there was not investment in capital goods which are needed to make consumer goods.
5. The answer is given immediately below the question, which gives an example for government. For individuals, an example of working hours versus leisure time might be appropriate. For firms, an example of increasing marketing spends versus investment in new technology could be used.
6. The photograph shows people entering a job centre which indicates there is unemployment so the economy is at point X in the diagram.
7. The answer is given immediately below the question.

Application task

The application task is based on the PPC diagram of capital and consumer goods in the Student's Book. Ask students to copy out the table. In the first column, they should place the movements on the PPC against the correct explanation.

Movement on the PPC above	Explanation of the movement
Z to Y	Increase in unemployment
Y to X	Increase in workers leaving the country to work abroad
Y to Z	Improvements in technology for factory machinery
X to Y	Spare capacity in factories gets used up and now factories are working at full capacity

Suggested answer to in-text question 8:

The answer is given immediately below the question.

Case study

China

- Use question and answer to review understanding of the impact of growth on the PPC.
- Discuss why countries like China have experienced high growth rates.
- Some students might need help in identifying in the case study factors that have encouraged growth.

Suggested answers

1. China's PPC has moved outwards, which is a sign of economic growth.
2. There are a number of factors which explain why the PPC has moved outwards. Investment in industry and new technology, improving technology and improving the skills base of the country through education along with investment in infrastructure, such as roads and railways.

APPLYING

Project work

For this project students are to use the internet for their research. Students should use the experience of previous project work research to take on more responsibility for their own research. However, you should prepare sources of information for students who might struggle completing their own research. This should cover:

- data about economic growth
- data on output of goods and services
- data on employment and unemployment
- information on use of automation and robotics in factories
- helping students to interpret the statistics that they discover as well as terms that they come across such as gross domestic product.

It would be useful to use the information to write a report and give guidelines on how the report should be presented. The following headings could be used.

- Changes in economic growth
- Goods and services output
- Employment, unemployment and migration
- Use of advanced technology and robotics
- Implications of advanced technology on the PPC

Expected outcomes

- Presentation of data on growth, employment and output.
- Presentation of information regarding the use of advanced technology in factories.
- A decision as to which direction the PPC is shifting with an explanation. For example, it is shifting outwards because there has been investment in new technology which has led to efficiencies and economic growth.

Knowledge check questions

Ask students to complete the knowledge check questions at the end of Unit 1.4 in the Student's Book.

Checking progress

Ask students to complete the Check your progress section in the Student's Book.

Chapter review

Ask students to complete the Chapter review questions at the end of Chapter 1 in the Student's Book.

2.1 Micro economics and macro economics

Learning objectives

By the end of this unit, students should be able to:

- explain the difference between micro economics and macro economics
- identify the decision makers involved in each.

Key terms

Micro economics; macro economics

STARTING POINT

Place the students into pairs and ask them to discuss together all three questions. After allowing time to complete the tasks, invite pairs to go through their answers. Write responses on the whiteboard to capture all new points.

- The demand for cars will depend on a number of factors. Businesses buy cars for their fleet vehicles, such as taxi firms, car hire businesses as well as company cars. Demand will depend on how successful these buyers are. For private motorists, the level of real incomes will be important as well as the availability of credit (motor finance). Costs of running a vehicle, such as fuel costs, might affect the type/brand of car bought. Another important determinant of demand is consumer confidence, but this is difficult to measure.
- Answers could include: the workforce involved in car manufacture will benefit and have greater job security; unemployed workers could get jobs; suppliers to the industry would see orders increase; shareholders in the car industry could benefit from increased profits; shops near the factories have increased trade.
- Government might make lower benefit payments as unemployment falls and receive more tax as more workers are employed.

EXPLORING

The exploring questions could be run as individual tasks, pairs work or group discussion. It would be useful at the end to run a plenary session to go over key issues.

- For individuals, savings provide a buffer against uncertain times allowing people to smooth out their consumption when times are tough and allow people to reduce debts and save for retirement.
- They could save up for a purchase or a holiday and it might mean that they do not have to borrow money and get into debt.
- If everyone saved more, that would mean they would spend less and retailers could face a fall in sales and profits.

Extension question

What is meant by the paradox of thrift?

The exploring questions are leading to the concept of the 'paradox of thrift', which was popularised by the economist John Maynard Keynes. It states that individuals try to save more during an economic recession, which essentially leads to a fall in (aggregate) demand and also in economic growth. It is a paradox because individuals saving is a good idea but in an economic downturn savings has an adverse effect on the economy.

DEVELOPING

Teaching tips

- It is important to link economic theory to current actual examples in the business world and the wider economy as this is far more interesting to the student.
- An issue to be aware of is that some students tend to think of micro economics as theory and macro economics as practice.

- While micro and macro economics appear to be different, they are interdependent and complement one another since there are many overlapping issues between the two fields. For example, increased inflation (macro effect) would cause the price of raw materials to increase for companies and in turn affect the end product's price charged to the public. It is important that students are aware of this.
- One way of approaching micro economics and macro economics is that micro takes a bottom-up approach to analysing the economy while macro takes a top-down approach. Micro tries to understand human choices and macro tries to answer such questions as "What stimulates economic growth?"

Suggested answer to the Application task

Economics studies the effects of the following	Micro economics or macro economics?
Bad weather affecting the rice harvest	Micro economics because rice farmers and consumers are affected. It only affects one market and not the whole economy
Unemployment increasing	Macro economics because unemployment affects the whole economy, as government has to pay more in benefits and demand might fall for goods and services
The exchange rate for your economy increasing in value	Macro economics because the whole economy could be affected as it could affect prices and demand for exports and imports
Your father's wage has increased	Micro economics because only one household's income has increased
The government raises income tax	Macro economics because a rise in income tax will affect all taxpayers and could impact on the demand for goods and services
A new machine is invented to clean floors more quickly	Micro economics as it affects one market but not the whole economy
Wages are rising for all workers across the country	Macro economics because wages are a cost of production leading to wage inflation and so affects the whole economy
The price of cocoa increases	Micro economics because only cocoa farmers and consumers are affected. It only affects one market and not the whole economy

Additional activity

Micro and macro economics

Collect past copies of newspapers. Divide groups of students into pairs. Give each pair some of the newspapers, flip chart paper, glue, scissors and pens. Ask them to draw a line down the middle of the flip chart paper and write the heading 'micro economics' on one side and 'macro economics' on the other. Students are to look through the papers and find appropriate stories that illustrate micro and macro economics and cut out and stick them under the correct heading.

When completed, each pair should attach their flip chart paper to the wall.

Invite pairs to give examples.

Case study

Housing market in Singapore in 2017

- Review typical micro and macro issues in a question and answer session.
- Discuss what might influence property prices in countries generally and then specifically in a crowded island such as Singapore.

Suggested answers

The case study questions ask to identify microeconomic and macroeconomic issues from the case study. They could present these in a table. Run a plenary after students complete to ensure understanding. Explain that the inter-relatedness of micro and macro means that costs of labour, for example, could be both a micro and a macro issue.

1. Micro issues
   - In the private residential property market, there has been an increase in house purchases.
   - House prices have been rising.
   - Singapore Press Holdings is planning to reduce its workforce by 10% over the next two years.
   - Wage increases are low (could affect one firm or one market).

2. Macro issues
   - Prices
   - Economic growth
   - Job losses – the Government has warned that unemployment may increase
   - Wage increases are low (could affect all firms)

APPLYING

Project work

- This project asks the student to use the internet to record inflation rates in your own country. Apart from statistics from your own country, the World Bank website is a useful source of data as it provides inflation data on all countries. You need to be aware that the way inflation data is presented can be confusing for economics students. A variety of measurements are used and these are calculated differently, so guidance will have to be given.
- Students are asked to identify microeconomic decision makers affected by changes in the inflation rate. These could include individuals who make economic decisions as consumers every day about how to spend their income and whose buying decisions are affected by inflation. It also includes business owners such as a farmer who might face rising costs for animal feeds.

Expected outcomes

- Presentation of inflation data over a five-year period
- Identification of microeconomic decision makers affected by inflation and the nature of the impact

Knowledge check questions

Ask students to complete the knowledge check questions at the end of Unit 2.1 in the Student's Book.

Checking progress

Ask students to complete the Check your progress section in the Student's Book.

2.2 The role of markets in allocating resources

Learning objectives

By the end of this unit, students should be able to:

- explain what is meant by the market system
- describe how markets determine the allocation of resources
- describe the economic problem
- explain how the price mechanism determines the answers to the following key questions about resource allocation:
  - what goods and services to produce
  - how these goods and services should be produced
  - who should be able to purchase and consume these goods and services.

Key terms

Market economy; planned economy; mixed economy; the economic problem; economic resources allocation of resources; markets; price mechanism; equilibrium price; market equilibrium; market disequilibrium

STARTING POINT

Place students in their pairs to answer the starting questions, which introduce the student to markets being any place where buyers and sellers meet. Ask selected pairs to provide their responses, writing key points on the whiteboard. They are likely to mention that fruit and vegetables can be bought in a market and supermarkets or from farm shops. Some students might know that in some countries and cities online retailers now offer food deliveries. Currency, for example, US dollars, can be bought at banks, currency exchange shops/kiosks, post offices etc. Tickets for a sporting event can be bought at the venue, online or through agencies. A football shirt can be bought online, in sports and clothes shops or direct from a football club.

EXPLORING

After allowing time for the pairs to complete the questions, invite selected pairs to give their responses. Note these down on the whiteboard or ask the selected pairs to come to the front of the class and present their answers. One of them can write their key points on the whiteboard while the other talks.

Answers for the set of questions are likely to be that price would rise. This price rise would encourage the wooden toy manufacturer to supply more so they would need more wood. There is an increase in demand for wood. Some students might point out that the price of wood could rise which could lead to an increase in costs for the wooden toy manufacturer. There could be a variety of responses to what happens to workers who are employed by the toy manufacturer. Some may say it depends as their firm might ask them to produce more in the same time, or that they might get offered overtime so their incomes might rise. If the firm operated a profit share scheme, they could benefit from profits rising.

DEVELOPING

Teaching tips

- Check understanding of the economic problem at the start of the work on the price mechanism.
- Think of a wide variety of examples for students to explain the process of moving towards an equilibrium.
- Divide things into logical stages and explain why one action has knock on effects.
- Observing or discussing what happens in an auction is a useful example.
- At this stage do not be afraid to answer the question of whether markets do in fact act in this way and the barriers that are used to interfere with the workings of the price mechanism. These points are examined later in the book.

Suggested answers for in-text questions

1. The photograph is a picture of a market and this is a good place to sell products because the market brings buyers and sellers together.
2. Prices in a market are determined by the price mechanism. As above, this market brings buyers and sellers together. If a trader priced too high, then they would not sell any goods (especially if there are a lot of market stalls selling the same products). They would have to lower price to persuade people to buy the products. If they were selling out fast, they would put up the price as they could sell the remaining stock at a higher price.
3. If buyers want to buy a greater quantity of a chocolate bar than sellers are offering for sale, you would expect the price to rise.
4. If there is a greater quantity of chocolate bars offered for sale than the quantity of chocolate bars wanted by buyers, you would expect the price to fall.
5. If there is more quantity supplied than quantity demanded, this will either lead to the lowering of the price or unsold supply (excess supply). Lowering the price of a good encourages consumers to purchase more and suppliers to produce less.
6. The numbers of sellers would fall.

Additional activity

What should they do?

This activity asks students to look at a number of scenarios. It is based on discussion stations related to the workings of the price mechanism.

Explain to the students that they will be visiting discussion stations and responding to different scenarios. Divide students into groups. Explain that groups will be rotating around the room to different stations. At each station are pieces of chart paper with a statement or scenario. Students will read the statements and respond in writing with their own thinking, analysis, or questions. They may also respond to other students' comments. They should use their knowledge of the price mechanism as well as other economic knowledge.

Allow 3–5 minutes at each station. When each station has been visited by every group, allow 5 minutes for the students to revisit stations and see what new thinking or questions have emerged since they were last at the station.

Invite several students to share what they learned or how their thinking changed during their visits to the information stations.

The scenarios are as follows.

1. A video games shop responds to an increased demand for a popular game by keeping the price the same and selling on a first come first served basis. Is this the right way? What does economics suggest should happen?
2. A bakery shop notices it sells out all its bread within a couple of hours and decides to issue a coupon to regular customers and will only sell to customers with coupons for the first two hours. Is this the right way? What does economics suggest should happen?

3. A firm making glasses for use in bars and restaurants has seen sales fall as bars switch to plastic. 20% of their workforce are not needed. What should the owners do? What does economics suggest should happen?

Notes:

In your plenary discuss each situation. Get the students to explain how the price mechanism should work.

Reflect that owners are likely to do what they think best even if it is not the wisest thing to do. The video shop could put up prices as a response depending on whether there is any competition. The bakery could increase production of bread or put up prices. The firm making glasses should lay off workers and/or switch to making products that their customers want.

Extension question

Some people say that the consumer is sovereign. Find out what this means. Do you think the consumer or business is more powerful in deciding what is produced?

Guidance on extension question

The idea that the consumer is sovereign is more than the idea that the customer is always right. It is that by buying goods and services, consumers are in a way voting those products and services into power. Firms can research a new product and spend millions on marketing but if the consumer doesn't like it there is little the firm can do. An example is the TouchPad, introduced in July 2011, which was Hewlett Packard's attempt to compete with Apple's iPad. With powerful video capability and impressive processing speeds, the TouchPad was widely anticipated to be among the only products that could compete with Apple. Despite large-scale press events and promotions, the HP TouchPad was a colossal failure and was discontinued almost immediately. As a result of the TouchPad's failure, the company wrote off $885 million.

Support question

If there is a greater quantity of ice creams offered for sale than the quantity of ice creams wanted by buyers, what will happen to price?

Guidance on support question

This support question allows you to check on understanding of the price mechanism. The answer is that you would expect price to fall. It might be useful to get the student to go further and add an explanation.

Case study: Silver is losing its shine!

Before setting the case study, it might be useful to have a discussion on the impact of changes in demand on price and quantity bought and sold as well as the impact on suppliers of raw materials.

Suggested answers:

1. The demand for silver ore is a derived demand from use in photography and jewellery. If the demand for these products falls, less silver ore is needed.
2. Incomes have risen and the case study suggests that consumers have switched to other products and services which they can now afford, such as luxury designer goods and travel.
3. Facing falling sales, silver jewellery producers would cut back on production and reduce their number of staff. Whether the wages of the remaining workers would fall is less certain but there would be a downward pressure on wages.
4. They would cut production and look for alternative products.
5. Luxury designer goods and travel.

APPLYING

Project work

In this project, the student has to give example of firms that face falling sales or increasing sales and to find out information about these firms. It would be useful to prepare this work to ensure that information is available on firms. You could give a number of firms that you have explored and allow the students to choose from these; this would help those students who find this type of research challenging. Students might need assistance in explaining why sales have fallen or risen. The one issue that you need to deal with and explain is that market sales for a good might be falling but an individual firm's sales might be rising because they are more efficient and competitive. For example, sales for a supermarket chain might be falling because their customers might have switched to a competitor.

Explain what is expected and the format of a report.

Expected outcomes

- Profile of a firm whose sales have fallen with an explanation and details of sales, the number of employees, number of factories/retail outlets etc.
- Profile of a firm whose sales have risen with an explanation and details of sales, the number of employees, number of factories/retail outlets etc.
- Findings presented in a written report

Knowledge check questions

Ask students to complete the knowledge check questions at the end of Unit 2.2 in the Student's Book.

Checking progress

Ask students to complete the Check your progress section in the Student's Book.

2.3 Demand

Learning objectives

By the end of this unit, students should be able to:

- define demand
- draw a demand curve and illustrate movements along the curve
- understand the link between an individual's demand and market demand
- explain what causes a shift in the demand curve and show this on a diagram.

Key terms

Demand; effective demand; demand schedule; law of demand; extension in demand; contraction in demand; ceteris paribus; demand curve; increase in demand; decrease in demand; conditions of demand; substitute good; complementary good

STARTING POINT

Use these questions in a class-wide plenary introductory session to demand. Write their responses on the whiteboard. A variation of this would be to ask them to write lists of: (a) five things they would like to buy and can afford; (b) five things they would like their parents to buy them that their parents could afford; and (c) five things which are more of a dream. This could prepare the way to an understanding of willingness and ability to pay.

EXPLORING

- People might have an increase in income and so they can afford more expensive fruit or buy more fruit and vegetables. The price of alternatives to fruit and vegetables, such as convenience foods, might have fallen and so people switch away from fresh fruit and vegetables. There might have been a health campaign to persuade people to eat more fresh fruit and vegetables.
- It depends on whether meat is a close substitute to fish. If it is, then as the price of fish increases people would buy less fish and buy more meat.
- There could be a variety of responses. Some students might say that as income rises then more vegetables would be bought, others might say that there could be little impact if they already have enough vegetables. Others might consider that some people would switch the type of vegetables they buy to more expensive items they could now afford.

DEVELOPING

Teaching tips

- Question and test your students often. The theory of demand and supply is a building block that underpins a lot of the students' study in the course.
- Students need to practise drawing demand curves and the changing conditions which would shift a curve.
- Some good Mathematics or Science students might want an explanation of why economists deviate from mathematical and scientific conventions by putting price on the vertical axis. There is a more complete explanation but the easiest way to explain this is that it is a historical convention.

Suggested answer in-text question 1:

As the price of a good rises, consumers buy less as they switch to other items that are not rising in price so much. This is called the substitution effect. Rising prices also cause consumers to buy less because they cannot afford to buy as much. This is the income effect.

When the price falls, the substitution and income effects will cause demand to rise. Consumers will substitute cheaper products for the more expensive ones. They will also buy more because of the income effects, as they can afford to buy more at the cheaper price.

Application task: The market for coffee

This asks students to plot a demand curve of coffee from data provided (see Figure TG 2.3.1 below). Ensure that students use the correct axes. Students should explain that as the price of coffee falls, the quantity demanded increases.

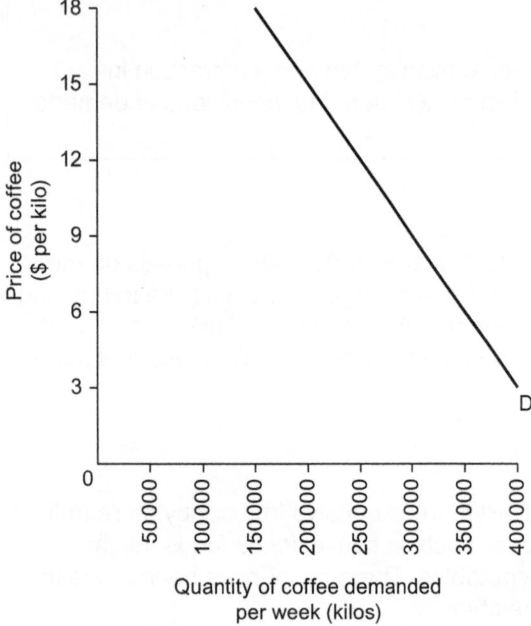

Figure TG 2.3.1

Suggested answer in-text question 2

The question is based on a conditions of demand table. Students are asked to come up with their own examples. This task could be set as individual work or as plenary discussion. Further examples are shown below.

Factor	Example and effect
Real disposable income	Income tax rises, leading to less money available to spend and there will be a decrease in demand for most goods, such as a decrease in demand for holidays
Tastes and preferences (fashion)	Publicity/photo shoot for the clothes a celebrity wears leads to an increase in demand for the fashion brand
Population	An ageing population leads to increase in demand for hearing aids
Prices of substitute products	Price of pasta falls leading to a decrease in demand for rice
Prices of complementary products	Increase in price of knives leads to reduced demand for forks

Additional activity

Auction to illustrate demand

This activity introduces students to demand and supply in an engaging way.

Equipment required:

- A block or bar of chocolate (or several) or some other healthier item of value that students may like to buy
- Whiteboard
- Counters to be used as money. Each counter represents 50 cents

Write a list of prices on the board, usually starting from a low price – such as 50c, and ending with a very high price, such as $4. (Usually at least 8 different price options is best: 50c, $1, $1.50, $2.50, $3.00, $3.50, $4.00 $4.50). Distribute the money in sealed envelopes. Not everyone will get the same amount. For example, if the class size is 28, distribute as follows:

$4.50 0 envelope

$4.00 1 envelope

$3.50 2 envelopes

$3.00 3 envelopes

$2.50 4 envelopes

$2.00 5 envelopes

$1.50 6 envelopes

$1.00 7 envelopes

Tell the students that the supply of items is fixed. Once the items are sold they are gone.
Hold up the chocolate bar/s or other item/s and asks the class 'Who is willing and able to buy this X for … (the price)?'.

Write the quantity demanded next to the price, and proceeds to do this for each of the possible prices listed.

You need to impress upon students that they are indicating their willingness and their ability to purchase the chocolate at that price. Explain that what the class has created together is called a 'demand schedule'.

Work with the students to unpack the ideas behind demand for a product including:

- that demand indicates a willingness and an ability to purchase
- that the demand schedule represents all the quantities demanded at all possible prices
- that this demand schedule can be used to create a demand curve/graph.

You can then ask a student to come up to the whiteboard and plot the graph, having shown that the price is plotted on the y (vertical) axis and quantity demanded on the x (horizontal) axis.

The results can be used as a basis for discussion of how and why the demand curve is downward sloping, and also the utility and benefit gained from purchases. It can also be used to discuss factors affecting demand.

Extension question

Can you think of any products where an increase in price might lead to an increase in demand?

This extension question is partly about Giffen goods. A Giffen good is typically an inferior product for which, when there is a rise in price, demand rises. Robert Jensen and Nolan Miller, two Harvard professors, have shown that poor Chinese consumers purchase more rice or noodles (their staple foods) as prices go up.

People need a certain amount of calories to survive. People can either get that by consuming rice and perhaps some vegetables alone, or by eating rice, vegetables and a few pieces of meat. As the price of rice goes up, they cannot afford to supplement the rice with meat and end up buying more rice.

Another example is the status or rare goods where high-priced items are sought after purely because of the status attached to them. In 2015, for example, Rolls Royce reported increased sales despite price rises and a recession.

There are other explanations including an increase in income inequalities and the growth in average incomes in particular parts of the world such as South East Asia.

Application task

Students have to put a tick in the box to show whether the change will lead to either a contraction or extension in demand (a movement along the demand curve) or an increase or decrease in demand (a movement of the whole curve). The correct answers are shown in the table below.

Change	Extension in demand	Contraction in demand	Increase in demand	Decrease in demand
Price of oranges increases		x		
Orange juice drinks become more popular			x	
A popular new film has been released – how will the cinema market be affected?			x	
Price of jeans decreases	x			
How does a decrease in income tax affect the demand for holidays?			x	
There is an increase in the number of babies born. How is the demand for nappies affected?			x	

Case study

Coffee

One way to prepare students to discuss demand factors is to start with another example. Ask what determines the demand for going to watch a film at a cinema. What would cause more people to go to the cinema? What would happen to the demand for ice cream and drinks if more people went to a cinema?

Suggested answers

1. The question is based on coffee. Initially the students are asked to plot a demand curve on the diagram they drew in the application task.
2. The second question asks for three factors that have led to more people visiting coffee shops and so to an increase in demand for coffee. Examples answers are: coffee shops offer a wide range of drinks which appeal to people's tastes; coffee shops are comfortable meeting places where people can talk; people can use the internet without extra charge in coffee shops for work and leisure purposes.
3. The third question asks whether increased demand for coffee might affect demand for tea and hot chocolate. This will depend on whether they are close substitutes and also what is happening to their prices. Some students might say that as coffee shops such as Starbucks sell coffees, teas and hot chocolate then more people going to these outlets might mean the demand for other drinks such as tea and hot chocolate might also increase.

APPLYING

Project work

The project work asks the students to investigate using airline flights to four other countries. They will find out price variations during the year. It would be useful to undertake some preparation investigating a variety of airline websites as well as online agencies. It might be useful to suggest a number of countries or names of airports. Travel websites sometimes request inputting the names of airports rather than countries. Prices might also vary from airline to airline.

Students might observe that buying a long time in advance will mean that flights will be cheaper. Friday flights are often more expensive as business customers often return home on Fridays. Tickets vary in price depending on the type of ticket. There is a hierarchy of prices from the cheaper Economy to the more expensive Business Class and First Class. Holiday seasons will tend to lead to higher prices. Flights around Chinese New Year from London to Beijing, for example, are very expensive compared to other times of year.

Expected outcomes

- Presentation of research of price of flights to four countries including price variations at different times of the year such as school holidays
- Explanation of price variations

Knowledge check questions

Ask students to complete the knowledge check questions at the end of Unit 2.3 in the Student's Book.

Checking progress

Ask students to complete the Check your progress section in the Student's Book.

2.4 Supply

Learning outcomes

By the end of this unit, students should be able to:

- define supply
- draw a supply curve and illustrate movements along the curve
- understand the link between an individual's supply and market supply
- explain what causes a shift in the supply curve and show this on a diagram.

Key terms

Supply; supply schedule; law of supply; supply curve; extension in supply; contraction in supply; increase in supply; decrease in supply; conditions of supply; indirect tax

STARTING POINT

Place the students in pairs and ask them to discuss the starting point questions. Get pairs to present their choices to the rest of the class noting down on the whiteboard the most popular choices. Lead a discussion on the top three choices as to why these were chosen. They might mention that they chose on the basis of trying to make as much money as possible for the charitable event and so chose items that they know they would be able to sell. Others might say they chose low-priced items as they would be more likely to sell these.

EXPLORING

Place the students in pairs and then invite comments in plenary session. Students could refer to profitability, the demand for products and prices.

DEVELOPING

Teaching tips

- Students often have a greater problem understanding supply than demand as they are not used to looking at the world from a producer's point of view. Students can think that a determinant of supply is demand as no one would produce anything if it was not wanted. It is important that students quickly realise that price is the independent variable and quantity supplied is the dependent variable. It might be necessary to relate this to the issue of causality.
- It is useful to relate the positive slope of the supply curve to the positive relationship in the law of supply.

Suggested answer to in-text question 1:

Wanting to supply is not the same as supply. This is because it is possible to want to supply a particular good but the price is not sufficient to make a profit and so a particular seller might decide it is not worthwhile. Other things being equal, the supply provided by producers will rise if the price rises because all firms look to maximize their profits.

Application task: The market for coffee

Students will draw a supply curve from the data supplied and indicate that as price rises suppliers will want to offer more coffee beans to the market place.

Take the opportunity to deal with possible confusion of students at this point. They see that as price rises producers supply more. Some students think that the price going up will reduce demand resulting in a surplus in the market. They need to understand that the supply curve just shows the relationship between price and quantity supplied. It becomes easier to understand when they examine equilibrium.

In addition, some students forget that what is driving an upward sloping supply curve is the law of increasing costs. This is the same phenomenon that causes the PPC to be bowed outwards. If they imagine some producers having lower costs than others (for example, because their land is more fertile, their oil is nearer the surface or their workers are more productive) then students begin to understand why the S curve slopes upwards.

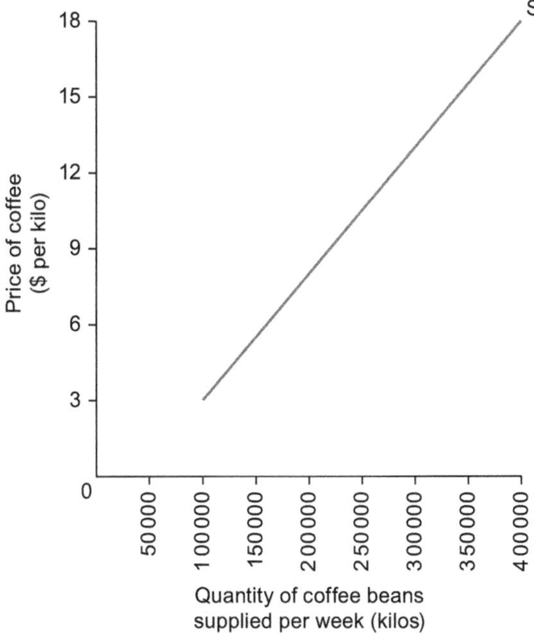

Figure TG 2.4.1

Suggested answer to in-text question 2:

The supply curve would shift to the left.

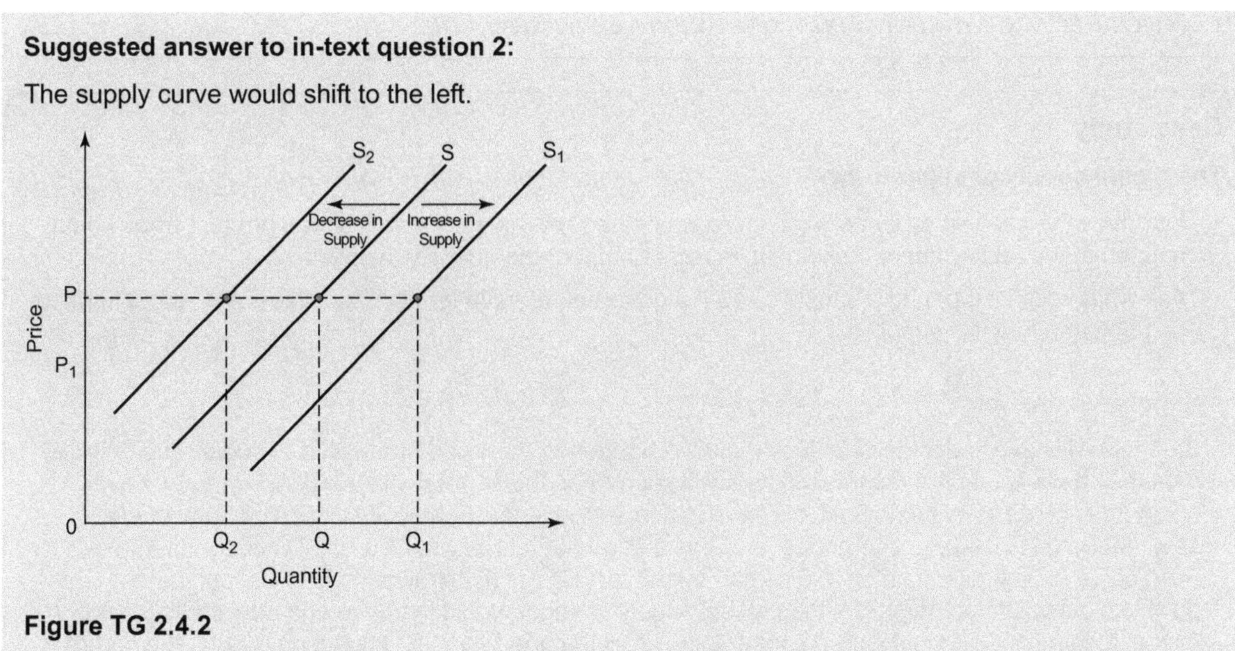

Figure TG 2.4.2

Suggested answer to in-text question 3:

The answer is below the question in the Student's Book

Application task

Students need to put a tick in the box to show whether the change will lead to either a contraction or extension in supply (a movement along the supply curve) or an increase or decrease in supply (a movement of the whole curve). Students should only tick *one* of the four options. The correct answers are shown in the table below.

Change	Extension in supply	Contraction in supply	Increase in supply	Decrease in supply
Price of tea increases	x			
Wages of tea pickers increases				x
A more efficient machine is developed to process tea leaves			x	
Very hot weather causes a poor harvest				x
Government increases a subsidy on tea				x
An increase in the number of growers harvesting tea	x			

Additional activity

Market stall

Use Activity sheet 2.4.

- This activity is based on running a market stall in a busy market. Students are stall holders selling fresh fruit and vegetables. Hand out the instructions to this activity which provides a number of scenarios which the market stall holder has to respond to.
- This activity can be an individual piece of work or students can work in pairs.
- After the activity, run a plenary session and compare answers.

Case study

The global supply of sugar in 2017

- Introduce the case study by asking if there was a bad harvest for an agricultural product what would happen to the supply curve. Ask about impacts on price and quantity supplied.
- Ask what would happen to a supply curve if a government gave farmers subsidies. Ask about impacts on price and quantity supplied.

Suggested answers:

Students will have to decide what they think will happen to the world production of sugar. The only data they have is that the Mauritian output will fall by 7% due to poor weather conditions. However, no figure is given as to the impact this would have on the global supply of sugar. The case study said that Brazil is the largest producer and has a good harvest, as has Russia. Whether incentives have come in time to impact on Indonesian output for 2017 is not known. If students feel that the positives outweigh the negatives then global supply of sugar would increase and they could reflect this on a supply curve shifting to the right. If they feel that the Mauritian impact outweighs the others then they will have a supply curve shifting to the left. Some students might point out that there is insufficient data to state what impact there would be on the global supply of sugar as no relative figures are given. If they argue this case they would be unable to draw a diagram.

APPLYING

Project work

Students will need to be directed to appropriate websites to obtain this information. Students need to be aware that oil supply figures are often given in barrels. A barrel of oil is equal to 159 litres, 42 US gallons or 35 imperial gallons. Statistics tend to be for crude oil. Crude oil is refined to make a number of products including petrol and this is the focus of the extension question.

Out of every 42 gallon barrel of crude oil:

- 20 gallons is distilled to make petrol
- 11 gallons is distilled to become diesel or heating oil.

Students could cover factors such as the policies of OPEC, the demand for fuel from China, political factors such as wars and civil unrest in oil producing countries, some oil fields running out, or new fields being found.

Expected outcomes

- Research notes on the supply of oil
- Presentation of factors that influence the world supply of crude oil with up to date information
- Data on the world supply of oil in the last five years
- Newspaper article on changes in the world supply of oil

Extension question

When crude oil is distilled, a variety of products are produced, including gasoline/petrol, naphtha for making chemicals, kerosene for aircraft fuel, diesel oil for cars, lorries and buses and bitumen for roads and roofs.

What problems would it cause crude oil suppliers and refiners if the demand for bitumen for roads and roofs increased dramatically? How would this impact on the supply of the other crude oil products? Are there any solutions to the impact?

Students could point out that if there was an increase in demand for one product, such as bitumen, this could lead to an increase in price and more being supplied. However this means that more crude oil would have to be produced which would mean the supply of all the other products would increase. Solutions might include new technology and improvements in the cracking process or storing the extra supply of the other products rather than putting them on the market.

Knowledge check questions

Ask students to complete the knowledge check questions at the end of Unit 2.4 of the Student's Book.

Checking progress

Ask students to complete the Check your progress section in the Student's Book.

2.5 Price determination

Learning outcomes

By the end of this unit, students should be able to:

- define what is meant by market equilibrium
- draw demand and supply schedules and curves and identify the equilibrium price and sales in a market
- draw demand and supply schedules and curves to identify disequilibrium prices, shortages and surpluses in a market

Key terms

Surplus or excess supply; shortage or excess demand

STARTING POINT

Students could discuss this question in pairs and you could invite some pairs to go through their responses. Alternatively, you could lead a discussion. Students might refer to using online sites for selling used products where potential customers bid for items. This would also be a source of information on prices. Students might have looked in local newspapers where people advertised similar products to gauge the prices.

EXPLORING

- The exploring questions build on the additional activity in Unit 2.4 of the Teacher's Guide. Firstly, a fruit and vegetable seller can choose any price they wish to charge for their products but it is the consumer who will decide whether they are prepared to pay that price. If no or few products are being sold then it implies that they are pricing too high. Their price will be influenced by the amount they paid wholesalers as well as the prices that other fruit and vegetable sellers are charging for similar products.
- It is likely that they will see customers switch to other sellers and so revenue will fall. It will depend if all their prices are higher or just on some selected items. Also they might sell better quality produce than their competitors.
- It is likely that customers will switch to that seller depending on the price differentials and other variables such as quality.

DEVELOPING

Teaching tips

- Demand and supply is at the heart of the subject and understanding how prices are determined gives a good grounding for the rest of the course in areas such as wage determination, in product markets and exchange rate determination in currency markets.
- Understanding price determination is an example of logical thinking. It might be useful to undertake some logical thinking exercises before looking at theory.
- It is important to embed theory in real life examples. This will make it easier to grasp the importance and relevance of key concepts.

Application task: The market for coffee

Suggested answers:

- Students will complete the demand and supply schedule using the information given in Unit 2.3 and Unit 2.4.
- Students will draw a demand and supply curve based on the schedule they have completed. Ensure that the diagram is correctly labelled.

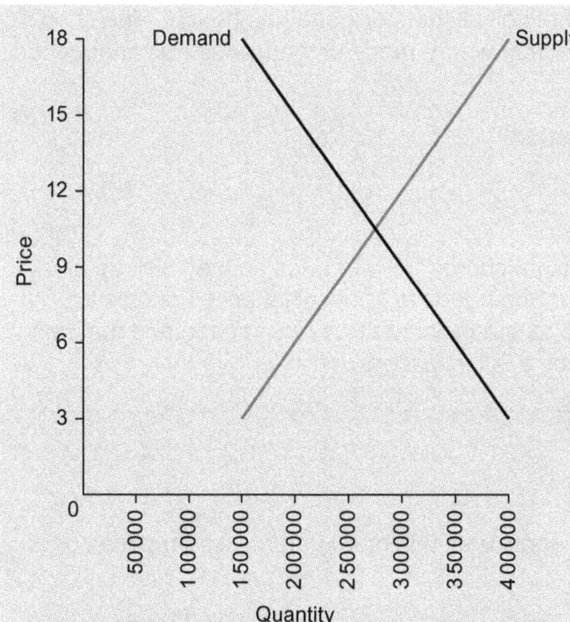

Figure TG 2.5.1

- The diagram shows that there is one price where the amount consumers are able and willing to buy is the same as the amount suppliers are willing and able to offer.
- At $18, 150,000 kilos would be demanded and 400,000 kilos would be supplied. Price is likely to fall as there is excess supply.
- At $6, 350,000 kilos would be demanded and 150,000 kilos supplied. Price would rise because of excess demand.

Suggested answer to in-text question 1:

The diagrams and explanation are provided underneath the question in the Student's Book

Additional activity

Use Activity sheet 2.5a

Price survey

- This activity could be set as a homework or you could organise a short field trip. If a field trip is organised then the institution's policy regarding the trip needs to be followed. As this is a survey of prices charged for items in shops, alerting your local shops would be prudent and timing the trip to times when the shops are less busy will be a good idea. On the activity sheet there are some suggestions for products that are to be surveyed but you could change these. Also, extra lines have been provided to add appropriate items.
- The field trip would be appropriate for pairs work. Ask the pairs to present their information in a brief report. Presentations could use tables and diagrams.
- Run a plenary to go over the main issues raised by the survey. One of the issues is that students faced with a demand and supply diagram view it as a static model rather than a dynamic model (they do not need to know these terms). Prices are constantly changing as markets are always on the move.

Support question

This support question is to enable you to identify whether some students have understood work on demand and supply to date.

You work at the weekend at a store selling computer games. There is another video games store opposite. Your manager is trying to decide what price to charge for a new video game that has had good reviews.

She is worried that if she priced it too high then she would not sell all the stock she has bought. The shop's customers are mainly in the 18–25 age range. Recently a factory where many of them work has announced that they have to reduce the hours of their workers.

- Why might the manager at the video games store be worried?
- What information might help her to make her decision?
- What do you think she should do?

The students could say that she is worried her competitor might charge a lower price so they pick up all the sales. If she priced low, then she would make less profit. She needs to know what prices people are prepared to pay for the game, whether the game is as good as the initial reviews have stated and that her customers who are mainly in the 18–25 age group might face a fall in income.

Case study

Food price controls in India, China and Venezuela

- It would be useful to check that students know how to show both minimum and maximum prices on a demand and supply diagram.
- Discuss the reasons why food price controls might be used. They are usually implemented as a means of direct economic intervention to manage the affordability of certain goods.

Suggested answers

1. Students will draw a diagram similar to that used in the Student's Book.

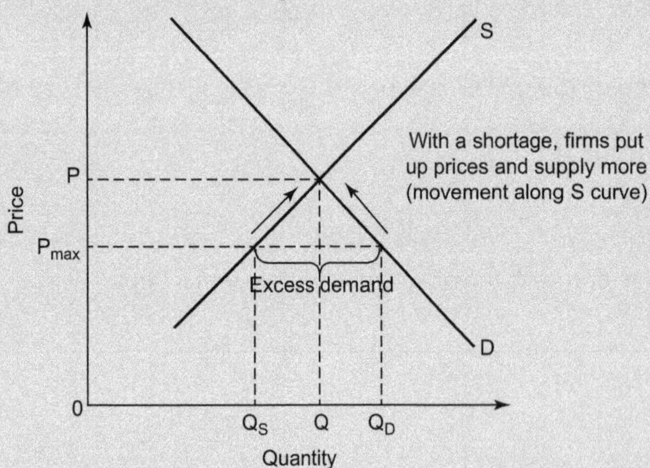

Figure TG 2.5.2

Government sets the price at P_{max}. At this price quantity demanded is at Q_D but the amount that suppliers are willing to sell is Q_S. This means there would be excess demand.

2. Producers might seek other markets for their products such as a nearby country which does not have price controls or switch to produce that does not have price controls. They would not sell price controlled items to supermarkets as profits and shelves would be empty of these items. Consumers would have to queue at shops or resort to buying on the black market. Some consumers would go without.

APPLYING

Project work

The project requires students to find examples of what happens when popular sporting events are sold out quickly and why the equilibrium price cannot be reached. Review source information before setting this project. Students are likely to comment that stadium capacity will limit tickets. Research might show that the consequences of this are that stadiums will set prices to ensure that all are sold. Popular football clubs can charge prices significantly above the average price for others in their league. For some events, a black market emerges (through ticket touts) where high prices are charged. Organisers try to prevent resale to stop this activity. Some students in their research might find reference to the supply curve becoming perfectly inelastic at capacity.

The extension question refers to ticket touts who buy tickets and then resell them at much higher prices. They can do this because for major sporting events demand exceeds supply. Many sporting events now prohibit the resale of tickets and refuse to let people in who are not the original buyers. This is to prevent this activity taking place.

Expected outcomes

- Examples of sporting events where tickets are sold out quickly
- Consequences in terms of prices that can be charged
- Existence of secondary black markets

Knowledge check questions

Ask students to complete the knowledge check questions at the end of Unit 2.5 in the Student's Book.

Checking progress

Ask students to complete the Check your progress section in the Student's Book.

2.6 Price changes

Learning outcomes

By the end of this unit, students should be able to:

- explain what causes the equilibrium price to change
- draw demand and supply diagrams to illustrate these changes in market conditions
- analyse the consequences of these changes in market conditions for the equilibrium price and sales.

STARTING POINT

Place the students into pairs and set the questions. Ask them to identify their three products. They might choose seasonal products such as fruit where price falls when there is plenty of fruit in the shops. Out of season prices might rise as the fruit would have to be imported. Students could refer to petrol prices which fluctuate when oil producers use cutting production to raise price.

EXPLORING

- This builds on the questions in Unit 2.5. When there is a popular sports event, as there is a set capacity for the event, demand outstrips available tickets. Popular football clubs, for example, can charge substantially more for tickets than less popular clubs.
- This is because households with children are limited to when their children are on holiday. This then creates a surge in demand for holidays when schools are closed. Prices are lower at other times to attract households which are not restricted by school holidays.
- If there has been good weather which results in a good harvest then more mangoes will be available. It is likely that if other things do not change prices will fall.
- It is likely that if a press report said mangoes contribute to a healthy diet and they are available demand would increase and price would rise.

DEVELOPING

Teaching tips

- Students need to practise diagrams as much as possible. One technique at the start or end of lessons is for you to suggest changes in conditions and to get students to come to the board and draw diagrams for those changes.
- When answering the questions in this unit, it is a good idea to ask the students to close their Student's Book.
- Encourage logical thinking by a step-by-step approach to changes in demand and supply curves.
- Use the 'What will happen?' additional activity as a discussion forum where rational ideas and consequences can be explored.

Additional activity: Shifts in supply and demand

Use Activity sheets 2.6a and 2.6b

This activity can be used in small groups, using Activity sheets 2.6a and 2.6b, or as a whole-class activity. For a whole-class activity, draw four supply and demand diagrams on the board each illustrating a different scenario (rightward shift in supply, leftward shift in demand etc). Each diagram is drawn using a different colour. Students each have four small coloured cards matching the four diagram colours. Read out a range of different scenarios (for example, impact of a rise in incomes on the market for luxury cars). For each scenario students hold up the coloured card matching the correct diagram.

Application task: The market for coffee

Students would draw the demand and supply curve from the data and then draw the new demand curve. Demand has shifted to the right. This means that equilibrium price has risen and more has been bought and sold.

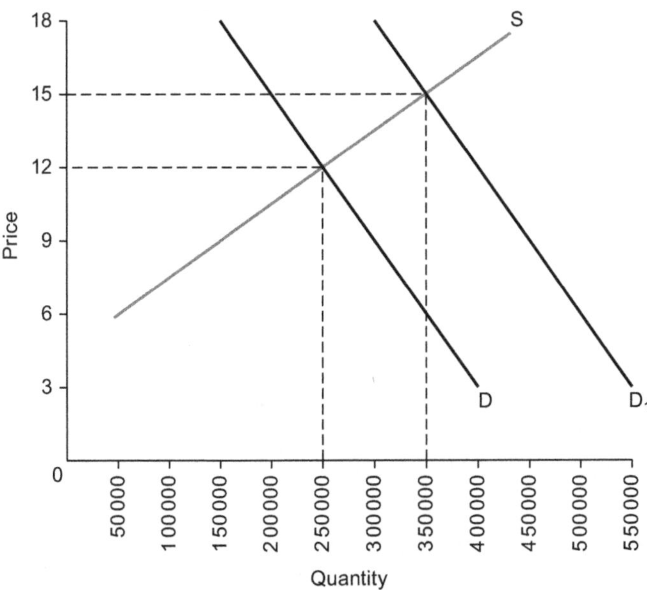

Figure TG 2.6.1

Suggested answers to in-text questions 1 and 2:

These questions come after an explanation for both the increase in supply and the decrease in supply. It would be useful to get the students to draw these diagrams without looking at their books. In their explanation, it could help them if they write it in numbered points or as a flow diagram such as: Step 1 Decrease in costs of production; Step 2 Supply curve shifts to the right so that more can be supplied at every price; Step 3 There would be excess supply at the previous price; Step 4 Price would fall and there would be a movement along the demand curve until a new equilibrium is reached. The same approach can be taken with the decrease in supply.

Application task: The market for coffee

After the increase in demand, the price rises from $12 to $15 and sales rise from 250,000 kilos per week to 350,000 kilos per week.

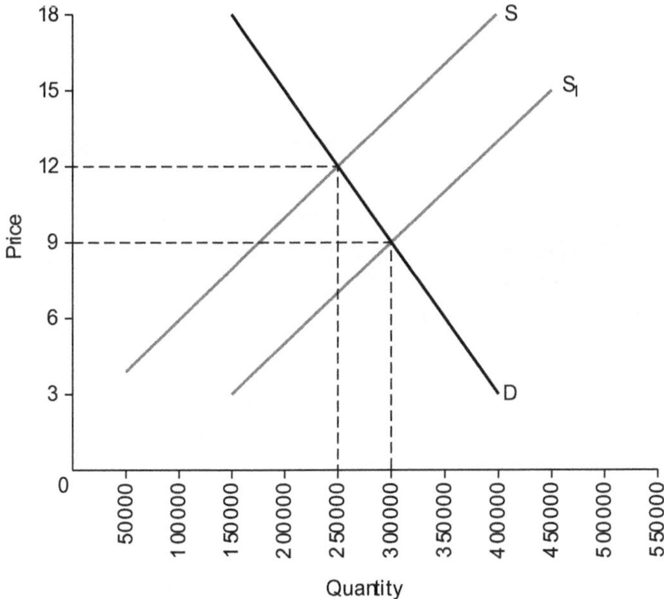

Figure TG 2.6.2

Suggested answer to in-text question 3:

The diagrams that the student needs to use are above the question in the Student's Book. You could provide some scenarios that students could use to provide a focus for their diagrams. For example the scenario could be that there is an advertising campaign for new trainers and the use of new technology brings down the cost of making trainers.

Case study

The price of rice

- Discuss why the supply and price of rice is important in many countries.
- Go over the relationship between good harvests and prices of agricultural products.

Suggested answers:

1. The world supply of rice is expected to increase because of good weather conditions. The supply curve would shift to the right.
2. Demand is expected to increase caused by an increase in population and a rise in incomes in developing countries. The demand curve would shift to the right.
3. The students would draw a diagram showing a shift to the right in the demand curve and a shift to the right in the supply curve.
4. The article suggests that prices are rising so this means that the shift in demand creating upward pressure on price is greater than the change in supply caused by good weather. Their diagram could show this. If price in their diagram falls, it means their diagram shows that the impact on supply is greater than the impact on demand.

Additional activity: What will happen?

Use Activity sheet 2.6c

This activity can be completed towards the end of the unit. The activity should be set as an individual piece of work. Explain that they need to look at each statement on the activity sheet and explain what is likely to happen. They have a list of possible things that could happen but some of the examples are designed to generate discussion.

The responses will be useful for you to see students' use of logic and also common sense. They will also aid you in terms of checking understanding.

Suggested answers:

These are a range of possible responses. It is important to use the students' responses as a basis for discussion.

Statement	What will happen?
A shop selling sweets decides to drop the price of all its chocolate bars.	*More people would buy chocolate bars or are attracted in for the first time by the price drop – movement down a demand curve; people switch from other confectionary at the shop so there might not be a gain.*
There has been a very wet winter and the strawberry harvest is very poor.	*Supply is limited; the supply curve shifts to the left and, so other things being equal, price would rise; low quality strawberries might cause people to switch to other fruits.*
Incomes of 18-25 year olds have risen over the past year. What would this mean for the demand for salt?	*Salt is a cheap product and people's spending patterns of salt might not be influenced by a rise in income. There is only a limited amount of salt that people require.*
A new type of chip for use in mobile phones has reduced the costs of manufacture.	*A change in technology causing a fall in production costs would cause the supply curve to shift to the right. This would mean that price would fall. However, if demand for phones was also changing as a result of, for example, a rise in income then this could impact on prices.*

Incomes of people over 60 have risen.	*Demand for products consumed by over 60s would shift because of the rise in incomes. However, if they decide to save more, the impact on prices might be more limited.*
In the town, there are two fast food restaurants. One of these has distributed 20% off meals vouchers.	*A 20% voucher is an example of promotion (advertising); this should shift the demand curve to the right. However, there might be brand loyalty and people prefer the other restaurant or there might be quality issues. It also depends on whether the people who receive the vouchers want to use them.*
The government increases the tax on petrol.	*An increase in tax on petrol would shift the supply curve to the left and so prices might rise and less petrol might be bought and sold. However people might need to use their cars so there might not be a significant fall in demand.*
A fall in the birth rate means that the number of children under 12 has fallen substantially.	*The decline in the number of children under 12 would mean that there is a fall in population. Demand curves of products bought for children would fall. Prices should fall.*
As a result of increased paper costs, all newspapers produced in a country have faced an increase in their costs by 10%.	*The supply curve would shift to the left and so prices would rise; some newspapers might decide to absorb the price increase so as not to lose customers. For many newspapers, their circulation is important because of the advertising they are seeking to attract.*
Coffee shops are having to pay more for top quality coffee because of a world shortage of quality beans.	*An increase in the cost of quality beans would affect the coffee shops' costs and the supply curve would shift to the left and so prices would rise; however the shops could use lower quality beans instead.*

APPLYING

Project work

In this project, provide appropriate sources of information, especially regarding historical data. Initially, students need to define what is meant by price. Is it the price some mobile phone providers charge for a phone? For many contracts the phones are 'free'. Is the price of a phone not part of a contract? Also students might observe that the same model is available at different prices from retailers. Students might explain that when a new phone model is introduced, price is initially high but this comes down over time. Others might point out that mobile phone manufacturers might discount models before a new model is introduced. Students should also use demand and supply analysis discussing the status symbols of some models or the impact of advertising on demand (tastes), or the impact on supply of new technology causing costs of production to fall. Some students might combine an increase in demand with an increase in supply and show that despite an increase in demand there is still a fall in price. Students should be encouraged to use diagrams in their explanations and present all the information in a report. Discuss the attributes of a news report and the differences between a news report and an essay. Remind students that it is important to write with the audience in mind. Consider making this a joint project with the English department.

Expected outcomes

- Comparisons of prices of different models
- Historical data of model prices over the last two years
- Analysis of changes in price using demand and supply analysis and empirical evidence
- Script of a news report

Knowledge check questions

Ask students to complete the knowledge check questions at the end of Unit 2.6 in the Student's Book.

Checking progress

Ask students to complete the Check your progress section in the Student's Book.

2.7 Price elasticity of demand (PED)

Learning outcomes

By the end of this unit, students should be able to:

- define price elasticity of demand (PED)
- calculate PED using the formula and interpret the significance of the result
- draw and interpret demand curve diagrams to illustrate different PED
- explain the key influences on whether demand is elastic or inelastic
- explain the relationship between PED and total revenue, both in a diagram and as a calculation
- analyse the significance of PED for decision making by consumers, producers and the government.

Key terms

Price elasticity of demand; price elastic demand; price inelastic demand; unit elasticity of demand

STARTING POINT

These starting point questions lead the way to the discussion of price elasticity of demand. They start with an approach of helping the students to grasp the concept before they know the terminology.

After allowing time to discuss the questions, invite pairs to offer their responses and note key points on the whiteboard.

Suggested answers

1. Pairs are likely to suggest that if all prices increased by 10%, they might stop buying the drinks. If there were no other choices, such as free water, then they might have to pay the extra 10%. Some pairs might suggest that they would bring drinks from home or buy drinks at a lower price from a shop outside school. Some might say that it would have no influence as they do not buy drinks at school. This is a valid response as students will give a response based on their own personal experience. This would be an opportunity to ask those students to put themselves in the position of someone who did buy drinks at school.
2. Pairs might say that they might switch to a drink other than Pepsi or it depends on how much they prefer Pepsi to other drinks. Some might say they are not allowed to buy carbonated drinks anyway.
3. Pairs could state in the first question the price impacts on all drinks so you do not have much choice, but for the second the price impacts on only one. Others could comment that it might be influenced by how much they like Pepsi compared to other drinks, whether the other drinks on offer are appealing or whether they buy drinks in the first place.

EXPLORING

The exploring questions invite pairs to discuss the responsiveness of demand to changes in price for goods and services. It is important to run a plenary session to make sure that there is a good grounding before the concept of price elasticity of demand is investigated further.

- Pairs might suggest holidays, luxury foods such as expensive cakes or lobster, products such as televisions, music systems.
- Pairs might suggest 'essentials' such as basic foods, fuel for the home or car, childcare, rent for their homes.
- In the plenary, use students' responses to lead to a discussion. The starting point could be that basic foods are essential and that people **need** to eat, they **need** to get to work, they **need** to ensure their children are looked after to enable them to go to work. Holidays, although welcome, are not essential: they are a luxury.

DEVELOPING

Teaching tips

- Try to give students as much practice as possible in working out price elasticity of demand.
- You might have to revise how to calculate percentages.

Suggested answer to in-text question 1:

If a business discovers that consumers are not sensitive to changes in the price, they should increase the price as demand is price inelastic. The change in demand is proportionately smaller than the change in price and so revenue will rise.

Suggested answers to Worked Example questions:

- Worked example 1: PED is –0.5, which means that the percentage fall in demand is smaller than the percentage increase in price. This shows that consumers are not sensitive to price change. This firm should increase its price as revenue would increase.
- Worked example 2: PED is –2.5, which means that the percentage fall in demand is greater than the percentage increase in price. This shows that consumers are sensitive to price changes. This firm should decrease its price as revenue would increase.
- Worked example 3: PED is –1, which means that the percentage decrease in demand is the same as the percentage increase in price. There is no point in changing price.

Suggested answers to in-text questions 2–6:

2. Price increases by 50% in the first example and by 0.1% in the second example. Quantity decreased by 33.3% in the first example and by 10% in the second example.

3. Revenue has increased so much because, with the PED of oil being only –0.2, the demand for oil is not very sensitive to price changes, in other words demand is very inelastic.

4. You would raise price because this would result in an increase in revenue.

5. The revenue would remain the same because the percentage change in price is matched by an equal and opposite change in quantity demanded.

6. Knowing the price elasticity of demand shows what happens to revenue when price changes. This is vital to a firm to help them with their decision making as well as understanding the possible impact of decisions.

Application task

The application task asks the students to calculate price elasticity of demand for coffee, tea and iced coffee. It is useful to provide opportunity for students to practise calculations. Practise calculation of percentages and ensure that everyone is able to do so before answering these questions. Remind students that it is good practice to show their workings when undertaking calculations. If students have practised these calculations, you could set these questions under test conditions.

Students should start with the formula they are going to use for the calculations:

$$\text{PED} = \frac{\text{percentage change in quantity demanded}}{\text{percentage change in price}}$$

$$\frac{\text{change in quantity demanded}}{\text{original demand}} \times 100 \quad \text{and} \quad \frac{\text{change in price}}{\text{original price}} \times 100$$

Question 1:

Coffee:

$$\frac{50}{1000} \times 100 \quad \text{and} \quad \frac{0.22}{2.20} \times 100$$

5% fall in demand, 10% increase in price. PED for coffee = **–0.5 (price inelastic)**

Using the same technique, the students would calculate:

Tea: There is a fall in demand of 12.5% and **PED = –1.25 (price elastic)**

Iced Coffee: There is a fall in demand of 10% and so **PED = –1 (unity)**

Question 2:

The question looks at the effect of a price decrease:

Coffee: There is a 5% increase in demand so **PED for coffee = –0.5 (price inelastic)**

Tea: There is a 25% increase in demand so **PED for tea = –2.5 (price elastic)**

Iced Coffee: There is a 5% increase in demand so **PED = –0.5 (price inelastic)**

Question 3:

Students would state that if they want to increase revenue they should **raise** the price of coffee as it is price inelastic. Revenue would rise from **$2200 to $2299.**

They should **lower** the price of tea as it is price elastic and revenue would rise from **$1600 to $1800.**

They should leave the price of iced coffee **unchanged.** When price increases, price elasticity of demand is unity and so the price increase will have no impact on revenue. If they lowered the price it becomes price inelastic so that revenue would fall if they lowered price.

Total revenue before price changes is **$5050.** Total revenue after price changes is **$5349.**

Suggested answer to in-text question 7:

Students could mention services where there are few alternatives such as commuting to work or the provision of water services when there is just one provider. Students would then consider products they might buy even if prices increase. These could include going to a music event or sports event, for example.

Additional activity: Charlie's

Use Activity sheet 2.7.

This activity looks at Charlie's, a petrol station and café.

- Before looking at the data, **Question 1** asks the student to give advice. They could say that as there are no other petrol stations, people might have to fill up and so he might be able to increase petrol prices. Some might say that petrol is an inelastic product so that he will see an increase in revenue if people have no choice. They might say that the café faces competition from a fast food restaurant and so customers might be more price sensitive and so if prices are elastic then he should not increase price.
- **Question 2** requires the student to work out at least the percentage changes. For petrol, there is a 32% increase in price and a 25% fall in demand, so demand is price inelastic and revenue would increase if price increased. For pizzas, there is just over a 9% fall in price and a 50% increase in demand. Demand is price elastic and so a fall in price will lead to an increase in revenue.

Extension question

Charlie is thinking of offering loyalty vouchers. He is considering offering a 50c voucher for people who buy petrol to be used in the café or a 50c voucher to be used for petrol if people buy a pizza. What should he do?

Support question

Charlie also sells ice creams.

These ice creams sell for $1 and he sells 100 a day. As a trial, he reduced price to 50c and sells 300.

a) Has this price change been worthwhile?

b) Is the demand for ice cream price elastic or price inelastic?

- With the **Extension question** students could say that it would be better to offer a 50c voucher for pizzas as they are price elastic. Using the voucher the other way round is not recommended as the demand is price inelastic.
- With the **Support question** a simple example is used. Students could point out that ice cream sales have gone up from $100 to $150 so it is worthwhile. The student does not need to work out the PED but to recognise that as revenue has risen after a price fall demand is price elastic for ice creams.

Case study:

Chocolate

- This case study asks the student to suggest what the price elasticity of demand for chocolate is. Make sure students know how changes in price impact on revenue when demand is price elastic or price inelastic. A review of the determinants of price elasticity would be useful.

Suggested answers:

1. The article states that the demand for chocolate has grown due to the worldwide popularity of chocolate and the perceived health benefits of chocolate. It suggests that chocolate consumers are price insensitive which indicates that chocolate is price inelastic despite consumers thinking it is a luxury item.
2. If chocolate is price inelastic then raising price would increase revenue as the percentage increase in price is greater than the percentage fall in demand.
3. This will depend on the respective PED for the different chocolate bars rather than chocolate as a whole and whether the bars are close substitutes. If the PED for the bars produced by the firm is identical to all the other firms then it would be worth increasing price. Should one firm put up its prices for chocolate bars while the rest of the firms in the market leave their prices unchanged?
4. This is unlikely. Chocolate bars vary – some are luxury high premium brands while others are economy brands. Brand loyalty could be a factor. Firms try to differentiate their chocolate bars through adding flavours or fruit and nuts. It is likely that firms will face different PED.

APPLYING

Project work

The project work asks for students to advise the school on pricing decisions for sales of food and drink. Suggest a research method and also work out how they can interact with their classmates. Although designed as an individual piece of work, this could be adapted for pair or group work. Students should be encouraged to use key terms in their presentation.

Expected outcomes

- Research data which contains food and drink, price information and responses
- Summary of research
- Recommendations for price changes with justifications
- Use of economic terminology
- Presentation of findings and recommendations to the class and explanation of impact on revenue.

Knowledge check questions

Ask students to complete the knowledge check questions at the end of Unit 2.7 in the Student's Book.

Checking progress

Ask students to complete the Check your progress section in the Student's Book.

2.8 Price elasticity of supply (PES)

Learning outcomes

By the end of this unit, students should be able to:

- define price elasticity of supply (PES)
- calculate PES using the formula and interpret the significance of the result
- draw and interpret supply curve diagrams to illustrate different PES
- explain the key influences on whether supply is elastic or inelastic
- analyse the significance of PES for decision making by consumers, producers and the government.

Key terms

Price elasticity of supply; price elastic supply; price inelastic supply; unit elastic supply; short term; long term; mobility of factors of production

STARTING POINT

The starting point questions could be answered in pairs. Alternatively, if you think it more appropriate, use the questions to lead a class discussion. Write key points on the whiteboard. If pair work is used, invite selected pairs to respond and write key points on the whiteboard. Follow this up with a class discussion.

For these questions, the expected response is that the school has given facilities and a given number of teachers so they might be unable to accept more students. Be prepared for responses such as it depends on how many. If it is a few then the students could be accommodated. If your school has a selection test for entry, students might comment that these students who want to come to the school must meet the academic requirements. These comments are of course valid and should be encouraged. In the discussion, emphasise that time is a factor. Some resources, such as teachers, can be recruited more easily in the short term but new classrooms would take longer to resource. This introduces students to the concept of **short and long term.**

EXPLORING

The exploring questions develop understanding of short term and long term. Invite selected pairs to come to the board and present their answers. One can talk while the other writes on the whiteboard. Invite comments from the class and add any points to the whiteboard.

The comments below are an approach to get students to think of logical consequences but also to think creatively. For the question about the bicycle factory, it will depend on spare capacity. If they are not using all their productive capacity in the factory, they could make more bicycles. They could offer existing workers overtime while they try to recruit more workers. Their ability to recruit more workers will be influenced by the level of employment in the area. The other determinant would be whether they can access materials to make the bicycles quickly.

The farmer has a greater problem as farmers are limited by the harvest of yams. They would have to make the decision months in advance to increase their production. The restaurant has a set amount of tables so this limits their ability to serve more customers. They could take short-term measures such as increasing opening hours or start a delivery service. Some restaurants change their layout and make small changes so that they can add more tables.One long-term possibility is to build an extension. Some restaurants respond to their popularity by opening more restaurants.

DEVELOPING

Teaching tips

- Students need to practise calculations and drawing of diagrams as much as possible.
- Provide as many real world examples as possible.
- Farming is a useful start for students to understand elasticity of supply before moving on.
- Encourage students to use economic terminology in all their answers.

Suggested answer to in-text question 1:

The value for price elasticity of supply is positive while price elasticity of demand is negative. This is because changes in price and quantity supplied go in the same direction which means that an increase in price will lead to an increase in supply or a decrease in price will lead to a fall in quantity supplied. It also means that if price increases, revenue will increase, and if price falls, revenue falls.

Suggested answers to worked example questions:

Worked Example 1: The PES is inelastic because it is less than 1 and so the firm cannot easily or quickly increase the supply of paint.

Worked Example 2: The PES is elastic because it is greater than 1 and so the firm can easily or quickly decrease supply.

Worked Example 3: The PES is unit elastic and so a 20% increase in the price of bread would lead to a 20% increase in quantity supplied.

Suggested answers to application questions:

1. Price change is 33%. Supply change is 20%. PES = 0.6 inelastic
2. Identical price and supply changes. PES = 1
3. PES = 0 perfectly inelastic
4. PES = 3 elastic

Application task:

The application task asks students to write a report on how quickly the supply of coffee in the Philippines could be increased to respond to increases in world prices. It is important that students can access information about coffee and any relevant information about the Philippines coffee industry. The key facts about coffee are that the coffee tree will grow fruits after three to five years, and will produce for about 50 to 60 years (although up to 100 years is possible). The fruit takes about nine months to ripen. Their report should discuss the consequences of the length of time it takes for trees to bear fruit and the length of time current crops take to ripen.

Suggested answer to in-text question 2:

Increasing the supply of copper will depend on whether more can be obtained from existing mines by working longer hours. It will depend on whether there are easily accessible copper ores that have not yet been exploited. Further shafts might need to be created which could take several months. If new mines have to be established, this would take a considerable time.

- The supply of wooden furniture would be influenced by availability of wood. Most manufacturers of wood can easily source more wood. This means that timeframes to increase supply are quite short. Other influences on how quickly supply can be increased include the availability of spare capacity in the furniture factory and having the skilled workers needed.
- Building yachts takes a long time. A large luxury yacht can take up to three years to build so it is not easy or quick to increase supply.

Application task:

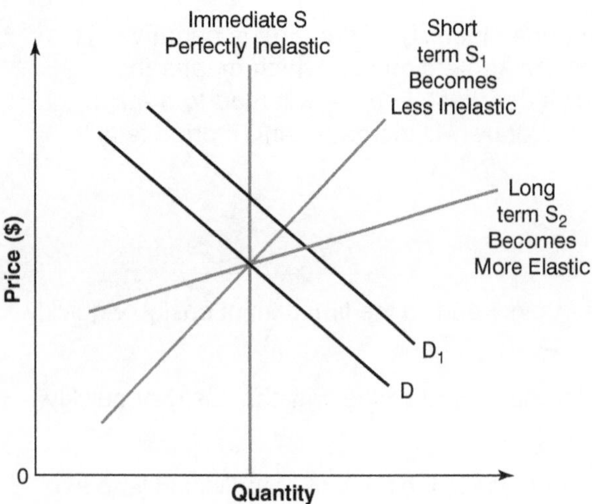

Figure TG 2.8.1

Case study: High demand for Google's Pixel smartphone

- This case study is based on the launch of the Pixel smartphone. It might be useful to provide some background information on the smartphone industry and Google's interest in this market. Some terminology might need to be explained such as configuration as well as explaining the company Verizon. Verizon are also known as Verizon Communications, Inc, an American multinational telecommunications conglomerate and the largest US wireless communications service provider.

Suggested answers:

1. The case study suggests that elasticity of supply is inelastic.
2. This is because stocks are low or have run out at both Google and Verizon outlets and it is taking time for shipments to be made.
3. Factors that could affect the PES are as follows.
   - The amount of stock (inventories) or ability to store the stock (inventory). This is low for the phone which implies PES is inelastic.
   - Level of spare capacity. If all the machines are being used and the factory has no space left to add more machines or workers then supply will be inelastic. This is because the firm is at full capacity and cannot quickly increase supply of the products.
4. It means that they cannot meet consumer demand for phones which will frustrate their customers who might switch to competitors' products.
5. They should have built up greater stocks before releasing to the market or invited pre-orders so that they could see the level of demand and change their production plans accordingly.

Additional activity

This activity should be undertaken at the end of work on elasticity of supply. It is a group activity with each group taking a scenario and then presenting the question in the scenario to the class. Students need to refer to elasticity of supply but should also be encouraged to use their knowledge of supply and demand theory.

Suggest to groups that they can use appropriate presentation techniques. Explain that they can make controversial points and that there is not necessarily a right answer. The important thing is the arguments they use to support their views.

Encourage students to use economic terminology including: demand, supply, changes in demand and supply, price elasticity of demand, price elasticity of supply, price inelastic, price elastic, mobility of factors of production, spare capacity, spare stocks.

Scenario 1

Incomes are rising in your country. This has led to a significant increase in demand for products and a rise in prices. Unemployment is at an all-time low. Would you rather own a factory producing ice creams or own a factory producing bricks for construction work?

Scenario 2

There has been a succession of bad harvests due to bad weather. Would you rather own a factory processing food (a company that uses meat and vegetables to make convenience food and tinned goods) or own a farm?

Scenario 3

There has been a large rise in tourism both within the country and from visitors from other countries. Would you rather own a group of hotels or own a business which sells high quality meals from its fleet of mobile kitchen diners?

Extension question

If there was a series of bad harvests do you think the government should intervene? What could they do?

Support question

An ice cream maker in a small shop sells 300 ice creams a day at $2 per ice cream. Demand increases and so the ice cream maker raises the price. However, the ice cream maker owns one machine that makes exactly 300 ice creams a day. Is the supply of ice cream from this shop elastic or inelastic? What could the owner do to supply more ice cream?

APPLYING

Project work

It is important to explain to students what you expect them to research. Prepare some sources of information to provide assistance, especially for those who find this kind of research difficult. Employment data such as job vacancies figures as well as unemployment figures should be available. However, some of these data sources can be quite technical. There is one key issue that needs to be explained: you can have unemployment and unfilled vacancies at the same time because the skills of those who are looking for jobs might not be the skills that firms are looking for. Articles in newspapers and magazines on skills shortages could be a good source of information.

Expected outcomes

- Presentation of research data on job vacancies in a country
- Explanation of problems for firms, such as they cannot meet customer demand and could lose out to competitors
- Explanation of problems for government, including that the economy might not be as competitive as other countries. There might be a need to invest in education and focus on filling the skills gaps but this takes time

Knowledge check questions

Ask students to complete the knowledge check questions at the end of Unit 2.8 in the Student's Book.

Checking progress

Ask students to complete the Check your progress section in the Student's Book.

2.9 Market economic systems

Learning objectives

By the end of this unit, students should be able to:

- define market economic system
- identify the difference between private and public sectors
- explain the advantages and disadvantages of the market economic system
- explain how market economic systems work in a variety of different countries

Key terms

Market economic system; private sector; public sector

STARTING POINT

The starting point questions provide the basis of examining the market economic system. Remind the students of the work they have done previously on public and merit goods. After allowing time for the pairs to answer the questions, run a plenary session discussing in particular those products and services provided only by the government and those provided by both government and businesses.

In Question 1, students are likely to mention products and services such as consumer durables, food, financial services and hairdressers. In Question 2, students might mention law and order and defence, education and health services. In Question 3, they might identify police, fire services and street lighting while in Question 4, the list could include health, education and broadcasting services.

EXPLORING

These exploring questions could be set as individual or pair work or could be used as the basis for class discussion. Question 3 would form a good class discussion. Use local examples to show that when there is direct competition firms have to think of the implications of charging a higher price than competitors. This is why, even when products are very similar, firms use marketing to create a brand image or try to differentiate in other ways such as better customer service.

DEVELOPING

Teaching tips

- It is important in topics such as economic systems that students focus on the economic dimension to these topics and not on other aspects such as politics. It is important that students understand the economic dimension to this topic. Try to ensure that all discussion on this topic focuses on economic issues relevant to the syllabus.
- However, at the same time encourage students to come to their own personal opinions that they can justify with use of economic arguments and respond to the criticisms of other students.
- These topics are useful for class discussions and the additional activity tries to encourage this.
- It would be useful to remind students how to interpret and devise pie charts.

Suggested answers to in-text questions:

1. This question looks at some of the advantages and disadvantages of the market economy and how it can reward enterprise and innovation. The rewards for the founders of Amazon, Apple, Facebook and Microsoft have been great. However, those who work for a firm and become unemployed because of falling sales or who care for children, sick relatives or the elderly will struggle to make ends meet. Inequalities can be significant as a result.

2. Students might state that if firms are left to themselves they are only interested in private costs. They do not have to consider the social costs of polluting a river. However, their action might affect the private costs of firms lower down the river who need to use the water from the river for their products and services.
3. This question is useful as a basis for class discussion. Governments vary in the balance they want between private and public sectors. French governments in the past have tended to intervene in the economy to be a catalyst for economic growth. Countries like Finland have a tradition of a more equitable system with generous pension provision and social care programmes. In countries like the USA and Japan, we see a balance towards the private sector to encourage innovation and growth with fewer restrictions on the business community.

Additional activity: Group discussion using T-charts

Use Activity sheet 2.9

This activity is a group discussion on private and public sectors using T-charts. It builds on the issues covered in the unit as well as encouraging use of existing economic knowledge.

Display four sheets of flip chart paper around the room, prepared as T-charts and labelled with the following headings:

- The public sector should provide most products and services in an economy.
- The private sector should provide most products and services in an economy.
- Private sector firms can be trusted to act fairly and do not need supervising.
- Large inequalities do not matter.

The two sides of the T should be labelled “we agree because” and “we disagree because” (see Activity sheet 2.9 as an example).

Divide students into four groups and ask each group to visit one of the flip chart sheets. Ask the group to spend five minutes discussing how they might deal with the issues shown on the flip chart, considering both the left and right side of the T-Chart. Ask the group to write their ideas on the flip chart.

After the five minutes, ask the groups to move on to the next flip chart. Each group should look through the ideas that the previous group has identified, then add their own **NEW** ideas to the chart (students should not just repeat ideas that the previous group identified for that chart). Repeat this process twice more so that all groups have visited each flip chart.

At the end of the activity, lead a discussion with the whole group.

An alternative would be to provide Activity sheet 2.9 to the students to complete independently.

Extension question

Choose one of the countries in Table 2.9.1 in the Student’s Book. You are not allowed to choose your own country. Write a short profile of the country and analyse the level of government spending.

Students might need support in identifying sources of information.

Support question

Do you think that a government should provide health care? Explain your answer.

If the student answers yes, they could point out that this would help people who could not afford to pay for healthcare and that it ensures a healthy workforce. If the student answers no, they could point out that people could take out health insurance and that the private sector in many countries delivers high quality healthcare.

Case study

Hong Kong – the world's freest economy

It would be useful to provide some background about the Heritage Foundation, including who they are and what their index is based on. This will encourage students to always check the data they are using. Discuss what 'freest' means in this context as well as other interpretations.

Suggested answers:

1. The case study evidence is the favourable business environment, free trade, simple and low taxes, law and order and a government that believes in close economic cooperation with major trading partners.
2. Advantages could include low taxes that encourage enterprise, innovation and investment. Encourage students to consider advantages not used in the data such as less 'red tape' which encourages firms to set up or expand.
3. Policies to promote a free economy could include lowering taxes or encouraging free trade by the development of free trade parks. Reducing government restrictions on things like planning permission could also be considered.

APPLYING

Project work

The project work asks students to research the goods and services produced by the private and public sector in their country and to use this information to draw a pie chart. Students need to decide where on the spectrum their country is. Are they closer to countries like Singapore or closer to countries such as Finland? Students might need help to identify sources of information and how to structure their answer to the question as to what extent their country can be considered a market economy.

Expected outcomes

- Data on public and private sector provision
- A pie chart illustrating this data
- An answer that analyses this data to see what the balance is between the public and private sector

Knowledge check questions

Ask students to complete the knowledge check questions at the end of Unit 2.9 in the Student's Book.

Checking progress

Ask students to complete the Check your progress section in the Student's Book.

2.10 Market failure

Learning objectives

By the end of this unit, students should be able to:

- define market failure
- define the following terms associated with market failure: public good, merit good, demerit good, social benefits, external benefits, private benefits, social costs, external costs, private costs
- explain how market failure can arise from public goods; merit and demerit goods; external costs and external benefits; the abuse of monopoly power; and factor immobility
- analyse the consequences of market failure with the overconsumption of demerit goods and goods with external costs
- analyse the consequences of market failure with the underconsumption of merit goods and those with external benefits
- analyse the implications of market failure on the misallocation of resources with either too many or too few factors of production being allocated by entrepreneurs to the production of these goods.

Key terms

Market failure; social optimum quality; merit goods; demerit goods; public goods (or services); private goods (or services); non-excludability; non-rivalry; external costs; private costs; spillover effects; social costs; external benefits; private benefits; social benefits; monopoly power; factor immobility

STARTING POINT

The starting point questions begin the process of considering interventions because without these interventions there could be harm. Either place students in pairs or run the starting point questions as a class discussion. Write the points that the students say on the whiteboard. Students might think of products such as eating vegetables and healthy foods. Some might mention services such as going to the dentist. Students might state that their parents want them to be healthy so they would encourage them to eat well. Students might consider products such as tobacco and junk food as being harmful.

EXPLORING

These questions could be set as individual, pair or group work. Using visuals of a road accident or a traffic jam caused by a road accident might act as a catalyst for students to consider the implications of a road accident such as injuries to people and damage to vehicles, the provision of emergency services and the cost of delays to individuals and firms.

1. Students could consider the cost of buying a car. The person might have borrowed money to buy the car which means a cost is the interest paid. Other costs would include car insurance, petrol, car servicing and road tax. Some might use their economic knowledge and refer to opportunity cost.
2. Students could refer to road congestion which could cause delays. This might have consequences such as being late for work, missing important appointments, or increased costs for haulage companies caught up in delays. Others might refer to pollution, global warming and health impacts caused by poor air quality due to the traffic.
3. Students could refer to those who have been injured or died in an accident. (Be sensitive in getting feedback on this question in class as students might have been affected themselves.) They would have the emotional costs of such traumas. Families could lose a breadwinner which could cause financial problems. Injured victims could face loss of income. There are the costs of emergency services dealing with the accident as well as the impact if long-term healthcare is needed. The effects for those caught up in delays caused by the accident could range from frustration to increased costs for haulage companies and those firms waiting for vital supplies.

4. This question focuses on why some of the effects are measured in money and others are not. This is because some are easy to measure. Some of the effects cost money, such as the cost of the emergency services and lost incomes due to increased costs for the haulage industry. Other costs such as trauma and bereavement are not money costs (although some economists do try to put a money value on them).

DEVELOPING

Teaching tips

- This unit covers a number of important concepts. It is important to check on understanding regularly as sub-topics are covered.
- The extension activity requires students to draw demand and supply diagrams which have not been practised. Either provide sources of information or show the diagrams to the students who are given the extension activity. The Extension activity is not suitable for students who struggle with the concept of demand and supply.

Additional activity – Types of market failure

Use Activity sheets 2.10a and 2.10b

This activity is designed to help students understand different types of market failure and ways the government can correct them.

Place the students in groups of three. Provide each group with a copy of Activity sheet 2.10a and Activity sheet 2.10b. Instruct students to categorise cards under the headings on the grid.

The first column on Activity sheet 2.10b contains the **explanations**, the second column the **examples** and the third column the **ways government can correct the market failure.** As this is group work, it would be useful to prepare by cutting up the activity sheets into cards. Make sure they have explanation on the back of the cards, an example and ways government can correct the market failure. Use large flip chart type paper for Activity sheet 2.10a. Students can then place the correct cards on the grid but also change them easily.

After allowing enough time for the groups to complete the activity, run a plenary session going through all the explanations and inviting groups to contribute. Each time ask if everyone agrees and respond to any misunderstanding.

Suggested answers to in-text questions

1. Students might explain market failure through examples to show the need for the country to provide merit goods such as healthcare to ensure that those who cannot afford healthcare can receive it. If people had to pay for healthcare, they might choose not to go to the doctor or inoculate their child. They may not understand the full benefits of inoculating their child nor the implication for society in terms of dangers of disease outbreaks. Others might refer to education: if left to the market, consumers might choose not to educate their children and this might lead to having an uneducated workforce.
2. Students could make reference to the fact it is not possible to know exactly when external benefits will arise. Inoculation against a contagious disease clearly provides protection to individuals and yields a private benefit. There is also an external benefit to other individuals who are protected from catching the disease from those who are inoculated. Students could state that individuals and families on low incomes are not likely to pay the full market price of merit goods and would under-consume.
3. Students could refer to:
   - public libraries and community spaces such as parks
   - state-financed museums and art galleries
   - subsidised bicycle programmes
   - free school meals
   - health services such as inoculations for children.
4. Students could consider demerit goods that could be over-consumed if left to market forces. Examples include tobacco and junk food.

Extension activity

1.

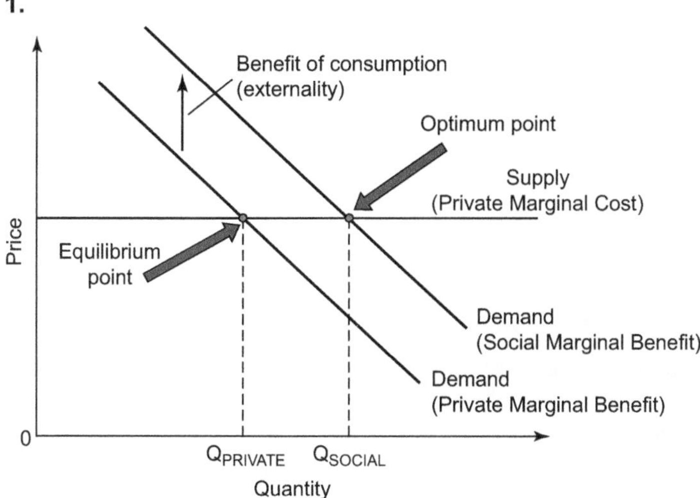

Figure TG 2.10.1

(a) The new demand curve is at a higher level than the original demand curve.

(b) The original equilibrium is at Q private and increases to Q social.

The output is at a higher level.

(c) There is under-consumption of the merit good as it is not known how beneficial it is to consume these goods and services so consumers demand them at the 'wrong' level. This is the wrong quantity because if consumers had all the information available then they would have a higher demand.

2. Demand and supply for a demerit good

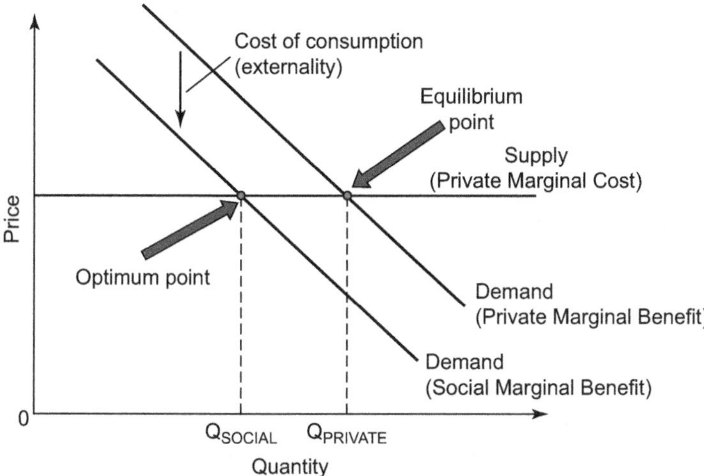

Figure TG 2.10.2

(a) The new demand curve is at a lower level compared to the original level.

(b) The original equilibrium is at point Q market and the social optimum is at Q optimum

The output is lower than the original equilibrium output

(c) There is over-consumption of the demerit good as it is not known how harmful it is to consume these goods and services so consumers demand them at the 'wrong' level. This is the wrong quantity because if consumers had all the information available then they would have a lower demand and the equilibrium price and quantity at the social optimum would be at lower sales in the market.

Suggested answers to in-text questions:

5. **(a)** Yes, because the shopkeeper will not allow someone to take away the jacket without paying.
   (b) It will depend. A private beach could exclude people if the owners control access. If access to a beach is not controlled, then anyone can consume the benefits of the beach.
   (c) If the film has been downloaded by someone else who has paid for it, you cannot be prevented from watching the film.
   (d) The ferry company could prevent someone from boarding the ferry without a ticket.
6. **(a)** If the hospital is considered a private good then consumers who have not paid will not be able to enjoy consuming the good or service. If the hospital bed is provided free, this would not arise as neither individuals would have paid. Access to the bed would be determined by the hospital.
   (b) Crime prevention by the police in your local area is an example of a public good and demonstrates non-excludability. If crime prevention was provided through the market, the people who have not paid towards it cannot be excluded from benefitting.
   (c) and **(d)** A book and a bicycle are examples of a private good. Consumers who have not paid will not be able to enjoy consuming the good or service. (Unless it is a library book available to everyone)
7. Defence is an example of a public good because it is non-rival and non-excludable. This means that individuals cannot be excluded from benefiting from defence. The services of a bodyguard are a private good. Individuals can be excluded if they have not paid.

Additional activity

This activity is a research activity which would be useful as a joint project with the science department or those who are responsible for health education in your school. This would mean that you could draw on the experience of staff who are used to talking about health issues with students and are aware of the sensitivities. If this is the case the other teacher concerned might want to add some additional health-related questions. Students could work in groups and present their findings.

If appropriate in your school, ask students to research the cigarette market in your country.

(i) How much does it cost to buy a packet of cigarettes in your country? If a consumer smoked 20 cigarettes a day, how much would they spend in one year?

(ii) What is the value of the total cigarette sales in your country?

(iii) How much does it cost the health service to treat smoking-related illnesses?

(iv) Analyse why the social costs of smoking are greater than the private costs.

(v) Who should pay for these external costs of smoking?

Students will need to be helped in accessing sources of information for the research into the cigarette market in your country to obtain information for (iii). With regards to (iv) the student could refer to the health costs for treating smoking related illnesses as well as the impact of passive smoking on non-smokers who cannot avoid breathing in cigarette smoke. (v) is more open-ended however students are likely to discuss that smokers should pay in higher tobacco taxes for the cost of healthcare.

Application task

1. The private costs include costs of construction such as materials, labour and capital equipment. The private benefits are the profits for the construction companies and the wages of their employees.
2. The external costs of the motorway would include impact on the environment such as loss of countryside, destruction of rare plants and animal habitats. There could be costs in terms of loss of income for shops in a town which is now bypassed. The external benefits include less congestion and the saving of financial costs. An area could benefit during the construction phase because of the spending of construction workers. Local people could be employed in the construction which would have positive knock-on effects in the area.

3. With this question, it would be useful to use pairs to consider whether the social benefits (private benefits and external benefits) are greater than the social costs (the private and external costs) and whether the building of the motorway will go ahead. There is not a right or wrong answer but there is a right or wrong problem-solving method. The right approach is to consider the costs and benefits then evaluate each one (for example, attempt to quantify and monetise their significance) then select on the basis of the balance between social costs and benefits.
4. *Extension*: You might need to help students identify sources of information for this question. Estimates for the costs of road use have been calculated. External costs of motorways are costs not borne by the road user. Costs can be estimated for the impact on noise pollution on people who live near motorways. Construction companies are often required to create banking to reduce noise. These will have a monetary value. Other costs such as a loss of a view are impossible to quantify. External benefits such as saving of time for the haulage industry can be quantifiable.
5. *Extension*: Cost benefit analysis (CBA) is used to decide whether a motorway is built. All costs and benefits are identified and a monetary value is assigned to each cost and benefit.

Private costs are direct (private) monetary costs.

External costs could be monetary, such as a new motorway may mean less money for train companies and non-monetary such as pollution, landscape and noise.

Direct benefits are the revenues for the construction company. Time saved for the new road could be given a value.

CBA suggests that if total benefits exceed total costs then the motorway should be built.

Case study

Soda and water usage

You could provide background information about the two companies and check students have a good understanding of private and external costs.

1. Fizzy drinks are produced because consumers demand the products and by selling them PepsiCo and Coca Cola can increase their profits.
2. Consumers, retailers, drinks companies, suppliers to the fizzy drink industry, employees of companies producing the drinks and people employed in the production and retail chain.
3. Indian trade associations, those whose water supply has been affected such as farmers, residents and firms that need water (such as the textile industry).
4. The private costs are the costs of producing the drink such as the factory and bottling, marketing costs etc. External costs are costs imposed on farmers who face drought conditions and might have to pay to bring in water for their crops and cattle.
5. Students need to come to their own conclusion but must back this up by using economic concepts.

APPLYING

Project work

You need to discuss sources of information. Global warming is a potential political debate and you need to be sensitive to all viewpoints. There may be students and families who will dispute whether the threat of global warming is as serious as some scientists suggest.

The advantage of an individual piece of work is that it allows the student to express their views backed up by evidence. Remind students they are economists and should think of this view with the experience of their knowledge of economics. An economist attempts to judge the evidence and arrive at a balanced conclusion.

Expected outcomes

- An explanation of what is meant by global warming
- An analysis of the causes of global warming

- Evidence of who the producers of global warming are (some students might say that all people in the developed world are producers of global warming, through their purchasing decisions)
- Analysis of the impact of global warming using economic analysis

The Extension question asks whether global warming can be stopped or reversed. There are a variety of approaches which could look at scientific suggestions, united actions by governments to encourage clean energy and a move away from fossil fuels.

Additional activity: The Debates!

Use Activity sheet 2.10c.

This activity takes the form of two debates. First, divide the class into two: Group A and Group B.

Subdivide Group A into two teams and subdivide Group B into two teams.

Provide the teams with the scenarios in Activity sheet 2.10c.

The teams within each group will prepare for a debate taking opposite sides. Each team needs to prepare to put forward their arguments using their knowledge of economics. Each team has a maximum of 10 minutes to argue their case. As well as putting forward their case, the teams need to appoint someone to introduce their case and someone to sum up at the end.

For the Group A scenario, Team 1 will argue for the building of the airport and Team 2 will argue against. Members of Group B will listen to the debate and ask questions, then vote for or against.

For the Group B scenario, Team 3 will argue for the ban and Team 4 will argue against. Members of Group A will listen to the debate and ask questions, then vote for or against.

Knowledge check questions

Ask students to complete the knowledge check questions at the end of Unit 2.10 in the Student's Book.

Checking progress

Ask students to complete the Check your progress section in the Student's Book.

2.11 Mixed economic system

Learning objectives

By the end of this unit, students should be able to:

- define a mixed market economic system
- explain the effects of imposing maximum and minimum prices on markets in various contexts, such as product, labour and foreign exchange markets
- define minimum and maximum prices
- draw and interpret diagrams showing the effects of indirect taxation, subsidies, and minimum and maximum prices in product and labour markets
- define government microeconomic policy measures of regulation, privatisation and nationalisation, and the direct provision of goods
- discuss the effectiveness of government intervention in overcoming the drawbacks of a mixed economic system.

Key terms

Mixed market system; maximum price control; minimum price control; fixed exchange rate system; indirect tax; subsidy; regulation; privatisation; nationalisation

STARTING POINT AND EXPLORING QUESTIONS

These questions are a good opener to the unit and you can use them as a question and answer session.

Examples of questions:

- When you came to school today, what did you use to walk, cycle or travel in?
- Who provides the road signs?
- Who provides the street lights?
- Who says you can't drive a car when you are eleven years old?
- What do you have to do before you are allowed to drive by yourself?
- Who decides this and why do they make that decision?
- Write the students' contributions on the whiteboard.

DEVELOPING

Teaching tips

- Students need to be comfortable with drawing demand and supply diagrams and showing changes caused by shifts in demand and supply diagrams.
- It would be useful to check on understanding of price elasticity of demand before starting this unit.
- There are many issues covered in this unit that are suitable for class discussion. Students need to use their economics in these discussions rather than giving an opinion.
- It would be useful to collect articles from newspapers and magazines that illustrate these issues, which can be used in your teaching and would also give a local context.

Teacher guidance for the in-text questions in this unit

Many of the in-text questions require students to use diagrams. To ensure students have access to accurate diagrams these are drawn underneath the in-text questions with an explanation. When this is the case there will be a reference to the Student's Book. One approach would be first to go through the diagrams and the explanations in their teaching of the topics and ask the students to practise the diagrams and explain them verbally. The in-text questions could then be set under test conditions.

1. The diagram and explanation on setting the maximum price below the equilibrium price is shown in the Student's Book.
2. The explanation is shown after the question in the Student's Book.
3. The explanation is shown after the question in the Student's Book.
4. The Student's Book suggests one response to this question. It comments that a government may want to stop very low wages being paid and therefore introduce a minimum wage to make all employers pay at least this decent wage rate to workers. This is explained in Figure 2.11.2. Students could consider other examples such as setting minimum prices for food to increase the income of farmers producing food. The EU had a Common Agricultural Policy which increased the income of farmers by setting minimum prices. As a demand and supply diagram shows, this would lead to oversupply and was criticised for being inefficient, led to higher prices for consumers and the imposition of tariffs on imports to keep food prices artificially high.
5. The student would need to refer to Figure 2.11.2 and the explanation in the Student's Book.
6. Although an explanation is provided in the Student's Book after the question, this is more suited to an in-class discussion question where students could mention unemployment. It would be useful for you to consider consequences in other markets such as using minimum prices for food.
7. This question could be used to check on understanding of elasticity. One method would be to get students to work in pairs on this question or get students to come to the whiteboard to draw the diagrams needed to answer this question. These diagrams can be found in Figure 2.11.5 in the Student's Book.
8. Students would need to recall their work on elasticity of demand. They need to mention that when PED is inelastic the percentage fall in demand is less than the percentage increase in price while when PED is elastic the percentage fall in demand is greater than the percentage increase in price. This means that by imposing a tax on a product which has an inelastic demand government would maximise revenue.
9. The standard answer would be that increasing an indirect tax on cigarettes would lead to an increase in tax revenues because it has an inelastic demand. Chocolate is perceived as having an elastic demand and so raising indirect taxes on chocolate would lead to tax revenue falling. However, some students might come to a different conclusion by pointing to evidence that demand for cigarettes at higher prices could become elastic. If governments wanted to stop people smoking they could increase indirect taxes to the point that demand becomes elastic. They could also increase taxes on chocolate or sugary drinks to reduce consumption. The analysis would then lead to a question about the purpose of the tax. Is the government using taxes to cut demand or raise revenue? It could be useful to have a class discussion on these issues. This would prepare the students for the next section in the unit.
10. An explanation is provided in the Student's Book after the question.
11. This could be used as a class discussion before looking at the section on Government microeconomic policy measures in Unit 2.11 in the Student's Book.
12. This could be part of the discussion referred to in in-text question 11. Suggestions are given in the Student's Book after the question.

Case study: Challenges in waste management for India

Students often do not appreciate the organisational issues behind rubbish collection. They tend to think of waste as something that is removed from the household. It might be useful to discuss the issue of waste management before setting the case study.

Suggested answers to questions:

1. Garbage is a problem for local governments as they have to deal with the increasing amounts of rubbish at the same time as keeping cities clean. As a result, local governments dump waste outside the city in landfill sites.
2. Consuming a demerit good creates negative spillover effects. The waste produced by individuals in a city will reduce the benefits to others in the form of rubbish outside people's homes, which is unsightly and unhealthy. This means that the local government has to remove and treat the waste which leads to residents paying for the service through their taxes.

3. The government is encouraging recycling which means that rubbish has to be sorted before it reaches the landfill site. The case study suggests that 80% of waste could be recycled.
4. Experience in some countries suggests that encouraging recycling does reduce the impact on landfill. However, recycling must be made easy to do for households and firms through the provision of different containers for household items such as paper, glass and plastics. Other countries encourage consumers to return their glass and plastic bottles to the shops where they bought them and they pay a bottle deposit which is returned when the consumer returns the bottle. Other countries fine households if they include recyclable items in their general waste. Without adopting similar schemes, it is unlikely to be effective.

Additional activity

Mixed market economy quiz

Students need to devise ten quiz questions with answers based on this unit. They must make sure their questions cover key topics. Divide the class into two groups.

Issue each student with ten blank cards. Each student should number the cards and write their name on one side. They then need to devise a two-part question for each card about a key topic relating to a mixed economic system. The first part of the question should ask for a fact. The second part should ask for an explanation or an example. On the reverse of the card, they should write an appropriate two-part answer to their question. An explanation should be short and concise. If examples are requested, the student must provide two or three alternative examples.

Example questions are:

- What are maximum price controls?
- What would be the effect of a maximum price on food?

It would be useful to divide up the learning outcome bullets amongst the students so that there is a spread of topics.

For the quiz, arrange students in two equal teams. Ask one student to keep score using a suitable score-card. Player 1 for Team A asks one of their questions to Player 1 of Team B, who needs to answer **both parts of** the question. Discuss the answer with the group and ask the group to determine if the answer is correct. If either part of the answer is not correct, the question passes to all players in Team B to answer.

Player 1 of Team A then confirms the answer they had devised. (Correct answers if the student's answer was not wholly correct.)

Under the appropriate team's score column, the scorekeeper records two marks for each correct part of the answer given by the original player answering the question. If play passes to the whole team, only one mark is recorded for each part of the question.

Play then passes to Player 1 of Team B, who asks their question to Player 1 of Team A, and so on.

Total the scores at the end of the quiz to see which team won.

After the quiz, collect students' question/answer cards and check that answers provided were correct. Return any incorrect answers to students and ask them to change their answer to the correct one.

APPLYING

Project work

The project work is based on investigating how countries such as China and Mexico deal with the problem of road congestion. You will need to help provide sources of information.

In China, after the famous 2010 gridlock, Beijing announced a series of drastic measures to tackle the city's traffic jams, including limiting the number of new plates issued to passenger cars to 20,000 a month and barring cars of non-Beijing plates from entering areas within the Fifth Ring Road during rush hours. In mega-cities like Mexico City, one of the world's most congested cities, more cars on the road bring greater traffic congestion, pollution and road safety challenges. Road traffic incidents were responsible for 954 deaths in Mexico City in 2012, while motorized vehicles are responsible for 49 percent of greenhouse gases emitted in the area. These problems are set to worsen as the city's vehicle ownership grows at 4.2 percent annually.

These problems are well-documented, but new research highlights another issue with Mexico City's car congestion: it creates economic costs to businesses and their employees.

Expected outcomes

- Analysis of road traffic congestion in China and Mexico
- Solutions to road traffic congestion in China and Mexico
- Analysis of effectiveness of solutions
- Commentary of applicability of solutions within your country
- Presentation of findings to the class

Knowledge check questions

Ask students to complete the Knowledge check questions at the end of Unit 2.11 in the Student's Book.

Checking progress

Ask students to complete the Check your progress section in the Student's Book.

Chapter review

Ask students to complete the Chapter review questions at the end of Chapter 2 in the Student's Book.

3.1 Money and banking

Learning objectives

By the end of this unit, students should be able to:

- describe the different forms that money may take
- explain the functions of money
- explain the characteristics of money
- analyse the role and importance of central banks for government, producers and consumers
- discuss the role and importance of commercial banks for government, producers and consumers.

Key terms

Money; barter; medium of exchange; measure of value/unit of account; standard for deferred payment; store of value; central bank; commercial bank; quantitative easing; lender of last resort; base rate; rate of interest/interest rate.

STARTING POINT

These questions are designed to get the students thinking about money. They encourage students to think about what money actually is, rather than thinking of money simply as something in their pocket that they buy things with. Place the students in pairs and ask them to discuss the four questions. Get the pairs to write the answers on a whiteboard/flipchart and discuss them as a class, aiming to achieve class agreement.

Suggested answers:

1. money: bank notes and coins, although allow gold bars; bank accounts and cheques are 'near money' (students do not need to use this term) which should lead to discussion as to the difference with money.
2. Likely suggestions could be: issued by governments; easily exchanged for goods; do not go bad; relatively scarce.
3. Likely suggestions: issued by the government/central bank; legally recognised.
4. Answers include: saving, investment, giving to charity/donations; giving as a gift.

EXPLORING

Ask the students to discuss the questions in pairs and then to present their ideas to the class.

For question 1, ideally the students could research this using the internet. If this is not feasible then they could be shown an actual note or a picture of one. With question 2 each pair needs to decide on just one idea and why they use the money in this way. For question 3 put the ideas on the whiteboard and then challenge them by asking 'why' or 'what problems might there be'.

Suggested answers:

1. Depending on the value of the note, you might have difficulty using it for public transport; in small shops and services such as cinemas. Other ideas should be allowed if valid.
2. Possible answers include: save, for instance in a bank account; spend on, for example, books, sport, leisure, food; give it to someone in need. Each pair must decide which they would ultimately do.
3. Possible answers include: offer my goods/services in exchange for what I want (barter, but do not expect this term at this stage).
4. Answers could include: to buy something you do not have enough money for; to set up a business; to bridge the gap between income and spending.

DEVELOPING

Teaching tips

1. As an introduction try to show the students different forms of money that have existed. If you are able to find pictures of unusual forms of money you could either display these on the walls or show them on a screen.
2. Students often confuse the four functions of money with the characteristics of money. Make sure students are confident about the differences. The Additional activity below (Red and green game) can be used. For the characteristics students could revisit notes made on the 'starting point' questions.
3. Students are less likely to be familiar with central banks than the banks they see in the local town. More time should be allocated to this part of the unit. One approach would be to start with a general session in which students suggest possible functions of the central bank. Ask them to complete the first part of the Project Work task 1: 'Research on the internet the central bank of your country. Find out its functions'. Encourage them to discuss what each function means to ensure understanding before they complete Task 1.
4. Although students may be more familiar with commercial banks, consider starting with a general session to check their understanding. It may be necessary to talk in more depth about some of the basic ideas such as taking in savings, lending money to individuals and firms or providing services to firms. If possible invite in someone from one of the local banks to talk about what the bank does. If there are several banks in your locality either yourself or some of the students could visit them and collect leaflets on what the bank offers. These could then be used to produce a display entitled: 'Similarities and differences between banks', so that all the students could see and use them.

Additional activity

Red and green game

The aim is to make sure that students are confident about the differences between the functions of money and the characteristics of money.

Create a series of flashcards, each with a function of money or a characteristic of money written on it. Use the lists of functions and characteristics of money in the Student's Book to create the flashcards.

Make red and green plain cards for the students. Make enough cards for each student to have one red card and one green card.

Procedure:

Give each student one red and one green card.

Show the flashcards in a random order to the class. Students hold up a red card if a function is displayed and a green card if a characteristic is displayed.

Additional activity

Functions of money game

Use Activity sheets 3.1a and 3.1b.

When students have completed work on the functions of money they can check their understanding by playing the 'Functions of money game'. The objective is to reinforce the learning on the functions of money.

This activity is to be completed in pairs.

PREPARATION

Make two copies of **Activity sheet 3.1a** for every pair of students in the class on card. Cut up the sets of cards and store in closed plastic wallets ready to distribute to the students.

Create a random selection spin wheel for each pair of students in the class. Do this by backing the spin wheel in **Activity sheet 3.1b** on cardboard and cutting it out. Then, using a split pin, make it so that they wheel spins freely.

PROCEDURE

1. Divide the class into pairs and distribute two sets of cut up currency cards and a spin wheel to each pair of students.
2. Students shuffle the cards and divide them up equally between them. They then place the cards face down in a pile on the table in front of them.
3. One student spins the wheel which randomly selects a function of money: medium of exchange; store of value; unit of account; standard for deferred payment.
4. Each player reveals the top currency card of their pile by placing it face up on the table in front of them. The player with the card which fulfils the selected function of money the best wins both cards and adds them to the bottom of their pile. Before taking the cards, the winning student must justify why their currency card is best making reference to the characteristics of money. For example, if the spin wheel picks 'medium of exchange' and players turn over currency cards revealing 'Cow' and 'Gold coins', the player revealing the 'gold coins' card wins as it more satisfactorily fulfils the function of a medium of exchange. The winning player could justify this by saying that gold coins are more likely to be *accepted* by more people than a cow, so it fulfils the function of medium of exchange better.
5. If players cannot agree on which currency card is better or if the cards are the same, they turn over the next card in their pile. You could also mediate and resolve disputes. The winning student is the player to accumulate all of the cards.

Suggested answers to in-text question 1:

Hopefully at this stage students will be able to make reference to the characteristics or functions of money. Students should be able to make comments on: the profitability of money as against having to carry goods around; money not requiring 'double coincidence of wants', students should explain what this means and the problems with it; and the problems of fixing values for goods and services unlike money which has a face value. They might also refer to the fact that money does not 'go off' unlike, for example, fruit.

Suggested answers to in-text question 2:

Standard for deferred payment enables people to borrow money and pay it back at a later date. This is one of the four functions of money. The other functions are: medium of exchange; measure of value (or unit of account); and store of value. Students need to judge 'to what extent' it is an important function. They might say that all the functions are important, and why. Alternatively, they might argue that the medium of exchange and the unit of account enable money to replace barter and for goods/services to be easily exchanged. To be able to buy now and pay later is perhaps less important, but without this function trade would be greatly reduced as people would always have to have the money before purchase.

Case study

Food as money

- If the students have not seen pictures of 'strange forms of money', provide some photos for them.
- Before starting the case study, check that the students have understood the types, functions and characteristics of money

Suggested answers:

1. Food would be an example of commodity money.
2. The only characteristics which can be accepted are: acceptable because it is possible everyone would accept it; divisible, possibly, if one could use portions of food and have bigger and smaller portions or devise a system such as ten grapes equals one orange; and recognizable as people would all know what an orange was.

3. The four functions of money are: medium of exchange; measure of value (or unit of account); standard for deferred payment and store of value. Answers must address the 'extent to which' food fulfills each function:
   - medium of exchange: this might be possible as goods could be paid for in food, but as it is, for example, not durable people might not be willing to accept it when it would fail
   - measure of value: this would be very difficult as food as money is not far from barter and would raise issues of how much or which food in exchange for a good
   - standard for deferred payment and store of value: these would be almost impossible as food deteriorates in value over time

   Problems such as the possible lack of scarcity (the ease of someone growing the food themselves) would render food as unsuitable for any of the functions.

Suggested answers to in-text question 3:

Students are only asked for the advantages. Independence means that the central bank is free from any political, legislative, or executive control by the government. It also indicates that it is free from private or group control and serves the needs of the country as a whole and not those of individuals. It is free to carry out its tasks without external pressure that may hinder economic progress and monitoring. Without independence, these tasks will be manipulated to suit individual government or political needs which could possibly lead to financial problems.

APPLYING

Project work

Tasks 1 and 2 can be integrated into the appropriate parts of the unit as indicated above.

Task 1: this could be divided into three separate tasks. In this case each group should make a presentation to the class.

Task 2: divide the class into however many banks are to be investigated. The groups should report back to the whole class. Write a summary on a board.

Extension: This question could be set as an essay or could be used for class discussion. Note that the question uses the wording 'how important' so a conclusion on this is required. Students could use the Student's Book to identify and explain the roles of the commercial banks, such as: taking savings; making loans; and transmitting monetary policy. As it says 'the economy', it would be expected that reference is made to individuals/households, firms and the government. Students should be encouraged to place the answer in the context of their country.

Expected outcomes:

- Familiarity with finding information on banks and banking
- Increased confidence and ability in presenting ideas and arguing for them

Knowledge check questions

Ask students to complete the knowledge check questions at the end of Unit 3.1 of the Student's Book.

Checking progress

Ask students to complete the Check your progress section in the Unit 3.1 of the Student's Book.

3.2 Households

Learning objectives

By the end of this unit, students should be able to:

- explain the factors that influence household spending, such as saving, borrowing, rate of interest and confidence
- explain how these factors may change over time
- analyse how these factors affect different types of households.

Key terms

Household; income; spending; saving; borrowing; rate of inflation; real income; direct tax; indirect tax; disposable income.

STARTING POINT

While all students are members of some form of household, they are unlikely to have given much thought to what influences spending, saving and borrowing. One approach would be to get the students to discuss the questions in pairs for about ten to fifteen minutes, then get feedback putting the answers on a whiteboard/ flipchart and discuss the similarities and differences. Alternatively, each pair could join with another pair and exchange ideas. The overall aim is to get the students to think about what they have done or would do before moving on to the content of the unit. There are no 'right' answers to the first four questions, but the responses need to be specific and able to be justified, for example: 'I would spend it on a new DVD, because I have been wanting to buy one, but have not had enough money and my parents would not give me any more money'. Question 5 does have specific answers: spending is related to medium of exchange, unit of account (sets the price of the good) and standard for deferred payment; saving to store of value; and borrowing to standard for deferred payment. Students can also suggest unit of account and medium of exchange.

EXPLORING

Again, working in pairs, the students should come up with ideas for these questions. Get the students to report back to the class on their ideas.

Suggested answers:

1. The basic answer is: increases until they retire then decreases as they use savings to support expenditure. With any response, challenge it with 'why'.
2. Students need to be able to justify where they are going to save the $1000. One approach is for each pair to put their idea and why on a sticky note and place this on the whiteboard. The class can then place the ideas in rank order to decide whether any one idea was better than the others.
3. If you use money in one way, then you have sacrificed whatever else you could have done with it: if you buy a DVD, you cannot go to the cinema, or if you spend it, you cannot save it and earn interest. One approach would be a class discussion which would allow both revision of opportunity cost and a chance to see how it can be applied in the use of money.

DEVELOPING

Teaching tips

- As a class, ask what big items of expenditure have their families bought in the last year. Make a list on the whiteboard. Ask them what influenced this spending and what they think would happen if their income rose or fell. This could be repeated in a similar way for saving.
- To help students understand 'deciles', you could use a real example, such as class marks in a previous exercise or the amount they spent last week.

- Changes in spending over time: ask students to find out from any adults they know what they spent their money on when they were the students' age. Ask them to draw up a table to show spending patterns and then to explain why there have been changes.

Additional activity

Survey of household expenditure

Use Activity sheet 3.2

Before starting this unit, ask the students to collect information on what their household has spent money on in the previous week. You could use the survey sheet in Activity sheet 3.2. Get the students to agree on the categories. Two have been inserted to give them a start.

Collate the information so that the students can see similarities and differences. Ask the students why they think these similarities and differences exist.

Suggested answer to in-text question 1:

Zero interest rates should discourage saving, as they have to pay money to banks in order to save, and encourage spending, both because saving is not worth doing and because borrowing money will be very cheap. However, zero interest rates could mean the Japanese economy is not doing well so people might save more because they are worried about what might happen (lack of confidence) and spend less. People would want to find institutions which offered positive interest rates or they might just save it at home. The effects might depend on factors such as age or total income.

Case Study

Increasing financial inclusion in Africa

- Make sure that the students know what is meant by mobile banking and that they understand there are different ways of doing this. Check they know what is meant by financial inclusion.
- Ask the students whether any of them use mobile banking or if their parents do. Do they use computers for this or smartphones and apps?

Suggested answers:

1. A chain of branch banks costs money to build and would take time. In rural developing countries where the population is scattered, it would be difficult for people to access the banks thus limiting customers. This could be because of poor transport networks.
2. 2011 – 42%; 2014 – 75%. Increase in percentage with access 33%. Percentage change between the two years:
   $\frac{33}{42}$ x 100 = 78.57%
3. Financial inclusion is enabling people to have access to formal financial services. Other ways could be setting up a chain of branch banks or providing bank vans to take branch banking to where people live – allow any valid idea, but as the question says 'best' there should be at least two other ways in addition to mobile banking. Students should set out the advantages and disadvantages of each method for their country, such as: branches allow people to talk through issues face-to-face, but are expensive to build and run; mobile vans bring banking directly to where people live, but depend on good roads and are expensive as they might arrive and find no-one wants to use them that day; mobile banking can reach everyone wherever they are, but it assumes people have the relevant technology and that they can get an internet connection.

Case study

Saving and spending variations

- Tell the students before they start that they are not expected to have knowledge of Latin America or Asia in order to answer questions 1 and 2. They need to provide sensible suggestions which are explained.
- For question 3 students can use the source of the case study or any survey produced by their country.

Suggested answers:

1. They have had to borrow large sums of money in the past to enable them to maintain expenditure and are now having to pay it back; or real income has fallen due to inflation; borrowing for housing is a bigger part of their expenditure.
2. Real incomes are higher so they can spend and save more; or goods are cheaper allowing more to be bought, but also more money left over to save; or borrowing is cheap so this increases spending power, while their culture encourages saving.
3. Having completed the research, students can produce a written account making sure they offer analysis and address 'the extent to which'. Alternatively, it could be used as the basis of class discussion.

Suggested answer to in-text question 2:

One pattern is that young adults may save more in order to afford their own housing; then spend most of their income as they have a family; save more when their children leave home; and finally spend more than they save after retirement. The key point is not the precise pattern, which depends on assumptions like having children, but to 'analyse' what factors, such as changes in income, influence the spending/ saving pattern.

Suggested answer to in-text question 3:

Although Group 10 people may spend more on individual items such as cars, housing, holidays, these are not everyday items. This gives them more money 'left over' at the end of a week/month to save. Group 1 spends more than its income, while Group 2 can only just cover their spending leaving only a little money for saving. This is because everyone needs items such as food or heating or clothes.

Suggested answer to in-text question 3 extension:

Students need first to research the savings rates of the population by income groups. This should be available online through government statistics (or use another country if this proves impossible). They then need to produce a graph similar to Figure 3.2.1 in the Student's Book.

Suggested answer to in-text question 4:

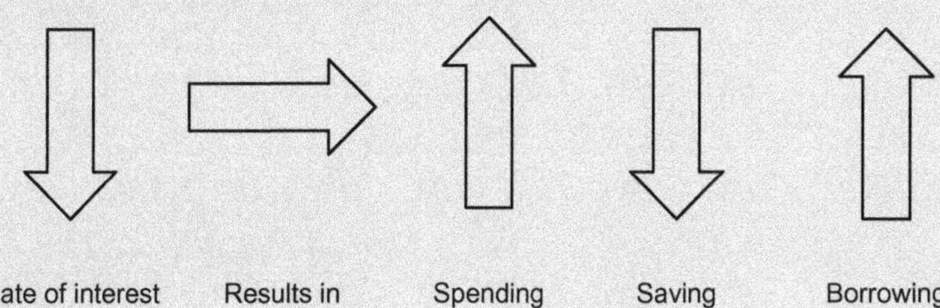

Figure TG 3.2.1

Explanation: this shows that as the rate of interest falls, people will spend and borrow more and save less. With lower interest rates, the opportunity cost of spending as against saving falls, saving becomes less worthwhile, and it is cheaper to borrow.

Extension activity

Ask the students to research the use of credit cards in your country:

- How many credit cards have been issued?
- How many different types of credit card are there, for example Visa and Mastercard?
- How much is owed on credit cards (that is, has not been paid off each month)? If this is difficult, then students could ask adults they know whether they normally pay off their credit cards every month.
- How widely are they used? Students could carry out their own local research asking adults such as parents, teachers and older friends/siblings.

APPLYING

Project work

This is an opportunity for students to focus on their country and changes over different periods of time. Some of question 1 may already have been covered, but now is the chance to bring it all together and to develop a whole class picture of the differences. The second question focuses in on their lifetime. The students could pool their findings, perhaps using graphical representations, and then discuss what has happened and why. Lastly, there is a chance to discuss as a class how spending changes in their country.

Expected outcomes

- Greater understanding of different spending and saving patterns across generations
- Being able to relate changes in interest rates to spending, saving and borrowing
- Being able to graphically represent data and interpret it
- Greater experience in discussion and creating a supported argument

Knowledge check questions

Ask students to complete the knowledge check questions at the end of Unit 3.2 in the Student's Book.

Checking progress

Ask students to complete the Check your progress section in the Student's Book.

3.3 Workers

Learning objectives

By the end of this unit, students should be able to:

- define what is meant by wages and non-wages
- explain how wages and non-wage factors affect choice of occupation
- analyse the determination of wages through supply and demand
- explain how relative bargaining power can determine wages
- analyse how the minimum wage influences wage determination
- explain how else government policy can help determine wages
- define earnings
- analyse the effects of changes in demand and supply on the labour market
- explain how changes in relative bargaining strengths, discrimination and government policy can all influence differences in earnings
- explain the advantages and disadvantages for workers, firms and the economy of the division of labour/specialisation.

Key terms

Wage; wage rate; salary; basic rate; earnings; non-wage factors; derived demand; minimum wage; living wage; division of labour; specialisation.

STARTING POINT

This is an opportunity for the students to start to think about another group of people, in this case workers. The first two questions should be done in pairs. In the case of the second question, the pairs could say which they chose. Once all of the decisions are in, ask each group to justify their choice. The third question could be the opportunity for a class discussion. Divide the students into two groups and give them some time to prepare their case. Tell them that extra credit will be awarded for the use of economic ideas. When both sides have made their presentation, open it out to general discussion. The main points made in the presentations and the discussion could be summarised on a whiteboard.

EXPLORING

Again, working in pairs, the students should come up with ideas for these questions. Get the students to report back on their ideas to the class.

Suggested answers:

1. Students may suggest ideas such as: pay, holidays, family tradition, couldn't think what else to do, wanted to work with children/young people, gained the right level of qualification. Put their ideas on the whiteboard. While you will undoubtedly be asked why you became a teacher, the purpose is to allow students to see that there are many different reasons why people might choose a particular job. Keep this list for use when discussing wage and non-wage factors.

2. Ask the students to draw a supply and demand diagram to explain their answer.

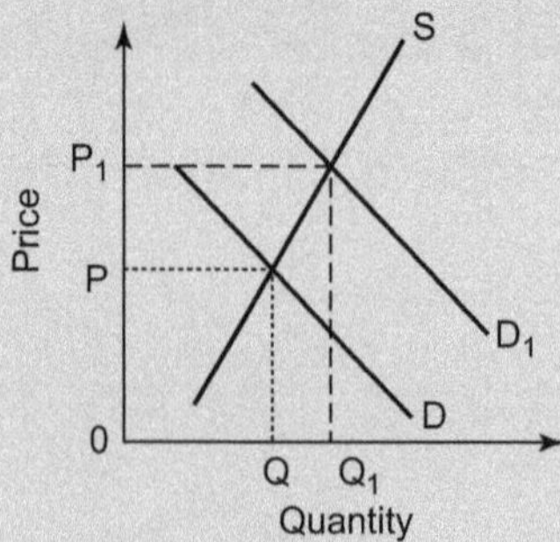

Figure TG 3.3.1

Increase in demand is shown by an outward shift of the demand curve from D to D_1. This results in an increase in pay from P to P_1 and an increase in the quantity of teachers from Q to Q_1. Ask one of the students to draw their diagram on the whiteboard and to explain it.

3. Students may suggest: greater demand; less supply; more skilled; more powerful trade unions; higher positions. Ask one pair of students to explain to the class their ideas then open it up for other suggestions. Create a list on the whiteboard.

DEVELOPING

Teaching tips

1. Use the list from 'Exploring question 1' to help students distinguish between wage and non-wage factors before starting the section on non-wage factors. Ask them whether they would consider non-wage factors when choosing a job and, if so, which ones and why.
2. It is very important that students feel able to use diagrams to explain changes in pay. Emphasise this skill on every relevant occasion. You could use Activity 1 below.
3. Students often confuse 'specialisation' and 'division of labour'. The Student's Book p 141 refers to these in terms of teaching. Get the students to extend this to the whole school so they have a clear pattern of who are specialists and where division of labour is used. They can then extend this to the economy and work as a whole.

Additional activity

Falal's and Antonio's pay

Use Activity sheet 3.3

This is designed to help students gain greater understanding of the difference between being paid a wage and a salary. Provide Activity sheet 3.3 for students to complete in class or as homework.

Answers

1. $\frac{42\,000}{12}$ = \$3500 a month (does not matter how many days there are in a month)
2. **a)** \$20 x 35 = \$700 a week x 52 = \$36 400

   b) \$700 x 4 = \$2800
3. Falal is paid more a year \$42000 against \$36 400 and also for a 4-week month \$3500 against \$2800.
4. \$25 x 120 = \$3000 + \$36 400 = \$39 400

Suggested answer to in-text question 1:

The question says 'to what extent', so students should carry out research in the school to find evidence for their answer. It would be good practice for them if they converted their responses into percentages before writing their answers. Alternatively, the students' information could be brought together through, for example, collating it on a whiteboard and used for a class discussion.

Suggested answer to in-text question 2:

A basic answer is shown in Figure TG 3.3.2 below.

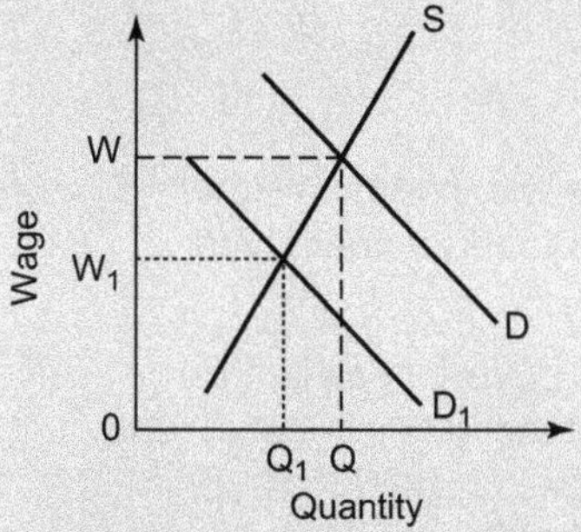

Figure TG 3.3.2

If the factory replaced labour with machines then the demand for workers would fall from D to D_1 leading to a fall in pay from W to W_1.

This answer can be extended by students arguing that while the above may be true, it may be necessary to employ highly skilled workers to control these machines. This is shown in Figure TG 3.3.3 below.

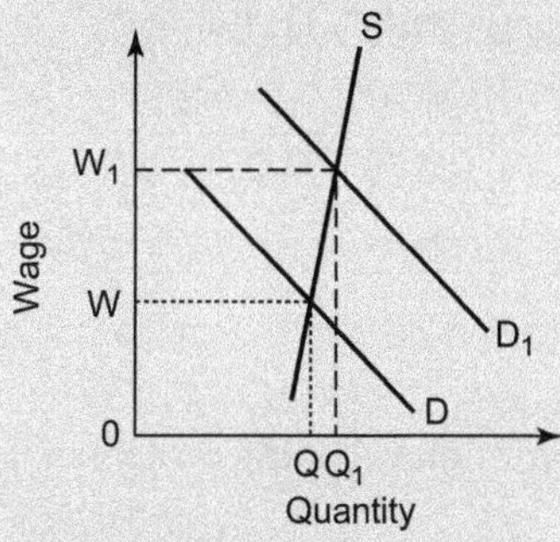

Figure TG 3.3.3

The highly skilled workers may be in short supply so their supply line is inelastic. This means that as demand increases, D to D_1, their pay increases by a large amount from W to W_1.

Suggested answer to in-text question 3:

This will depend on the country, but expect reference to some of: minimum wage legislation; direct employment which gives benchmarks for other employers and employees; wages councils; moral persuasion through statements/election promises; maximum wage levels. Each point needs to be explained, for example:

- Minimum wage legislation forces employers to pay at least that wage. It is likely that higher wage earners will demand more in order to retain the difference in wage rate. In this way many wage levels have risen.
- Government ministers can make statements expressing concern at the high pay of, for example, chief executives and threatening to bring in laws to regulate pay. This can lead to shareholders and customers putting pressure on firms to pay less or at least limit pay rises.

Case study

Guatemala increases minimum wage for agricultural workers

- Make sure that the students have a clear understanding of the idea of a minimum wage.
- Ask the students to find out what the minimum wage is in their country.
- Ask the students to find out how much agricultural workers in their country are paid.

Suggested answers:

1. The lowest wage level that an employer may legally pay their workers.
2. $\frac{5.03}{81.87}$ x 100 = 6.14%
3. Higher wages will lead to a fall in demand as employers replace workers with capital. Higher wages will allow workers to purchase more and/or better goods, such as food, so their lives improve.
4. Higher wages are likely to increase the costs of exports. This could lead buyers to switch to cheaper alternative supplies so the Guatemalan producers receive less income. This could lead to them making a loss and going out of business. In addition, higher wages for the lowest paid can lead to better paid workers demanding more money to maintain their differential thus pushing costs even higher. This would reinforce the loss of profit.
5. Extension: Note 'the extent to which' part of the question means that students need to come to a conclusion in terms of their economy. Benefits could include: workers might have a greater incentive to work hard thus increasing output, which could lead to greater sales at home and abroad; workers would spend more thus increasing consumption which would help the economy to grow; workers might spend more money on health care thus increasing the health of the economy and healthier workers are able to work more and take less time off work; could afford to send their children to school raising literacy rates and increasing the skills of the workforce. Problems could include: higher cost reducing exports and increasing imports; employers cannot afford the wages so make workers unemployed and/or go out of business or move abroad.

Suggested answer to in-text question 4:

Answers will depend on which two individuals or groups are chosen. The answer below is an example of how this question should be approached.

The Chief Executive of Z Motors is paid $1m a year. The workers making the cars are paid on average $40 000 a year. One reason is that there are relatively few people able to become Chief Executive of Z Motors, but there are potentially plenty of people able to become car workers. Another factor could be that worker representation is weak so workers are unable to get big pay rises, while the Chief Executive has greater power to get higher pay. In addition, the Chief Executive has far more responsibility than a car worker. If the Chief Executive makes a poor decision then the firm can lose millions of dollars and possibly go out of business. If a car worker makes a mistake it can be put right before the car leaves the factory so has fewer consequences. The Chief Executive is paid much more because of this greater responsibility.

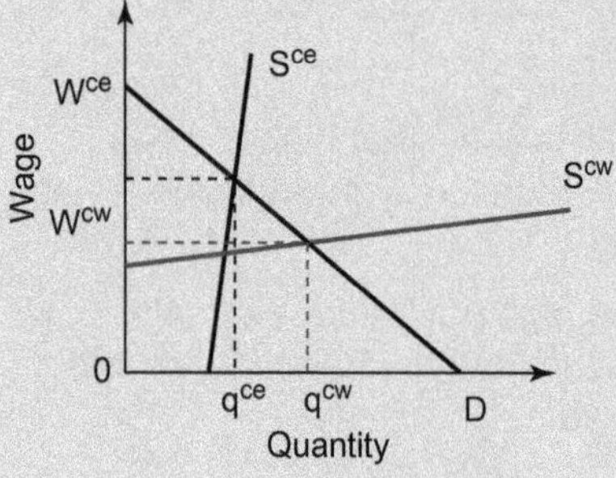

Figure TG 3.3.4

The diagram shows an inelastic supply of chief executives and an elastic supply of car workers. This leads to the former being paid w^{ce} while the car workers are paid w^{cw}.

Case study

Specialisation and the car factory

- Ensure students have a clear understanding of the division of labour – see Teaching tip 3 above.

Suggested answers:

1. The process by which each worker specialises in, or concentrates on, one particular task.
2. They are doing the same task every day so lose interest.
3. Tell the students they cannot repeat boredom. Answers can include: deskilling – by specialising, workers lose the skills to do other types of work and are less able to respond to changes in demand; lack of job security – if there is a fall in demand for a particular product, workers may find it difficult to get another job because they do not have the necessary skills or experience. This may also occur because their work can be replaced by machines.
4. Advantages include: higher output; higher productivity; higher quality; bigger market; greater revenue and profit; economies of scale; and time saving. Disadvantages include: a rise in costs; dependency; failure of exchange; and high labour turnover.

   Students should explain at least three advantages and two disadvantages and then say why the advantages do or do not outweigh the disadvantages.

Extension activity

Ask students to research a firm in their country which specialises. This could be in the production of a good or a service.

Students should then make a presentation to the class of their findings explaining why the firm specialises.

APPLYING

Project work

The first task involves individual work, but students could present their findings as a chart. With the second task, students should interview a different person from anyone interviewed in other activities in this unit. Note that the question asks about the adult's present job, not their choice of occupation. Ask students to feed back to the class in order to see what the factors were. With the third task, it is important for the students to use diagrams in their explanation. The extension task offers a good opportunity for a debate as to why there is a gap. Students could consider factors such as: opportunities; education; cultural expectations; full-time and part-time work; how appointments are made.

Expected outcomes

- Greater understanding of factors affecting pay in your country
- Increase in research and presentation skills
- Greater understanding of why men tend to be paid more than women

Knowledge check questions

Ask students to complete the knowledge check questions at the end of Unit 3.3 in the Student's Book.

Checking progress

Ask students to complete the Check your progress section in the Student's Book.

3.4 Trade unions

Learning objectives

By the end of this unit, students should be able to:

- define what is a trade union
- explain the role of trade unions in the economy, including collective bargaining, employment protection and influencing government policy
- explain the factors influencing the strength of trade unions
- analyse the advantages and disadvantages of trade union membership for workers, firms and the government.

Key terms

Trade union; collective bargaining; industrial action; health and safety; equal opportunities.

STARTING POINT

This is a good opportunity for the students to discuss these issues as a whole class or in groups of perhaps four or five. As trade unions often have some characteristics associated with clubs/societies, this provides a starting point for why people join organisations. From this, the students can consider whether as a member of a school they have any power or influence and thus how could they try to be more influential. Again, ordinary members of any organisation can struggle to make their voice heard. Lastly, the students consider the question of rules. Even the more powerful members of an organisation are bound by the rules. Either the members, or outside regulatory/legal bodies, can apply the rules to ensure that those running the organisation comply.

EXPLORING

Again, working in pairs the students should come up with ideas for these questions. Ask the students to report back on their ideas to the class.

Suggested answers:

1. Students are likely to suggest: Head/Deputy Head Teacher; other teachers; parents; governors/school owners; pupils; government. This could be seen as a pure discussion or the student pairs could first do some research and then bring their findings to a class discussion. Get them to think about the relative influence of the groups they identify.
2. Students may suggest among other ideas: new classroom furniture; new equipment such as computers; improved lighting, heating, ventilation; rearrange the seating in classrooms to ensure that all had good sight of the whiteboard; shorten/lengthen how long lessons last. Ask students who come up with ambitious ideas such as building a new school how long they think it will take and would it improve their conditions or those of the students following them.
3. A win-win situation is one that is good for everyone who is involved. All taking part feel they have made gains. All sides in a negotiation should aim for this as they can at least show to the people they represent that they have emerged from the negotiation with some benefits. The opposite is winner takes all. This is likely to lead to discontent from the losers and can cause problems in the future. It may be possible to link this with employer-employee negotiations.

DEVELOPING

Teaching tips

Students are likely to have little real knowledge or understanding of trade unions so it would help if you are able to invite in a trade union official to talk about their role. The local situation may make this difficult to do. A good point for this would be not at the very beginning of the unit, but after a few lessons when students have some knowledge from the course and are able to prepare some useful questions to ask.

At the start of the unit ask students to keep a diary based on what is reported in the media/on the internet about trade union activity. Towards the end of the unit ask the students to tell the class what they have found. Put the results on the whiteboard. What light does this evidence throw on the ideas mentioned in the Student's Book. While in some situations this may be a sensitive topic, try to encourage students to explore the benefits of trade unions.

Additional activity – Homework negotiation

Negotiate with the students when they have to produce a piece of work, for example one of the case studies. Give the students a short time period to decide what their position will be and to choose negotiators. Then carry out the negotiation. Remember to start from a position which is unlikely to be acceptable to the students, such as by tomorrow.

Additional activity – the Blue-Red Game

Use Activity sheets 3.4a and 3.4b

The purpose of the game is to help students understand that successful negotiation is based on the win-win approach and on trusting the other side to keep their word and play their part to achieve mutual success. Do not tell the students this before they play the game.

The students form pairs (teams) and join up with another pair at a table. These pairs are in competition with each other.

Provide each pair with one plain blue and one plain red card which are to be kept out of sight of the other pair and a score sheet.

The blue is a positive card signalling willingness to negotiate and to go for a win-win, while the red card is negative. As in real life, the side who takes a positive approach does not always win.

There are eight rounds of negotiation. Each time the pairs must decide whether to play the blue card or the red card. After Round 4 and Round 6 the two teams can decide to have negotiations (but do not have to) with their opponents. This involves one person from each pair moving to another part of the room for secret negotiations. The negotiators may agree to both play blue, but they may instead in their pairs decide to play red.

When they have decided which card to play, they tell the referee (you) who then informs each table of their outcome (see score sheet).

The winner is the pair in the room who has the most positive points (see score sheet).

At the end: ask the winners what their strategy was; and the team with the least points how this came about.

The winners are likely to be those who operated a win-win policy for all or most of the game.

Suggested answer to in-text question 1:

Unless the worker could not be replaced, it is likely that the employer would tell the worker no pay rise and if you go on strike you will lose your job. Again, unless the worker could get the backing of most of the other workers, the worker would not be able to gain what they had asked for.

Suggested answer to in-text question 2:

If the employers were confident that they could easily replace the workers, which could be the case if they were unskilled and there were many others unemployed, then the outcome would be similar to question 1. Otherwise, the employers will need to negotiate an outcome. This will depend on the relative strength of the workers and the employers.

These two questions could be the basis of a class discussion with half the class preparing question 1 and half question 2.

Case study

The role of trade unions in the Costa Rican banana industry

Ask the students to find out more about the Costa Rican economy.

Ask the students to find out about the banana industry.

Suggested answers:

The International Trade Union Congress has stated that 'In Costa Rica trade unionists are dismissed, intimidated and harassed and workers are strongly discouraged from even joining a trade union'. This type of anti-trade union action would put most workers off as they would fear losing their jobs and possible harm to their family. Due to this type of action, many workers may be unaware of their rights and/or existence of a trade union for them.

The case study says that '2017 has seen an increase in strikes and protests as unskilled workers strive for the opportunity to negotiate collective wages, working hours, working conditions and essential legal protection'. Trade unions could insist that the government enforces the International Labour Organization's 'decent work policy'. They could draw up a list of demands; if these demands were incremental, this could encourage more employers to put them in place. This would put pressure on other employers who are less willing. Industrial action could be effective as the banana industry is important to the economy. This would put pressure not only on the employers, but also on the government to intervene. Students should indicate which of the possible methods would be most effective and/or the order in which they should take place.

Extension task

Ask students to find out about the ILO's 'decent work policy'. Are employers in your country meeting these standards?

Suggested answer to in-text question 3:

Individual workers find it more difficult to improve their situation as they are often in a weak position compared to the employer. Students can make reference to the answer to question 1. In the individual's case, improvements are likely to depend on the goodwill of the employer or how keen they are to retain that worker. Those who belong to trade unions have the strength of the union behind them leading to collective bargaining. In this situation, the union always has the threat of taking industrial action if the employer is not willing to grant some improvements (win-win situation).

Case study

Trade unions in Indonesia

Ask the students what the picture in the case study shows.

Review with the students what is meant by a minimum wage. One of the students could be asked to draw and explain a minimum wage diagram.

Suggested answers:

The case study gives four examples (only two required): unions backing the loser in the presidential election; unions becoming divided; failure to improve working conditions; government excluding them from minimum wage decisions.

New unions have to use direct action as otherwise the employers may not realise they exist and ignore them leading to loss of members. Direct action also makes them seem more energetic than the existing unions thus encouraging people to join, making the union larger and more powerful.

The minimum wage is the lowest legal amount that a worker may be paid.

If trade unions are excluded from the setting of the minimum wage, it is likely that the wage set would be lower than if the unions were involved. This is because the government would be a less powerful counterweight to the wishes of employers which are always to keep costs down.

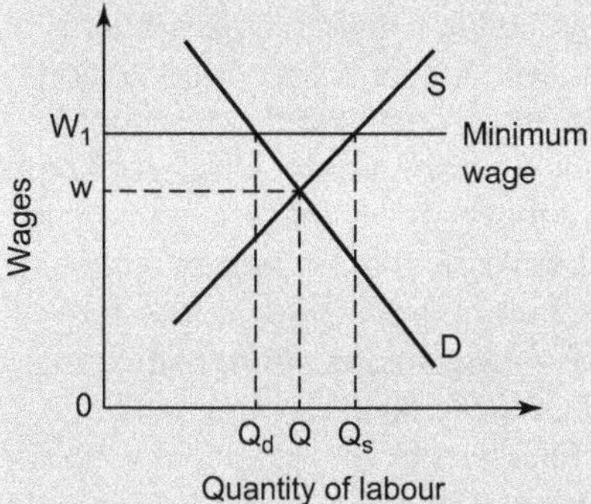

If the unions were involved, the minimum wage would be w_1. Without the unions, it would possibly be set at w, the equilibrium point, meaning no wage rise, or at a point between w and w_1 giving rise to a smaller wage increase than if the unions had been involved.

Suggested answer to in-text question 4:

Skilled workers are more difficult to replace, at least in the short-run, so they have an inelastic supply. The opposite is true for unskilled workers. The skilled workers' trade unions are therefore stronger relative to employers than the trade unions of unskilled workers. This results in employers being more willing to offer higher pay and better conditions to skilled workers. Students may also mention that the products produced by skilled workers are likely to be more valuable/command a higher price so it is easier for employers to pay higher wages and to pass the cost on to consumers.

Case study

Teachers' strike in Argentina

This strike was in March 2017. Ask the students to find out what has happened since then.

Make certain that the students are sure of what is meant by collective bargaining.

Discuss with the students why teachers might or might not go on strike in your country.

Suggested answers:

Collective bargaining is a process of negotiation over pay and conditions between a trade union, representing a group of workers, and employers. In this case, the employer is the government. On one side, therefore, is the government and on the other side are the teachers' unions. They have been negotiating so collective bargaining has been taking place.

Although the pay increase of 21% is very close to the actual rate of inflation, 21.9%, in June 2017, the previous year inflation was 40%. This means that since the last pay rise real wages have been eroded by far more than the current pay offer. Teachers want to both get a real increase in pay, higher than 21.9%, and make up for some of their lost real income from the previous year.

The strength of the unions' position is shown by the fact that the strike has lasted 16 days, demonstrating worker solidarity. This is likely to be supported by parents pressing the government to make an agreement so their children can return to school. The weakness is shown by their inability to make the government give in and the fact that teaching is not an essential industry, so a strike will not cause immediate damage to the economy. Students need to explain the two positions and then comment based on the explanation whether they think the unions have a strong or a weak position.

Suggested answer to in-text question 5:

One important advantage for workers is the role of trade unions in negotiating improved pay and conditions. Trade unions use collective bargaining so have greater power than individual workers. They are more likely, therefore, to be able to gain higher pay, better fringe benefits and working conditions. Collective bargaining is also an advantage to employers. Instead of negotiating with each individual employed, the employer can save time and achieve an agreed situation with just one set of negotiations. A disadvantage of this to the employer is that the pay rise agreed will push up costs leading to either lower profits or rising prices and possibly loss of sales. Workers also benefit from greater job security and protection from unfair dismissal as unions will intervene to try to prevent this or will represent workers in any legal case. Not only will this save workers money, but will make it less likely that an employer would act unfairly. A disadvantage to workers is that an active union could encourage employers to look for ways of substituting capital for labour, thus reducing job opportunities. Equally, unions often restrict entry to the occupation by either shifting the supply curve of labour to the left and/or making it more inelastic. This means that those looking for employment may not find any work. Finally, a major disadvantage to an employer is that a union may take industrial action, such as strikes, leading to the loss of production/sales.

APPLYING

Project work

The first two questions can be looked at together. Students can work individually or in pairs and then report back their findings to the whole class so a picture of union activity and effectiveness in their country emerges. Students could use the information about unions in their book as a starting point. In question 3, the information is shared by the students. The key questions for the discussion are: do there appear to be differences between countries; are there any links between countries with similar amounts/patterns of industrial action; and are there factors in common to explain these similarities/differences?

With the extension task, students need to try to find out about industrial relations within BP, or another multinational firm. Ask the students to look for: media reports and/or social media channels; any comments by BP or their unions; information in BP's annual report. Students should present their report to the class including why they think the unions and workers would, or would not, agree.

Expected outcomes

- Greater understanding of trade unions in their country
- Knowledge of why industrial action is often focussed on certain types of countries or industries
- Realisation that it is possible for firms and unions to have generally good relations even if in negotiations they are inevitably on opposite sides

Knowledge check questions

Ask students to complete the knowledge check questions at the end of Unit 3.4 in the Student's Book.

Checking progress

Ask students to complete the Check your progress section in the Student's Book.

3.5 Firms

Learning objectives

By the end of this unit, students should be able to:

- define primary, secondary and tertiary sectors
- define private and public sectors
- explain how firms are classified by relative size
- analyse the advantages and disadvantages of small firms
- explain the challenges facing small firms and the reasons for their existence
- explain the reason for the existence of small firms
- explain the causes of the growth of firms
- explain the advantages and disadvantages of different types of mergers
- analyse how internal and external economies and diseconomies of scale can affect a firm/industry as the scale of production changes.

Key terms

Primary sector; secondary sector; tertiary sector; private sector; public sector; profit maximisation; merger; takeover; horizontal merger; vertical merger; conglomerate merger; economies of scale; diseconomies of scale; internal economies; external economies; average costs

STARTING POINT

Although students are likely to have an idea what a firm is, they are less likely to have thought about who really owns it. These questions start at that point. Students need to be able to say how they know it is, for example, government owned. Car manufacturers, shipbuilders and oil refiners are all manufacturers in that they turn raw materials or components into a recognisable product that consumers and firms can buy. Firms can be larger or smaller while, within a firm, individual units can also be smaller or larger. For both the questions about the school the key question they need to answer is 'why'. Students will find that many of their answers to these starting points can be used to help their understanding while studying this unit.

EXPLORING

Again, working in pairs the students should come up with ideas for these questions. Ask the students to report back on their ideas to the class.

Suggested answers:

1. The key difference students should be able to identify is that a car manufacturer makes a car while the garage (where petrol is sold and repairs made) provides a service to motorists.
2. One important challenge is getting sufficient finance both to survive and to expand as larger firms find this easier. Secondly, they are often competing in selling similar products, but the large firm produces on a large scale and can afford to sell at a lower price than the small firm. The large firm can pay higher wages whereas the small firm may not have the money to do so. This means that the larger firm can attract higher-qualified staff. To compete, small firms can offer a better and more personalised service than larger firms. They can also offer more specialised products which a large firm may not want to do. (The answer will depend on the firm chosen).
3. This will depend on factors such as the type of school and its location. Students may suggest: build more classrooms so that more students can be accommodated; advertise more widely so that more people know about the school and its achievements; or improve its results so more students are attracted to it.

4. Younger students are taught a smaller range of subjects so do not need as many classrooms or teachers. Younger students are often taught nearly all their lessons by the same teacher in the same classroom so only one classroom is needed for each class. Older students have many lessons in specialist rooms so not all the rooms are used all the time.

DEVELOPING

Teaching tips

- Make the work in this unit as practical as possible. What this means will depend on your school. Get the students to try to classify the firms in your town/area/region by common characteristics before introducing terms such primary or private or small.
- If possible, ask the owner of a small business and/or someone from a large business to visit and talk about, for example, how their business survives and their advantages and disadvantages.
- When introducing economies and diseconomies of scale, you could build on the Starting point and Exploring questions. What are the advantages the students' school has over their primary/first school? What would be the disadvantages if the school grew much larger?

Suggested answers to in-text questions 1–5:

1. Education is a service provided to parents and students. It does not manufacturer anything (secondary) nor extract anything from the land or sea (primary).
2. Extension question: Oil extraction is in the primary sector because it takes oil from the land or the sea – it extracts. Oil refining takes the oil which has been brought to the surface and turns it into different products such as petrol – it makes things. A petrol station provides a service to the motorist by serving them petrol.
3. One definition of a small business is one with less than 50 employees and a turnover under £10 million. The bakery has only 10 workers and it is unlikely to have a turnover of £10m so it qualifies as small.
4. Size depends on the number of people employed, the turnover and the type of industry the firm is in. In many cases, 500 workers would qualify the firm as being large. If its turnover is under £10m then it could qualify as small. If it was a bakery then 500 workers would not be small. In the car industry, a producer with this number would definitely be small compared to firms such as Ford or Toyota.
5. An example response is: Zoe feels that although she cannot employ as many highly qualified people as she would like to, the personal contact that she and her staff have with the customers clearly outweighs this disadvantage. It allows her to know what the customers want and to be able to quickly respond to it.

   The answers will depend on the businesses the students choose for their examples, but expect to see contrasts between advantages and disadvantages with comment on the extent to which the advantages are greater than the disadvantages.

Case study

The Flipkart–Myntra merger

- Ask the students to find out what mergers or takeovers have taken place in recent times in your country.
- Ask them to take one example and to find out why this merger/takeover took place.

Suggested answers:

1. Although they are both in e-commerce, Flipkart's sales are largely electronics while Myntra concentrates on fashion. This points to it being more of a conglomerate merger than a horizontal one. (Ensure that the students explain their choice of integration).

2. The merger will allow the new firm to operate in different markets. This will give them risk-bearing economies of scale because if, for example, fashion sales fell they would still have electronics. Another advantage would be that it would increase the consumer base of the firm as it enables Flipkart to target electronic products at Myntra's customers. These advantages are likely to result in increasing economies of scale and lower average costs. Disadvantages include the difficulty of bringing together what may be two different ways of working. This is likely to be a costly process. Equally, decision making may be more difficult as the managers from the two firms will not fully understand each other's needs. Both of these could lead to diseconomies of scale and rising average cost.
3. Extension: consumers would gain from falling average costs as this could lead to lower prices. Consumers could also gain from having more goods available on one site thus cutting down time needed to find products. On the other hand, if the merger leads to diseconomies this could result in rising prices. Choice may also be reduced as Flipkart was starting to sell fashion items. Now they are one, the firm may concentrate on a more limited range. Students need to analyse two or three advantages and disadvantages and then decide whether or not the consumer would benefit and why.

Extension activity

Ask the students in pairs/small groups to research a merger/takeover in your country and to make a presentation to the class of the advantages/disadvantages to the consumer of this merger.

Suggested answer to in-text question 6:

Technology firms depend on employing well-educated people who will quickly understand the needs of the business. They would look, therefore, to locate in areas with top universities and good schools so as to be easily able to find suitable new employees. One example is the technology firms located near the University of Cambridge in the UK. Technology firms also need easy access to finance in order to be able to expand and launch new products.

APPLYING

Project work

All of the tasks are focused on your country. For the first task, students should compare the classification of firms used by their government with the classification of firms by size by the European Union presented in the Student's Book. Similarly, they should compare the problems faced in their country with the list of challenges facing small firms in the Student's Book. Hopefully, for the third task, students will be able to find examples of mergers in their country though a merger between a firm in their country and one abroad will be fine. If they cannot, then accept ones elsewhere. Concentration of firms can be either firms in the same/similar industry such as Silicon Valley in the USA, or firms where there is a high density of various industries. The advantages and disadvantages are likely to be external economies/diseconomies of scale.

For the first extension task, students may choose a firm of any size. If the students are investigating a wide variety, then this should result in some interesting comparisons resulting from the presentations.

For the second extension task, students need to consider the economy as a whole. This is where the World Bank's website will prove a useful starting point from which they could then conduct some primary research using local firms.

Expected outcomes

- Greater knowledge of firms in your country and in the local area
- Better understanding of mergers and takeovers
- Opportunity to see how economies and diseconomies apply to the real world
- Increase in their research and presentation skills

Knowledge check questions

Ask students to complete the knowledge check questions at the end of Unit 3.5 in the Student's Book.

Checking progress

Ask students to complete the Check your progress section in the Student's Book.

3.6 Firms and production

Learning objectives

By the end of this unit, students should be able to:

- define production
- define productivity
- explain what influences the demand for factors of production
- define labour intensive production
- define capital intensive production
- explain the reasons for adopting the different forms of production
- analyse the advantages and disadvantages of different forms of production
- explain what influences the levels of production and productivity.

Key terms

Production; productivity; labour productivity; efficiency; labour intensive production; capital intensive production

STARTING POINT

The first question is a chance for students to refresh their memory of the factors of production. If unsure, they should revisit Unit 1.2 in the Student's Book. The second question is an opportunity for students to check they are sure they understand how labour and capital apply to their school. This could lead to a class discussion. For the third question, first check that the students understand the idea of a PPC. One pair of students could be asked to draw the diagram on the whiteboard and to explain it.

EXPLORING

Again working in pairs, the students should come up with ideas for these questions. Ask the students to report their ideas to the class.

1. Students may suggest: number of students who 'graduate' each year; the IGCSE/other exam results; number of students picked for area/regional/national teams. As a class they may decide that all should be included and given different levels of importance or that only one or two criteria are important.
2. Answers could include: No, it would make no difference because two more could be fitted into the classroom and we have sufficient resources. Two more would not detract from the time we can have with our teacher; Yes, it would because our classroom is too small for the numbers we already have and we are short of textbooks so two more would lead to overcrowding and less access to the books. Two fewer: Unless our classroom was too small or we were short of books/computers it would make very little difference. Each pair needs to offer a reasoned argument.
3. If there were ten fewer students, it would mean that scarce resources such as the teacher's time would be shared out between fewer students so we could all get more help. It would be possible to borrow resources more easily. As a result, this should improve our performance. If there were ten more students, it would lead to overcrowding of the classroom, lack of resources such as books, and could make getting individual help from the teacher more difficult. Again, each pair needs to offer a reasoned argument.

DEVELOPING

Teaching tips

1. Revisit Unit 1.2 before starting this unit to ensure that students have a firm grasp of the factors of production.
2. Production and productivity are often confused by students who think they are the same. Ensure that candidates are very clear about these concepts before leaving this unit.

3. While covering labour and capital intensive production, revisit 'starting point number 2'. Discuss with the students whether they wish to change their answers or not, and why.
4. Try to arrange a visit to either a labour-intensive firm or a capital-intensive firm, or invite someone in from one or other of these. In both cases talk about why they are, for example, capital intensive and how the firm seeks to improve output and productivity. This will help with the project at the end.

Additional activity – The box game

This activity is designed to help students have greater understanding of production and productivity.

For teams of 4–6 people.

(This activity could be adapted to show the benefits of specialisation by having a preliminary round where all students work individually, with exactly the same quantity of resources available as for this group version.)

You will need: paper and/or card; scissors; glue or other sticking agent; rulers; and possibly staplers.

Aim: for students to produce boxes which you are prepared to buy.

Your firm wishes to purchase standard size and well made boxes, 14 cm square, and is prepared to pay $10 for each with the possibility of bonus payments if the teams can meet any additional requirements you may make, for example a design on the box. Boxes with very minor faults are bought for $5. Any not up to standard are rejected.

Cost of supplies to the teams:

Paper $1 per A4 sheet

Card, if used, $2

Glue – to be decided depending on what is available

A pair of scissors $10

A stapler $20

Staples $20 per 100 staples

All of the supplies to be bought from you, or if possible an assistant/s. If you have assistants, it is a good idea to 'set up shop' in another room.

The teams must purchase the equipment, make the boxes and sell them to you.

At the end:

Add up the number of boxes you bought from each team and how much you paid. This will give the result. Put this on a board.

Ask the teams:

1. How did they organise production?
2. How did they try to improve output?
3. How did they respond to the extra demands you introduced?
4. If they played the game again, what would they change to improve their performance?

Suggested answer to in-text question 1:

Capital-intensive production is where a high level of investment is required and equipment used compared to the other factors of production. Agricultural work is often low paid, while small farmers make only a small amount of money from their farm. As countries become wealthier, people are thus attracted from the land to work in other industries where they earn more money. The population can also afford more food and thus demand rises. This favours larger farms where output is higher. These farms need to gain economies of scale and, to do so, substitute machinery for labour.

Case study

The advantages to India of labour-intensive production

- Students should have gone through the worked example in their book and have had a chance to discuss it as a class.
- Ensure that students are clear as to what is labour intensive production.

Suggested answers:

1. Labour intensive production is where the production of a good or service depends more heavily on labour than the other factors of production.
2. If labour is easily available, then it can be employed at relatively low cost. This means that production costs will be low so prices can be kept at a competitive level. Labour is more flexible than capital as it can move from the production of one good to that of another reasonably easily and thus changing consumer demands can be met.
3. An example response is: My country is a developed one with low unemployment. This means that if the demand for labour increases, the wage rate rises considerably. The scarcity of labour points to greater use of technology and machinery. This also has the advantage that labour can only work legally for so many hours and are entitled to holidays and a range of benefits. Machinery can work 24 hours a day, every day, and can increase the productivity of the people employed. We should only look to use labour intensive methods if unemployment rose dramatically.

   An alternative answer could be: My country is less developed and many people are out of work. If demand for labour rose, more could be employed without a rise in wages. This will favour labour intensive methods, especially as labour will be cheap while machinery is expensive to buy.

Suggested answer to in-text question 2:

In many towns land is a scarce resource as demand exceeds the amount available. To build outwards means a lot of land is needed for the buildings. Air costs nothing so the same number of offices or housing can be fitted in a much smaller area of land if built upwards rather than outwards. This will save the builder money as they need to pay for less land.

APPLYING

Project work

Students may be able to visit small firms individually or you could organise a group visit or bring someone from a firm in to talk to them. If students are doing independent research, then they should present their findings to the class. In the case of the third task, the whole class could bring their ideas together and then make a presentation to a suitable group. Students could suggest ideas such as: provide all students with their own computer/tablet; provide more books; increase/decrease the length of lessons. In doing this, they need to think what questions may be asked of them and how they would respond. This would enable students to be more prepared when doing the extension task where again the emphasis should be on the quality of: the research; the presentation; and ability to answer questions.

Expected outcomes

- Greater knowledge how firms operate
- Increased understanding of productivity
- Increase in presentation skills with emphasis on ability to answer questions

Knowledge check questions

Ask students to complete the knowledge check questions at the end of Unit 3.6 in the Student's Book.

Checking progress

Ask students to complete the Check your progress section in the Student's Book.

3.7 Firms' costs, revenue and objectives

Learning objectives

By the end of this unit, students should be able to:

- define the costs of production
- calculate total cost, average cost, fixed cost, average fixed cost, variable cost and average variable cost
- analyse how change in output affects the costs of production
- define revenue
- calculate total and average revenue
- analyse the influence of sales on revenue
- explain the objectives of firms.

Key terms

Total costs; average cost; fixed costs; average fixed costs; variable costs; average variable costs; total revenue; average revenue; sales (revenue) maximisation; survival; social welfare

STARTING POINT

The first three questions are focused on the students' experiences. The first question should lead to the idea that while it is clearly cheaper in terms of total cost to feed one person, the average cost of feeding several may well be less. Similarly, with the second question, students should realise that buying in bulk is cheaper and that this is because the seller will give a discounted price. This revisits the work on economies of scale. If any of the pairs have not sold anything, it might be useful to link them to a pair who have. Lastly, they need to recall the four factors of production.

EXPLORING

Again, working in pairs the students should come up with ideas for these questions. Ask the students to report back on their ideas to the class.

1. Students should undertake some research to find out how much their household spends on food each week. If they already have a younger brother/sister they must consider the extra cost for an additional one (one extra).
2. Try to get the Bursar or Finance Manager to come to talk to the students. Students could suggest a range of cost reductions: fewer staff; larger class numbers; not providing meals. The important part is for the students to be able to decide what the consequences would be and whether these would have further effects, for example: reducing the number of teachers and making class numbers bigger would save money, but might lead to poorer results. This could then mean that parents find other schools for their children leading to lower numbers and income.
3. If the Bursar has given a talk to students, hopefully some/all of the information needed will have been gained. Possible ideas include: government policy; results; work of parents/teachers to raise money; number of students.
4. Students could generate ideas in pairs and then as a class and put a presentation together to give to the Bursar. At this stage of the course, allow any ideas which would increase income even if they are not really revenue raising ideas.

DEVELOPING

Teaching tips

1. Many students may find this unit challenging as it involves a lot of numerical work and diagrams. In order to help students, you could:
   - ensure that students are very clear as to the difference between, for example, the different cost concepts and how to do the calculations before moving on (see the Additional activity below)
   - provide the students with more calculation questions so they are confident in the work. You could use the Application tasks in the Student's Book as templates.
2. If you can, invite a business owner to talk about the objectives of their firm to help students understand this part of the unit.

Application task

Farah's costs

Farah has taken over a shop previously owned by a relative. The relative has left her some information, but not all the information needed.

Output	Fixed cost	Variable cost	Total cost	Average cost
0	100	0	100	–
5	**100**	40	**140**	**28**
10	**100**	**70**	170	**17**
15	**100**	110	**210**	**14**

1. The missing numbers are shown in **bold.**
2. As AC is still falling, Farah should think about increasing output to gain more economies of scale. Farah must be aware, however, that VC are starting to rise at an increasing rate which will eventually increase AC leading to diseconomies of scale. Farah should increase output, but by only a small amount.

Suggested answer to in-text question 1:

Average fixed cost (AFC) is the fixed costs per unit. As fixed costs are costs the firm would incur even if it produced nothing, then as output increases the same cost is being divided by an ever increasing number. This will lead to AFC continuing to fall as AFC = $\frac{\text{Fixed cost}}{\text{output}}$

Output units	Fixed cost $	Average fixed cost $
0	400	–
5	400	80
10	400	40
15	400	26.66
20	400	20

As can be seen, as output increases in units of 5, AFC falls, but at each increase the fall is less than before.

Suggested answer to in-text question 2:

Total revenue [TR] is equal to PxQ. Average revenue [AR] = $\frac{TR}{Q}$ which is the same as P.

Thus, as price falls so does AR while as AR rises so does P. This can be seen in the diagram below.

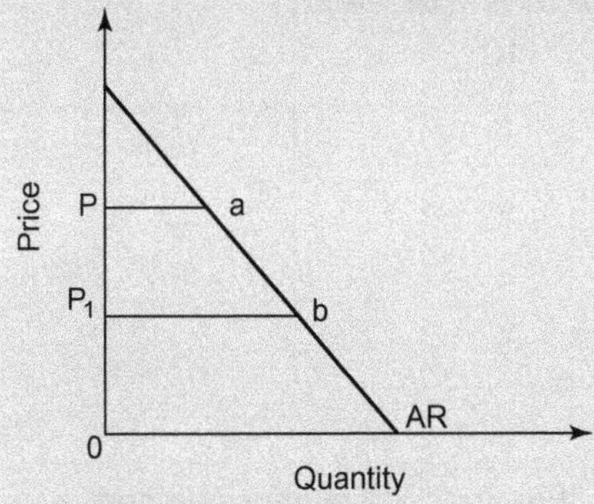

If price falls from P to P_1 then AR declines from a to b; whereas if AR rises from b to a then price increases from P_1 to P.

Additional activity – Calculating costs and revenue

Use Activity sheet 3.7

Answers:

Output	FC	AFC	VC	AVC	TC	AC
0	200	–	0	–	200	–
10	200	20	200	20	400	40
20	200	10	360	18	560	28
30	200	6.67	550	18.33	750	25
40	200	5	800	20	1000	25
50	200	4	1200	24	1400	28

1. See above. Award 1 mark for each correct column [6]
2. AFC is falling [1] by a decreasing amount/more slowly [1]. AVC is falling at first [1], but then rising [1]. AC is falling and then rises [1], but rises after AVC increases [1]
3. The diagram should look similar to the one below

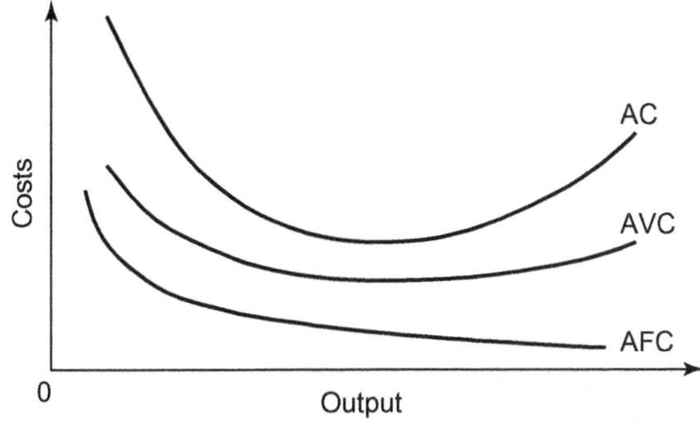

Award 1 mark for each curve correctly plotted/drawn [3]. Award 2 marks for labelling the axes correctly [2]. Award 1 mark for each correct labelling of the lines [3].

Application task

José's Garden Centre

PRICE ($)	Sales (plants)	Total revenue ($)	Average revenue ($)
10	50	500	10
8	72	576	8
6	90	540	6
4	110	440	4
2	125	250	2

1. The calculations for TR and AR are shown in the table above.
2. Up to sales of 72 plants a week Jose is increasing his total revenue. If he tries to sell more he can only do so at a lower price, but if he does so total revenue falls, for example, by cutting price from $8 to $6 his sales increase from 72 plants to 90 a week, but his total revenue falls from $576 to $540.

Extension activity

1. Calculate the PED if price fell from: i) $10 to $8, and ii) $8 to $6.
2. Using the calculations, what do they tell us about the elasticity of the demand line?

Answers

1. **i)** % change in quantity = $\frac{22}{50} \times 100 = 44\%$: % change in price = $\frac{-2}{10} \times 100 = -20\%$

   $$\text{PED} = \frac{\text{Percentage change in Q}}{\text{Percentage change in P}} = \frac{44}{-20} = -2.2$$

   ii) % change in quantity = $\frac{18}{72} \times 100 = 25\%$: % change in price = $\frac{-2}{8} \times 100 = -25\%$

   $$\text{PED} = \frac{\text{Percentage change in Q}}{\text{Percentage change in P}} = \frac{25}{-25} = -1$$

2. As price falls, so does the value of PED. This follows from the idea that the PED declines as we move down the demand line. At –2.2 the demand is elastic, while at –1 it is unitary. Below this point demand will be inelastic.

Case study

Greta and Lorenzo

- Ask the students if they can think of any local businesses which might have 'survival' as a main objective. Why have they suggested those firms?
- Ensure that the students fully understand what is meant by fixed and variable costs.

Suggested answers:

1. If total revenue is equal to or exceeds total cost then a business can continue to survive as it is not making a loss (breaks-even) or makes a small profit.
2. The takeover would allow a forward vertical merger to take place so that they would have a direct outlet for their produce while the retail part would be guaranteed supplies. Marketing campaigns could be for the whole firm leading to marketing economies of scale. This would lead to lower average costs allowing prices to fall resulting in increase in sales and market share. The disadvantages could include: diseconomies of scale as the two sets of managers find it difficult to agree procedures or operational methods leading to time wasting and rising average costs. Overall, the potential advantages outweigh the disadvantages because the latter can be overcome by proper planning and consultation, while the former would give the new firm permanent gains.

3. Extension: Secondary sector businesses manufacture products. To do so they are likely to need considerable capital equipment, like machines, and buildings. Both of these are fixed costs in that their cost does not vary with output. There is a large outlay before manufacturing can take place. Many of these businesses are capital intensive. The service sector is usually labour intensive. A legal firm has a building and some equipment such as computers, but they employ a lot of people to carry out the work so have large variable costs. Shops are similar in that the amount of stock carried and people employed varies with the demand.

APPLYING

Project work

There are two tasks here for the research. The first is a group activity. Assuming your school is able and willing to provide the information, the students need to: gather the information; analyse it in terms of costs and revenue, think about the implications of student numbers increasing, but not the buildings or rooms; and make a presentation, hopefully, to members of senior management or the finance team. The second task is for individuals or small groups. The students select a business they have some links with either as consumers or because a relative/parent works for it. They have to try to find out what the objectives of the firm might be based on its activities, for example: a firm which has opened new premises could have growth and profit maximisation as objectives, while a firm which has cut prices could be looking to maximise sales. The students should share their findings with the whole class.

Expected outcomes

- Greater understanding of the costs and revenues of a business
- Better understanding of the objectives of businesses
- Improvement in presentation skills

Knowledge check questions

Ask students to complete the knowledge check questions at the end of Unit 3.7 in the Student's Book.

Checking progress

Ask students to complete the Check your progress section in the Student's Book.

3.8 Market structure

Learning objectives

By the end of this unit, students should be able to:

- define what is meant by a competitive market
- define what is meant by a monopoly
- analyse the effects of competition on price, quality, choice and profit
- describe the characteristics of monopoly markets
- discuss the advantages and disadvantages of monopolies.

Key terms

Competition; competitive markets; barriers to entry; product differentiation; monopoly; consumer sovereignty

STARTING POINT

Students start by thinking about competition. In addition to the two parts in question 1, ask the class as a whole how they would define competition. Put ideas on the board and try to decide which one is best. If the definition chosen is clearly wrong, you will need to discuss this with them to ensure greater understanding. The second starting activity links the first and the last. Students could opt for choice or the ease of having only one. Ask the students which option they went for. If everyone goes for choice, then explore why this was. If there were differences of opinion between the students, ask the students to explain their option to those who decided on the other option. For the last activity, ask the pairs to put their ideas on the whiteboard. Did they go for different ideas: if so, why?

EXPLORING

Again, working in pairs the students should come up with ideas for these questions. Ask the students to report back on their ideas to the class.

1. Students may suggest: advertising, or other marketing methods; price cuts; higher quality; better customer service; specialist products; being more efficient. Ask the pairs why they chose those methods.
2. Students may suggest: customer service; personalised service; specialist products; higher quality. The important point is to challenge any suggestion that would be unlikely, such as cutting prices.
3. Consider discussing this question as a class. Students could suggest: too powerful in relation to the government; to protect consumers; to help small firms.

DEVELOPING

Teaching tips

1. Students should have some experience of how firms compete for customers, for example different shops in the same town selling the same product, online retailers.
2. If you have a market near you, either take the students and ask them to observe how competition takes place, or you could ask the students to do this for homework.
3. Ask students to make note of what brands are bought for their household's use and to find out why they or their parents choose, or do not choose, well known brands.
4. Invite in someone from a local firm to explain how their firm competes and why the firm uses those methods.

Suggested answer to in-text question 1:

Advertising allows firms to tell people about their product and thus to inform them about their choices when selecting which product to buy. Some consumers may not have known about the product so this could increase sales. Advertising also allows firms to persuade consumers that their product is different from or better than those of their rivals, even if it is basically the same.

Additional activity – Advertising

For homework, ask the students to look at or watch adverts:

- on television, in the cinema, or online
- in newspapers or magazines
- on billboards or posters besides the roads they travel along
- on buses, trains or other forms of transport.

Students should: make a list of the companies or products advertised; decide if they think the advert is effective or not and why.

Students bring the research to class and discuss their findings. If they are able to see similar adverts in different formats, as above, then which did they feel worked better and why?

If you are able to download/stream any adverts from television or online, this could provide an introduction to the activity.

Suggested answer to in-text question 2:

Advertising is only one way in which firms compete. Students must look not only at adverts, but also consider some of: price; other marketing methods; quality; customer service; specialist products. They should include in their work at least two ways in addition to advertising. This will then form the basis for discussion focused on why firms use these methods and how effective they are.

Suggested answer to in-text question 3:

Large firms have more resources, including finance, than small firms. They can afford to cut prices by larger amounts and for longer, so the outcome of a price competition between small and large firms is usually that the small firm loses. One example of this is where a large firm will sell a product below the price it cost them to buy/make it in order to gain customers (so-called 'loss leaders). Small firms usually cannot afford to do this.

Case study

Problems for traditional clothing manufacturers in the UK

- If your country exports low-cost clothing, provide a list of the major countries to which this goes.
- If your country is an importer of low-cost clothing, provide a list of the main sources.

Suggested answers:

1. Low-cost clothing producers can sell their products at a lower price and still make a profit. Where this clothing is in competition with that of traditional producers, they are then forced to cut their prices. The alternative is to lose sales and to risk going out of business.
2. One factor is that low-priced products have used poorer quality materials such as the cloth which could mean the clothes not lasting as long as their higher-priced rivals. Another is that production uses cheaper, but inferior, methods which lead to lower quality in things like zips/buttons breaking or coming off or seams coming apart.
3. Competition has resulted in prices falling which means consumers can afford to buy more clothes or have more money to spend on other products. It can also increase the variety of clothes on offer thus increasing consumer choice. This means that consumers can have a different look to that of their friends or work colleagues. On the other hand, competition could result in some manufacturers going out of business thus reducing choice. This could also deny consumers the brands that they want to buy. This could result in either less choice or having to buy clothes of a lower quality. Some consumers, however, may be willing to pay more for quality clothing, and for their favourite brands, so competition may have a limited effect depending on who the consumers are and what they want from the clothes they buy.

Suggested answer to in-text question 4:

Monopolies, as sole providers of a good or service, will normally have a fairly inelastic supply curve.

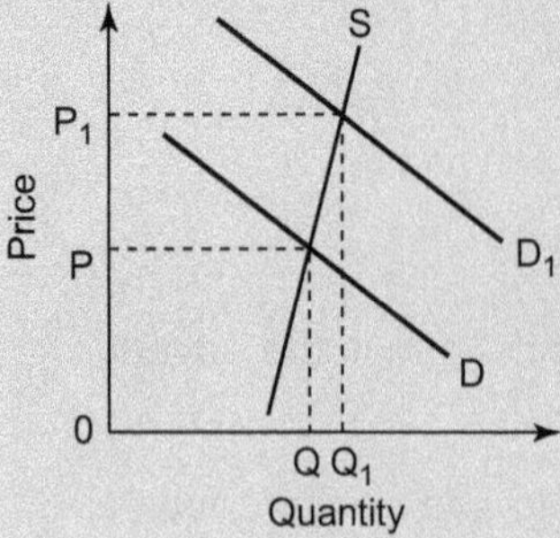

As can be seen in the diagram, an increase in demand from D to D_1 will lead to a large rise in price, P to P_1, and a smaller increase in quantity from Q to Q_1.

An answer that does not refer to PES, but says that both price and quantity would increase, would be a basic answer.

Additional activity – Product differentiation

Use Activity sheet 3.8.

Discuss with the students what is meant by product differentiation and ask them to suggest examples of it.

Use Activity sheet 3.8 as homework to extend this activity.

Case study

The European Union (EU) takes on Google

- If students are not familiar with the EU, use a map so they can see which countries are members.
- Provide some background on the EU, for example, size of population.
- Make sure that students understand that in the EU a firm is a monopoly if it has 25% or more of the market. It does not have to be the only firm.

Suggested answers:

1. The EU argued that 'It denied other companies the chance to compete on the merits and to innovate.' 'It denied European consumers a genuine choice of services and the full benefits of innovation.' It did all of this by ensuring that consumers saw the products of firms that Google wanted to promote. This reduces choice which is one of the things a monopoly does.
2. The advantages include: consumers can easily find what they are looking for thus saving both time and potentially money as they are not wasting time going to different sellers. It still gives consumers choice, but limits it so they are not confused. The disadvantages include: reducing choice because consumers see a choice that Google want you to see and not the choice a consumer might make, thus resulting in less price competition and so higher prices for consumers.

Extension activity

Students could research whether other search engines use similar or different methods to those of Google.

Do you think it is important that your choice may be limited by the owners of the search engine?

Make a presentation of your findings to the class and explain why it does/does not matter to you.

APPLYING

Project work

The first activity could be linked to activities earlier in the unit. Students could put a display of their findings in the classroom to enable everyone to see the evidence before discussing the findings. Findings should include addressing any links between prices and advertising. The second activity could lead to either a presentation to the class or to a piece of written work. Students may need some guidance, such as percentage share of the market, as to whether a firm is a monopoly. The extension activity could lend itself to small group work with each taking a different firm leading to a number of presentations. Students should refresh their memories of what is meant by non-price competition.

Expected outcomes

- Understanding of how advertising often affects prices
- Greater understanding of what a monopoly is
- Better understanding how non-price competition can be used

Knowledge check questions

Ask students to complete the knowledge check questions at the end of Unit 3.8 in the Student's Book.

Checking progress

Ask students to complete the Check your progress section in the Student's Book.

Chapter review

Ask students to complete the Chapter Review questions at the end of Chapter 3 in the Student's Book.

4.1 The role of government

Learning objectives

By the end of this unit, students should be able to:

- identify and describe the types of goods and services provided by government
- describe the role of government locally, nationally and internationally.

Key terms

Private benefits; external benefits; social benefits; public good; non-rivalry

STARTING POINT

The starting point questions use stimulus pictures to introduce the role of government. An alternative to pairs would be to use the photographs in a class discussion.

1. The services shown are
   - rubbish collection
   - defence
   - fire services
   - education.
2. The services shown in the picture would vary from country to country as to whether they are provided by local or national government. In a lot of countries, rubbish collection would be provided by local government and in all countries defence would be provided by national government.
3. Students could mention that it would be difficult to charge users of fire services and defence for example. Some might mention that education is a right and should be provided to all irrespective of income so that the nation has an educated and skilled workforce. If rubbish collection was left to the private sector, what would happen if some people in a street refused to pay. Rubbish would collect in the streets and be unsightly and a health hazard.

EXPLORING

It would be useful before setting these questions to discuss what the term 'effectively' means. The principles of economic efficiency are based on the concept that there are scarce resources. There are not enough resources to have all aspects of the economy functioning at their highest capacity at all times. The scarce resources must be distributed to meet the needs of the economy and it is related to the welfare of the population as a whole. It is government's role to ensure that this happens.

1. Students could provide a number of points which could include:
   - benefits to ensure there is a safety net for individuals
   - taxation to pay for government services and to redistribute income and wealth
   - managing the economy to reduce inflation and unemployment
   - helping industry to invest so the economy can grow
   - encouraging firms to export.
2. At a local level, this could be investing in social housing, repairing roads in the town, managing refuse collection, providing services such as sports centres. At a national level, this could be providing health care, education and other essential services and managing the economy to achieve growth by keeping inflation low and encouraging investment as well as investing in infrastructure such as roads and railways. At an international level, governments could negotiate with other countries to reduce barriers to trade.
3. The students could provide a list which includes: civil servants, police, fire fighters, teachers, doctors and nurses, refuse collectors, street cleaners.

DEVELOPING

Teaching tips

- Economics can be confusing! There is a huge variation between countries on the role of government in the economy. What is considered a merit good in one country might not be in another country. Economics provides analysis and explanation of the economic consequences of the decisions that are made.
- Getting students to look at government spending by % of GDP will show the variety of approaches to the role of government. Taiwan (19.41%) and Singapore (19.87%) have the lowest % of GDP. Finland (53.84%), France (52.71%) and Denmark (52.16%) have the highest. Other examples are the UK (39.17%) and the USA (39.39%). [Source: IMF World Economic Outlook Database 2017 prediction].
- For the extension question in the knowledge check questions, the student should be helped to find sources of information regarding the provision of healthcare. It would be useful for the student to answer the question in the context of their own country. Also the debate in the USA on healthcare could provide students with materials they could use in their answer.

Additional activity – Group categorising

Use Activity sheet 4.1

The aim is to help students identify and describe some of the goods and services produced by government. It is intended to be a relatively quick interactive activity to get students using some of the key economic terms presented in the unit.

1. Explain to students that they are going to take part in a group categorising activity.
2. Divide the class into groups of three and hand each group a set of three cards (Activity sheet 4.1).
3. Tell students that you are going to call out a good or service and they must decide whether the good or service identified is produced in the public sector (by the government), private sector or both.
4. Once students have agreed on the correct response in their groups, they should hold up the corresponding card.
5. Emphasise that this is not a competition and you will allow them up to 30 seconds to agree on the best response. Let them know that they may be asked to justify their selection.
6. Demonstrate the activity for students using the first item in the list below.

List of goods and services

Good or service	Category	Justification
Education	Both	Merit good, but also a private good (excludable and rival so private producers can profit from providing it).
Street lighting	Public sector	A public good that only the state can provide
Car insurance	Private good	Merit good but excludable and rival
Health care	Both	Merit good but excludable and rival
Dental care	Both	Merit good but excludable and rival
Defence	Public sector	Non-excludable and non-rival
Museums and galleries	Both	Merit good, but excludable and rival
Bottled water	Private	Excludable and rival
Fire services	Public sector	A public good that only the state can provide

Suggested answers to in-text questions

1. This question follows a table which shows the range of goods and services and asks students to identify three goods or services which fall under more than one of the classifications. Students could refer to public services such as the Police and fire services which are examples of public good, merit goods such as education and health which could be classified as public services and roads which are investment in infrastructure and could also be classified as public services.
2. The answers will vary from country to country but could include provision of social housing, encouraging sport through sports centres and financing Olympic teams, public broadcasting, postal services.

Additional activity

Presentation by students

This activity is based on a presentation by students on the role of government. Students should work in groups of three or four. Give out a question to each group from the following list. You should choose carefully which question goes to which group.

- Is a lighthouse a public good?
- What are the private, external and social benefits of providing fire services?
- Is education a public or a merit good?
- Why do some countries provide a national health service while others do not?
- Is it better for governments to provide as little as possible and so keep taxes low?

Guidance notes for students

You need to develop a short presentation on a question given to you by your teacher and deliver this to your class. You will have one week to prepare your presentation. Your presentation should not contain more than ten slides.

Before you begin to prepare the presentation, agree with your group on how you are going to approach the question and what research each of you will focus on.

Make sure you prepare an introduction to your presentation and a conclusion. Use one slide for each of these. For the remaining slides, make sure you use bullet points. You should prepare separate notes to help you deliver your presentation. Do not just read the text from the slide.

You should aim to include at least two graphics (pictures or diagrams) in your slides.

You will be asked questions about your whole presentation. Make sure you can answer questions on your own slides and on your partner's slides.

Guidance notes for teachers

A week before the presentations are to be given, give students a copy of the guidance notes. Answer any questions they may have about their task. Support the students' research by recommending websites, textbooks or other resources they could use for their research. Check in advance that no students are struggling with the task.

The presentations should be no longer than 10 minutes. Students should use notes they have prepared and should not just read from the slide.

You should complete an observation sheet to record how successful each student was at presenting their information.

Case study

Government-funded mega projects in Thailand

Before setting the case study, provide the students with a map of Thailand and the surrounding countries. Discuss what infrastructure means and the possible benefits of improved infrastructure.

Suggested answers

1. There are four elements to the infrastructure and students could deal with each in turn.

   The high speed link with neighbouring countries could help trade with these countries as well as encourage tourism. The metropolitan rail system in Bangkok will reduce traffic congestion, benefit commuters and the firms they work for as well as reducing pollution. The development of ICT would provide the necessary skills as well as technical infrastructure which would help firms be competitive. Fibre optics can significantly increase bandwidth potential. Fibre optic internet is many times faster than copper. This will improve productivity.

2. Students can provide a list connected to the examples:
   - construction workers – engineers, labourers, railway designers, architects
   - railway staff
   - computer engineers
   - train construction workers.

Extension task:

Ask students to find an article from a newspaper or news website about a good or service produced by the government. They should read the article and answer the questions below.

1. Identify the good or service mentioned in the article.
2. Explain what type of good or service it is.
3. Explain why the government provides it.

Identify one type of occupation the government may need to employ to provide the good or service.

APPLYING

Project work

The project is based on an article that the student has chosen. You could provide a bank of articles which you know would enable the questions to be answered and also be suitable for the extension question. Articles need to include goods and services provided at a local, national and international level. You could amend the task so that students use articles at each level rather than writing on one only.

Question 3 asks about benefits to society: students could comment on the benefits of government providing public and merit goods. They could also mention a public service which is considered to be essential for a modern society to function effectively.

For the extension activity, students might need some tips on how to summarise an article.

1. Skim the article, thinking of the focus while you are reading.
2. Consider the most basic questions: Who? What? When? Where? Why? How?
3. Read thoroughly and take notes and highlight as you read.
4. Take note of the subheadings.
5. If there are no subheadings, divide the article into sections in your mind.
6. Outline the article and write down the support points using your own words.
7. Start by telling the reader what you are summarising and provide any necessary background information.
8. Use summarising language such as 'the article claims' or 'the author suggests'.
9. Conclude with a final statement and summarise what the author wanted to get across.

Expected outcomes

- Description of good and service illustrated in the article
- Explanation of how society benefits
- For the extension question, students will produce a summary of an article

Knowledge check questions

Ask students to complete the knowledge check questions at the end of Unit 4.1 in the Student's Book.

Checking progress

Ask students to complete the Check your progress section in the Student's Book.

4.2 The macroeconomic aims of government

Learning objectives

By the end of this unit, students should be able to:

- describe the aims of government policies, such as economic growth, full employment/low unemployment, stable prices/low inflation, balance of payments stability, redistribution of income
- explain the reasons behind the choice of aims and the criteria that governments set for each aim
- analyse the possible conflicts between aims, including:
  - full employment versus stable prices
  - economic growth versus balance of payments stability
  - full employment versus balance of payments stability.

Key terms

Macroeconomic aims; economic growth; living standards; inflation; balance of payments; current account; exports; imports; trade deficit; trade surplus; unemployment rate.

STARTING POINT

The starting point questions begin the journey of understanding the variety of possible macroeconomic aims of a government. Divide the class into pairs or threes. Give each group three large pieces of paper, for example flip chart paper, and ask them to label them 'Strong Economy', 'Growth' and 'Barriers'. Allow 15 minutes for the groups to discuss the three questions. Ask them to put their flip chart paper on the walls. Invite different groups to read through their bullets and run a plenary discussion.

1. The students might refer to low unemployment, low inflation, exchange rate stability, competitive trading position. Responses could include that a strong economy enables high-quality health care and education to be provided as well as social factors such as reducing poverty and removing slum areas.
2. The students might suggest economic conditions that encourage businesses to invest, the availability of skilled workers, a supply of raw materials that are in demand and good infrastructure.
3. There are a possible range of points that students might suggest, including a list of economic factors such as: high inflation, competitiveness, dependence on few products for exporting and lack of investment. Others might point to political stability and corrupt practices. While these issues are relevant, the focus of the discussion should be on the economic factors.

EXPLORING

The three exploring questions require knowledge of your country. You could prepare a fact sheet about the country which could help students explore the economic issues facing their country. The World Bank databank would be a useful source for the fact sheet. It is good to embed these discussions in economic knowledge rather than rely on impressions. To answer question 2, students need information about other countries. You could prepare a fact sheet using the same headings on a selected group of other countries or ask pairs to use the internet to research other countries. You might suggest a list of countries that they research. After the first two questions, invite selected pairs to present their response, writing key points on the whiteboard.

As an alternative to answering Question 3 in pairs, this could be the focus of a class discussion which would enable you to build on the comments made. Students could consider economic growth, reducing inflation, reducing unemployment, encouraging international trade, redistribution of income and wealth.

DEVELOPING

Teaching tips

- Macro economics is an area of study with precise aims attached to it. Understanding the indicators used in macro economics to measure the success in these areas is important. Underpinning the understanding of macroeconomic aims is the ability to explain the various types of inflation, unemployment and economic growth. It would be useful to check on understanding at the start of this unit.
- A useful resource would be to collate key economic indicators from a variety of countries as well as cuttings from newspapers and magazines or text from blogs on the macro data from your own country.

Suggested answer to in-text question 1:

One approach is to give students a copy of a summary table (see below) with the macroeconomic aims and get students to pick the one they think is most important and provide an explanation. You could put a large version of the summary table and collect 'votes' before discussing student responses.

Macroeconomic aim	The most important is:	Because:
Economic growth		
Full employment		
Stable prices		
Balance of payments stability		
Redistribution of income		

Case study

Export-led growth in China

- Prepare students for the case study by asking them to note down the macroeconomic objectives they think are most important for China. You could supplement the case study by preparing a single sheet of paper with data on the Chinese economy.
- Ask one or two students to share their ideas with the class. Encourage them to elaborate on their opinions by asking questions but do not provide them with the answers at this stage.
- Ask students to read the case study to check whether the macroeconomic aims they have identified are the same or different from those mentioned in the text.
- Ask students to complete the focus questions individually or in pairs before discussing the answers with the class.

Suggested answers

1. Advantages
   - Higher economic growth (as high as 14.2%)
   - Rising incomes and higher standards of living for the population

   Disadvantages
   - Dependence on exports for growth and jobs
   - Rising pollution levels which is reducing quality of life for some members of the population
2. Accept any reasonable responses. These may include:
   - encouraging domestic consumers to spend more, perhaps by lowering income tax
   - encouraging foreign businesses to set up in China which may lead to an increase in production of goods and services and jobs for Chinese workers
   - encouraging tourism perhaps by easing visa restrictions which should create growth and jobs in the tourism industry.

Suggested answer to in-text question 2:

Students could explain that there are two elements to consumer spending as consumers could buy home produced goods or imported goods. If there was an increase in spending on home produced consumer goods, this would increase demand and have a positive impact for producers. Their profits could increase and more workers could be employed with knock-on effects. If there was a decrease in consumer spending or a switch to imports, this would mean that sales would fall for producers and lead to a fall in profits and layoffs.

Students need to explain the connection between consumer spending and producers.

Suggested answer to in-text question 3:

Students again might distinguish between spending on home produced goods or imports. If the fall in consumer spending was primarily on imports, the effect would not be as significant as a fall in spending on home produced goods. A fall in spending on home produced goods could mean that producers and retailers could make staff redundant and so unemployment might rise.

Suggested answer to in-text question 4:

Students will infer that a slowdown in economic growth is likely to lead to higher unemployment as fewer workers are needed when firms decrease their production. This generally leads to lower incomes and decreased consumer spending. If this is sustained over a long period of time, the living standards of the population are likely to fall.

Additional activity – Jigsaw reading activity

Use Activity sheet 4.2.

This activity requires students to identify an appropriate government macroeconomic aim for a country and justify their choice.

Teacher guidance

1. Tell students they are going to compete a jigsaw reading activity. They will each get a case study scenario for a different country. Using the information in the case study as well as their own knowledge, they should decide on the most suitable government economic aim for each country. They will then have to explain their choice to other students and justify their selection.
2. Divide the class into four equal groups and hand out a copy of Activity sheet 4.2 to each student.
3. Allocate a different case study (A, B, C or D) to each of the four groups.
4. Allow students a few minutes to read their case study and, working individually, note down a response to the question in the activity sheet. Next, give students five minutes to discuss their ideas with the other members of their group. They should try to come to a consensus on what the best government economic aim is for their country.
5. After students have finished discussing their case study, re-group students. Arrange it so that each new group contains at least one student from A, B, C and D.
6. Instruct students to share their case study and response to the question with the other members of their new group. They should justify their responses by saying why they think the aim they chose is the most important for the country in the case study. Encourage the other group members to ask questions and share their own opinions on the different case studies. Students may make notes if they wish but should be encouraged to engage in conversation over note-taking.
7. Once each student has discussed their case studies with their group, round off the activity by selecting a few students to share their opinions on the different case studies with the whole class.

Extension question

Ask more able students in the group to use the internet to investigate some of the reasons why their chosen countries are experiencing economic problems.

Support questions

a) Why is economic growth in a country seen as a good thing?

b) Why is high inflation in a country seen as a bad thing?

Case study

Inflation target set for India's central bank

- Ask students to recall the functions of a country's central bank.
- If necessary, refer students to Unit 3.1 to revise the functions of a central bank. In particular, discuss the role the central bank plays in using interest rates (monetary policy) to control inflation.
- Ask students to read the case study and individually respond to the focus questions before discussing the answers with the class.

Suggested answers

1. They need to refer to the conflict between low inflation and economic growth and the conflict between low inflation and low unemployment. They could also refer to interest rates and consumer spending.
2. Their responses should refer to the relatively high upper limit for inflation of 6% which indicates that the Indian government is willing to tolerate moderate inflation in order to achieve higher economic growth and low unemployment.
3. An upper inflation limit below 6% is likely to result in slower growth and higher unemployment. For example, an upper limit of 3% might force the central bank to take action to reduce consumer spending sooner by raising interest rates. This could lead to slower economic growth and higher unemployment. It might also indicate that the Indian government and the Reserve Bank of India are less concerned about the impact on international competitiveness of 6% inflation. This might be based on an analysis of the relative inflation rates of its trading partners or on price elasticity of demand for imports and exports.

Extension task

Ask students to research the aims of the government in their home country. They should:

1. identify and explain three economic aims of the government of their home country
2. explain how the government intends to achieve each aim.

Students could present their findings in the form of a poster or PowerPoint® slideshow which they could briefly present to their peers in the next lesson, either in small groups or to the whole class.

Note: The economic theory to answer question 2 is covered in Unit 4.3. Students may therefore find this question a little challenging. However, encourage them to do their best to answer it, as attempting it will help prepare them for the content of the next unit by providing them with a foundation on which they can build their understanding of government macroeconomic policy.

APPLYING

Project work

This project involves using the internet to research the economy of a country of the student's choice. They have to identify *three* macroeconomic aims which might be relevant to the government of the country they are investigating and explain why each aim is important. Students are to present their findings in the form of a poster or PowerPoint® presentation slide to present to their classmates.

You will need to discuss sources of research with students prior to undertaking this project work and how they can identify relevant macroeconomic aims from economic data. Encourage students to research comparative data from more than one year.

Expected outcomes

- Students identify three macroeconomic aims of the government of their choice. These may include any three of economic growth, full employment/low unemployment, stable prices/low inflation, balance of payments stability, redistribution of income. Other aims are also acceptable, such as a volatile exchange rate, level of government debt etc. but encourage students to focus on three of the five aims outlined in the Student's Book.
- Students describe each aim in the context of the country they are investigating – for example: Venezuela is currently experiencing its worst economic crisis in history. In 2016, Venezuela had an inflation rate of over 400% and negative economic growth of minus 8% and unemployment of 17%. Therefore, controlling inflation, positive economic growth and lowering unemployment are important aims for the government.
- Students explain why the aim is important for the country within the context of their research. For example, people in Venezuela are taking to the streets to protest the rising cost of living and high unemployment. High inflation has made it difficult to purchase imports including of food and medicine. There is therefore not enough food or medicine available for the population. The government must lower inflation and unemployment in order to solve these problems.
- Students are not expected to explain the causes of the economic problems at this stage, simply identify them and explain why they are important for the country they are investigating.
- Students should prepare PowerPoint® slides and speakers' notes or a poster to present to the class.

Knowledge check questions

Ask students to complete the knowledge check questions at the end of Unit 4.2 in the Student's Book.

Checking progress

Ask students to complete the Check your progress section in the Student's Book.

4.3 Fiscal policy

Learning objectives

By the end of this unit, students should be able to:

- define government budget
- describe the main areas of government spending and explain the reasons for and the effects of spending in these areas
- explain what is meant by taxation and describe the reasons for governments levying (collecting) taxes
- describe the different ways in which taxes can be classified, such as direct or indirect, progressive, regressive or proportional
- describe the qualities of a good tax
- analyse the impact of taxation on consumers, producers, government and the economy as a whole
- define fiscal policy
- explain tax and spending changes, in the form of fiscal policy, that cause budget balance or imbalance
- calculate the size of a budget deficit or surplus
- analyse how fiscal policy measures may enable the government to achieve its macroeconomic aims.

Key terms

Fiscal policy; tariff; income tax, corporation tax, value added tax (VAT); excise duty; progressive tax; regressive tax; proportional tax; multinational corporation; tax evasion; tax avoidance; redundant; black market; aggregate demand; consumption; investment; government spending; net exports; expansionary fiscal policy; contractionary fiscal policy; balanced budget; budget surplus; budget deficit; loan

STARTING POINT

a) The public sector refers to government owned organisations and government provided services such as the Police and fire services. The private sector refers to organisations that are not government owned and goods and services are provided outside of government. Companies owned by individuals are part of the private sector.

b) Goods are items you buy such as food and clothing. They are tangible objects. The typical service business provides intangible services that do not have a physical nature such as accounting, banking or hairdressing.

c) A consumer good is one that is purchased and used by consumers such as a TV and clothing. A producer good is one used by producers such as factory machinery.

d) Merit goods are products that are more beneficial to consumers than they realise and have benefits for those who are not involved directly. Left to the private sector too little gets consumed. Health care is an example of a merit good. Demerit goods are more harmful to consumers than they realise. They are over-consumed and over-produced. Smoking is an example of a demerit good as it damages health and also imposes costs on non-smokers.

e) A private good is a good that has to be purchased to be consumed. Its consumption by one consumer means that others cannot consume it. Private goods are rivalrous and excludable. An example is a take away pizza. If one person eats the pizza, no one else can eat it (rivalrous), and a pizza outlet can prevent consumers who do not pay for pizzas from consuming them (excludable). A public good is one that is non-excludable and non-rivalrous and individuals cannot be excluded from benefiting from it. Examples are street lighting where benefitting from a street light does not reduce light for others (non-rivalry). It would be impossible to erect a dam to stop flooding and exclude people from benefitting from it (non-excludable).

f) Externalities are costs or benefits that affect third parties who are not participants in the production or consumption of goods and services in a market place. A positive externality is a benefit that third parties enjoy as a result of a transaction, production, or consumption between the buyer and the seller.

A negative externality is the cost that a third party has to bear as a result of a transaction in which the third party has no involvement.

An example of a positive externality is the research into new and innovative technologies. The technological knowhow can greatly contribute to the benefit of an entire industry and can result in lower production costs, better quality and better safety standards that benefit the producers, as well as consumers.

An example of a positive externality is research into new technology by one firm. This can contribute to the benefit of lower production costs and improved quality. An example of negative externality is pollution. An organisation may pollute the environment by burning fuels and releasing poisonous fumes to the environment which can result in problems with public health.

EXPLORING

1. Working in pairs, ask the students to identify the areas of government spending shown in the pictures. Road Construction, Education and Defence.
2. A government finances its spending through taxation and also borrowing.
3. A government will decide on its priorities. Are more schools and hospitals needed? Is there a threat which means more spending is needed on defence? Is improving infrastructure such as roads, communications or railways needed to help the economy grow? A government knows it has limited resources so it needs to work out its priorities.

Extension activity

Ask students in their pairs to pick what they think are the three most important areas of government spending. Suggest that each pair should try to come to a consensus.

After a few minutes, ask the pairs to share their ideas with the class and ask whether it was easy to come to a consensus. Encourage students to develop their responses by asking questions such as How do you think government makes these decisions? What restricts the amount that governments can spend?

DEVELOPING

Teaching tips

- It can be helpful to use real data from your country to engage the students. This data might need to be simplified and produced in a clear and straightforward way. It would be useful to provide historical data so that changes in government spending and taxation over time can be shown. This will facilitate discussions on the reasons for the changes.
- Use media sources to compile a range of comments regarding government spending and taxation decisions. Views from a range of stakeholders can be included such as employer and worker organisations, political parties, economic journalists and charities.
- It is vital to give a balanced approach to government spending and taxation, remaining neutral.
- Emphasise that spending in one area can impact on other areas.
- Stress the limitations on government spending.
- Aggregate Demand is included in the Student's Book but is not on the IGCSE Economics syllabus. Students do not need to use the terminology, but can do so. While the concept itself is outside of the scope of the syllabus, students need to develop a conceptual understanding of 'total demand' in an economy in order to analyse the effects of demand-side policies, demand-pull inflation and a large number of other macroeconomic concepts. Making the concept of aggregate demand explicit may help students to grasp other important macroeconomic concepts and to distinguish between market demand and total demand in an economy. Although the term aggregate demand is not included in the IGCSE syllabus, it is fine for students to use it in response to a question as long as it is used in an accurate context.

Suggested answer to in-text question 1:

Responses should first summarise why government spends money:

- Reduce inequality for example, welfare payments such as unemployment benefit and pensions
- Provide public goods such as fire service, Police and national defence
- Provide important public services such as education and health
- Protect the environment
- Improve infrastructure such as roads and railways
- Aid industry and agriculture

It is important to advise students that when they choose an area of government spending as the most important, they need to do so in the context of the needs of their country rather than personal preference.

Good answers would then point out that spending more in one area would mean less for other areas and that this is the policy dilemma for government.

Additional activity: Where to spend

Use Activity sheets 4.3a and 4.3b.

In this activity students have to allocate spending to areas. The students should work in groups. This is a simulation activity based on an imaginary country. This will demonstrate the opportunity cost of decisions.

Instructions

Divide the students into groups. Get each group to think of a name for their country. Get the students to cut up their **token sheet (Activity sheet 4.3b).** These are the only available resources that their country has. Using tokens helps students to better appreciate the limited resources and gives a visual stimulus. Students could put the tokens in separate piles for each area of spending.

Hand out the decision sheet which has the previous year's spending. Distribute and go through **Scenario Handout 1 (Activity sheet 4.3a).** Scenario 1 includes some requests from different government departments and interest groups. Ask the students to come up with their government budget for Year 2 using the tokens as an aid. Emphasise there is not a right or wrong answer but they have to justify their decisions. On the flip chart paper they are to write three bullet points explaining their decisions.

At this point, get each group to present their decisions and their explanations. Highlight the main differences between the groups.

Give out Scenario handout 2 (Activity sheet 4.3a). Scenario 2 makes things more difficult as the budget has fallen by $10m. There are also additional events to take into consideration.

Groups are then to make their Year 3 decisions. On the flip chart paper they are to write three bullet points explaining their decisions.

As each group completes their presentation, write key points on the whiteboard, especially points of difference.

In a plenary after the activity ask students to comment on how consensus was achieved in their group. Encourage debate on each group's decisions. Discuss how in real life governments face similar issues. It would be useful to use news stories to discuss the issues surrounding government spending in your own country.

Extension question

What new demands on government spending are there likely to be in your own country over the next decade?

Suggested answer to in-text question 2:

The answer to this question could vary from country to country depending on the taxation regime. The emphasis should be on the types of goods rather than types of taxation. Students are likely to discuss goods like tobacco where taxes are imposed to try to affect demand. They should mention that demerit goods like tobacco could be harmful to consumers and this explains the use of these taxes.

A second type of good that could be taxed through tariffs and custom duties is imported goods. The impact would be to raise the prices of the imported goods. These would be imposed to protect domestic producers who might be less competitive than foreign producers or do not have the same advantages of economies of scale.

A third type of good that could be taxed could be consumer products such as petrol. The price elasticity of demand for petrol is inelastic and by imposing a tax on petrol the fall in demand would be smaller than the increase in price. The reason for taxing this type of good is to raise revenue. More able students should be able to illustrate this with an accurate supply and demand diagram. This taxation revenue can then be used for spending on provision of goods and services such as education and health care.

Suggested answer to in-text question 3:

The answer to this question will depend on the income taxation system in a country. The question limits itself to income taxation systems so any discussion of expenditure taxes would not be relevant. It is likely that a progressive tax system is used. A progressive tax is a tax in which the tax rate increases as the taxable amount increases. The word progressive refers to the way that a tax rate progresses from low to high. Some students might go on to explain that a taxpayer's average rate of tax is less than the person's marginal tax rate. Supporters of the progressive system believe that higher salaries enable rich people to pay higher taxes and that this is the fairest system because it reduces the tax burden on the poor.
A progressive tax system helps reduce income inequality. This is when one segment of the population controls a much larger share of the nation's wealth. By shifting the wealth of the society, the progressive tax system helps reduce inequality.

Some students might point out disadvantages of a proportional system which some interpret as punishing hard work and acts as a disincentive to people working hard. It might encourage high earners to leave a country.

Additional activity – Classification of taxes

Use Activity sheet 4.3c

Provide students with Activity sheet 4.3c, which will help them to understand classification of taxes. It will reinforce the distinction between progressive, regressive and proportional taxes.

Suggested solutions

Question 1

Income tax paid by Mr Rich

Mr Rich's income	Tax rate	Tax paid
$10000	10%	$1000
$90000	20%	$18000
$100000	30%	$30000
Total income = $200000		Total tax paid = $49000

Income tax paid by Mr Poor

Mr Poor's income	Tax rate	Tax paid
$10 000	10%	$1 000
$10 000	20%	$2 000
Total income = $20 000		Total tax paid = $3 000

$49 000 is **24.5%** of Mr Rich's income, whereas $3 000 is only **15%** of Mr Poor's income.

Therefore, the tax system is progressive as Mr Rich pays a higher proportion of his income in tax than Mr Poor.

Question 2

Tax on food of 20%

	Mr Rich	Mr Poor
Total income	$200 000	$20 000
Spending on food before tax	$10 000	$2 500
Spending on food after tax	$12 000	$3 000
Cost of the tax	$2000	$500

$2000 is **1%** of Mr Rich's income, whereas $500 is **2.5%** of Mr Poor's income.

Therefore, the tax is regressive as Mr Poor pays a higher proportion of his income in tax than Mr Rich.

Question 3

Flat income tax rate of 20%

	Mr Rich	Mr Poor
Total income	$200 000	$20 000
Income paid in tax	$40 000	$4 000

$40 000 is **20%** of Mr Rich's income and $4 000 is **20%** of Mr Poor's income.

Therefore, the tax is proportional it takes an equal proportion of the incomes of Mr Rich and Mr Poor.

Suggested answer to in-text question 4:

The Student's Book goes into detail looking at the impact of an increase in direct taxation. It is important that students understand that the question asks for who would benefit from **a decrease** in direct taxation. It would be useful for students to use the structure of the impact of an increase in direct taxation table in the Student's Book for their response.

Benefits to individuals (consumers and workers) Increase in consumer spending – a decrease in income tax would increase consumers' disposable income. As a result, consumers will have more money to spend which may result in higher standards of living. Reduced incentives to work – a decrease in income tax may increase an individual's incentive to work. Some individuals may therefore choose to work fewer hours or not work at all.

Benefits to producers Lower profits – a decrease in corporation tax would have the effect of increasing the after-tax profit received by business owners. Increase in the incentives for entrepreneurs – Higher profits may increase the incentives for entrepreneurs to start up new businesses.

Benefits to the economy A fall in direct taxation is likely to mean a fall in revenues and the government has less money to spend. However, assuming that consumers spend as a result of the lowering in income tax rather than save, this could have knock-on effects and a positive impact on the economy. Some students might point out that it might also depend on other tax rates remaining the same such as indirect taxes and that government spending does not fall. Some students could refer to the impact on inflation which might reduce the benefits of lowering taxes.

Suggested answer to in-text question 5:

The Student's Book goes into detail looking at the impact of an increase in indirect taxation while this question looks at the impact of a **decrease** in indirect taxation. Students should start by defining indirect taxation. The lowering of indirect tax would have benefits for the following.

- Individuals (consumers and workers). Lowering indirect taxes could lead to lower prices and increased consumption for goods and services. As consumers are paying less taxes on their spending, this increases their disposable income which could lead to more consumption.
- Producers would also benefit from a fall in their costs of production and an increased demand for their goods and services.
- The economy would also benefit in that there is less inflationary pressure.

Case study: 'Fat tax' introduced in India

This case study examines the imposition of a tax on unhealthy food. Discuss why more governments in the world are intervening in this way. Discuss how consumers might react.

Suggested answers:

1. A fat tax would make people pay the social cost of unhealthy food. Consumption of foods such as burgers, pizzas, doughnuts and other junk foods have external costs. Eating unhealthy foods is a significant contributor to the problem of obesity. Obesity causes health problems such as heart disease, angina, diabetes and strokes. There is also an impact on productivity with days lost through illness. Increasing the cost of unhealthy foods would reduce demand and play a role in reducing obesity levels. Making people pay social cost would achieve a more efficient allocation of resources. A tax on unhealthy foods would encourage people to choose healthier foods which would lead to improved health and would help reduce related disease. A fat tax would also encourage producers to supply foods lower in fat and sugar. Fast food outlets would have an incentive to provide a wider range of foods. A fat tax also raises revenue which could be used to help with the additional costs of health care or could be used to offset other taxes. The drawbacks of a fat tax are that it is difficult to know which foods deserve a fat tax. Many foods could contribute to obesity if consumed in sufficient quantities. Obesity is caused by more factors than just over-consumption of 'high fat' or high sugar foods. It includes issues such as size of portions, levels of exercise and genetic factors. The administration costs in collecting tax from unhealthy foods can be high. The case study also shows that people might switch to alternatives which are just as unhealthy.
2. A tax is one way of approaching the problem of obesity. It could lead to a fall in demand for junk food, but those who are not obese but occasionally eat junk food or include high fat items in their diet have to pay higher prices. There is also the issue of what foods should be included in a fat tax. Health awareness education programmes could be created for schools and the workplace. They could focus on healthy lifestyles, nutritious and healthier diets and physical activity and exercise. A tax alone will not change attitudes or show people the positive benefits of a healthy lifestyle. One possibility is to use revenues from the fat tax to pay for these education programmes.

Suggested answer to in-text question 6:

It is believed that reducing income tax rates (marginal tax rates) would have a positive impact on economic growth. Lowering income tax rates will give people more after-tax income (disposable income) and this could be used to buy more goods and services which would lead to an increase in aggregate demand. However, some consumers might save instead of spend so that would reduce the impact on aggregate demand. Another factor is that aggregate demand has elements other than consumer expenditure. Lowering income tax could mean less revenue for government and lead to a fall in government spending which would have an impact on aggregate demand. Consumers might spend their increase in disposable income on buying imports which could also mean that the increase in aggregate demand is not as high as hoped.

Suggested answer to in-text question 7:

Inflation means rising prices. Fiscal policy involves the government changing tax or spending levels in order to influence the level of demand in the economy. To reduce inflationary pressures the government can increase tax. This will reduce people's disposable income so they will spend less. This will make it harder for firms to sell their output, leading some to lower their prices and others to not increase prices. This helps to lower the inflation rate.

Case study

Obama's fiscal stimulus package

Discuss what is meant by a fiscal stimulus. Table 4.3a from the Student's Book could be used to remind students of the effects of fiscal measures.

Suggested answers

1. This recovery package played a role in boosting economic growth. Tax cuts increased consumers' disposable income which caused spending on goods and services to rise, which has knock-on effects for business. By investing in infrastructure projects such as roads and public buildings, this boosted the construction industry. More workers were needed which also boosted spending in the economy. Firms needed to invest in new equipment which had positive knock-on effects on the capital goods industry. The result was that there was a rapid decline in unemployment.
2. The stimulus package is likely to have caused an increase in the budget deficit in the short term Lowering taxes and increasing spending will mean that government borrowing will increase. However, as the economy grows the government receives more tax revenues. More people in jobs and less unemployment means those extra people in jobs will pay taxes. Increased sales will mean that expenditure tax revenues will also rise. Increased profits will mean that more corporation tax will be paid.

APPLYING

Project work

It is important to provide clear instructions and parameters. It would be advisable to produce a list of possible government funded projects. This would help less able students in particular. Stress that students can investigate projects that are not on the list but they need to check with you before proceeding that it is a government funded project. Go through the research method required and the importance of researching views from more than one perspective. Explain how the research should be presented. Ensure that students have access to recording facilities for the video clip. This does not need video equipment; recording on a smartphone could be a useful approach or they could produce a script for the radio broadcast. Discuss with students in advance the qualities needed for a one-minute video and the need to write a script which pulls together key aspects from their research report.

Expected outcomes

- Students identify a suitable government funded project and describe the project and the intended aims and objectives. Students should place the project in the context of government policy and show how the aims of the project would help to achieve government policy.

- Students need to investigate the costs of the project. The costs should include costs other than monetary ones, such as social costs. Social costs are the total costs to society. They should distinguish between private costs and external costs. For example, the private costs of building an airport are the cost of construction while the external cost of an airport could be the environmental impact in terms of noise and pollution to those living by the airport and the loss of landscape. Students should refer to the opportunity cost of the investment.
- Students need to investigate the benefits of the project. They should identify social benefits and discuss the favourable impact of the project on people or places. Reference could be made to possible multiplier effects of the project on the local and national economy.
- Students need to weigh up the costs and benefits of the project and come to a conclusion.
- The video script will summarise costs, benefits and impact.

Extension activity

Ask more able students to work together in pairs to discuss possible projects that the government should fund in the future that would have a positive impact on the local economy.

Knowledge check questions

Ask students to complete the knowledge check questions at the end of Unit 4.3 in the Student's Book.

Checking progress

Ask students to complete the Check your progress section in the Student's Book.

4.4 Monetary policy

Learning objectives

By the end of this unit, students should be able to:

- define money supply
- define monetary policy
- explain monetary policy measures: changes in interest rates, money supply and foreign exchange rates
- analyse how monetary policy measures may enable the government to achieve its macroeconomic aims.

Key terms

Money supply; monetary policy; interest rate; expansionary monetary policy; contractionary monetary policy; quantitative easing (QE); devaluation; revaluation.

STARTING POINT

This unit builds on Unit 3.1 where the functions and characteristics of money were introduced

1. Ask the students what they can do with money. They should respond that you can buy goods and services with it and also save money by putting it in a bank. Money facilitates transactions of goods and service as a medium of exchange. Money measures the value of various goods and services which are produced in an economy. Modern economic setup is based on credit and credit is paid in the form of money only. In reality, the significance of credit has increased so much that it forms the foundation stone of modern economic progress. It was virtually impossible to store surplus value under a barter economy; the discovery of money has removed this difficulty. With the help of money, people can store surplus purchasing power and use it whenever they want.

   The main characteristics of money are durability, divisibility, portability, acceptability, recognisability, stability of supply, stability of value, limited supply and uniformity.

2. Money facilitates trade because it is a medium of exchange. The use of a medium of exchange allows for greater efficiency in an economy and creates more trade. In a traditional barter system, trade between two parties could only occur if one party had and wanted what the other party had and wanted, and vice versa. But the chances of this occurring at the same time are minimal.
3. Money is anything which is generally accepted as a means of payment for goods and services. It consists of notes and coins and bank deposits in the forms of both current and savings accounts. Cheques, debit cards and credit cards are not money. The first two allow money in the form of bank deposits in current accounts to be transferred between buyers and sellers. Credit cards enable the holder to spend money now and to pay it at a later point in time.

EXPLORING

These exploring questions are suitable for individual or pair work.

1. Ask the students to write a list of goods and services and also to put them into categories. In a plenary capture the categories and write them on the whiteboard.
2. Question 2 looks at the knock-on effect of spending. Suggest to students they use a spider diagram to capture as many knock-on effects as possible. In a plenary invite a pair to draw and talk through their spider diagram.
3. Students should be able to describe the impact of a fall in consumer spending as this was covered in Unit 4.2. Falls in consumer spending will reduce flows of payments to business which might react by cutting staff and so the cycle would continue.

DEVELOPING

Teaching tips

- It is useful to embed monetary policy concepts with local information as this will give a context and shared experience.
- Get students to put together a cuttings file from newspapers, newspaper websites and financial journalists' blogs. Divide the class into groups and ask them to collect news stories on interest rates, exchange rates, inflation etc.
- Use diagrams such as flow diagrams when talking about processes or spider diagrams to consider knock-on effects. Students should rehearse these diagrams.

Suggested answer to in-text question 1:

Students should find out the current interest rate set by the central bank in their country. The answer to the second part of the question will depend on the direction of interest rates. If they are falling, then this might be part of an expansionary monetary policy to raise demand in the economy by the central bank lowering interest rates. Expansionary monetary policy is likely to result in lower unemployment and higher economic growth. If they are rising, this might be part of a contractionary monetary policy and the central bank can achieve this by raising interest rates. This can reduce consumption and investment and demand in the economy which will help to lower inflation.

Additional activity

Think – Pair – Share

This short activity is a collaborative activity on conflicts in using monetary measures. Display a slide or flip chart with the question:

What do you think is more important?

(a) *to use monetary measures to encourage economic growth and jobs, or*

(b) *to use monetary measures to influence the price and balance of payments stability*

Step 1 – Think

Working on their own, each student **thinks** about the question and makes notes of their responses or key points which they believe to be important.

Step 2 – Pair

For the next step, each student **pairs** up with a partner. The two students exchange their ideas and make further notes to add clarity to their own ideas.

Step 3 – Share

As a final step, invite different pairs to share the ideas they have discussed in response to the question.

In the plenary, go over the conflicts and why economists might differ in their opinions.

Support activity – What would you do?

This activity checks linking monetary measures with an economic problem.

In the table below there are different problems. Suggest one monetary measure that could be used as a solution.

Problem	Monetary measure
Inflation is too high	
Unemployment is too high	
Economic growth needs to rise	
Balance of Payments needs to be more stable	

Case study

QE – an alternative form of monetary policy

The study is based on quantitative easing (QE) in the USA and the UK. You could ask students to research other examples. For example, students could look at Japan, which has used QE several times since 2000. Some students might need some assistance with some of the terms used in the case study, such as bond certificates.

Suggested answers:

1. A simplified flow diagram can show the steps involved in QE leading to higher economic growth and lower unemployment

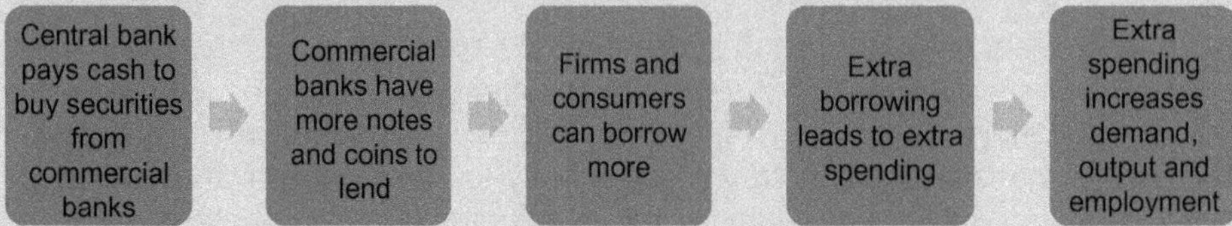

Figure TG 4.4.1

2. Countries give central banks slightly different roles. They are often the government's banker, the issuer of notes and coins and the regulator of commercial banks.

Suggested answer to in-text question 2:

It might be useful to give some background to rupee devaluation in 2017 before tackling this question. 2017 saw the rupee plunge to a nine-year low as the economy showed signs of stress. The International Monetary Fund had pointed out that the currency was overvalued by 20%, negatively impacting its exports. The position had been made worse by regional players devaluing their currencies including China, India, Turkey and Thailand which had given them a competitive edge over Pakistan.

Using this information, the student could conclude as follows.

- A devaluation reduces the price of exports and increases the price of imports. As a result, sales of exports are likely to increase leading to increased inflow of export revenue into the country from abroad. Furthermore, domestic consumers may switch away from purchasing higher priced imports towards relatively cheaper home-produced alternatives, reducing the money flowing out of the country.
- Devaluation would return Pakistan to the position before their international competitors devalued their currencies.

Suggested answer to in-text question 3:

Students could create a new table which highlights the conflicts in Table 4.4a.

Monetary policy measures	Policy conflicts
A fall in interest rates reduces the cost of borrowing	Low unemployment and economic growth vs low inflation and stable balance of payments
A rise in interest rates increases the cost of borrowing	Low inflation and stable balance of payments vs low unemployment and economic growth
An increase in the money supply using quantitative easing (QE)	Low unemployment and economic growth vs low inflation and stable balance of payments
An exchange rate devaluation (value of the currency falls)	Low unemployment, economic growth and stable balance of payments vs low inflation
An exchange rate revaluation (value of the currency rises)	Low inflation vs low unemployment, economic growth and stable balance of payments

APPLYING

Project work

This project asks students to investigate changes the central bank has made to interest rates in your country over the past year. Students might need help with finding their sources of information. If interest rates have not changed in the last 12 months, extend the time period. Newspaper articles are a good source of information particularly from financial papers and magazines.

You also need to point out what form the report should use:

- Introduction
- Use numbered points
- Sections for each question – where relevant this should include the extension question

Expected outcomes

- A copy of the report on central bank interest rate policy
- An explanation as to why these changes have taken place using economic terminology
- An awareness that expansionary or contractionary monetary measures have impacts on domestic consumers and producers
- For extension students, a discussion of how if interest rates rise this could cause an upward pressure on the exchange rate and if interest rates fall this could cause a downward pressure on the exchange rate. Some students might look at the knock-on effects of this.

Knowledge check questions

Ask students to complete the knowledge check questions at the end of Unit 4.4 in the Student's Book.

Checking progress

Ask students to complete the Check your progress section in the Student's Book.

4.5 Supply-side policy

Learning objectives

By the end of this unit, students should be able to:

- define supply-side policy
- explain supply-side policy measures: including education and training, labour market reforms, lower direct taxes, deregulation, improving incentives to work and invest, and privatisation
- analyse how supply-side policy measures may enable the government to achieve its macroeconomic aims.

Key terms

Supply-side policy; aggregate supply; productive capacity (or productive potential); labour productivity; deregulation; grant;

STARTING POINT

The starting point questions review understanding of the factors of production from Student's Book Unit 1.2.

You could use the questions as a basis for a class discussion rather than pair work. Write the key bullet points provided by the students on the whiteboard. Productivity is an important issue in supply-side economics. You need to be aware of a potential confusion between the terms production and productivity, as they are commonly used by students interchangeably, as discussed in Unit 3.6 of the Student's Book.

- Production is the total output of the goods and services produced by a firm or industry in a period of time. It records the total level of output produced regardless of the number of workers or machines employed to produce it. An example could be where a firm with 100 workers and output of 1000 units has the same production as a firm with 50 workers and an output of 1000 units.
- Productivity is a measure of output that takes into account the factors of production used to create the output. The productivity of labour can be measured by dividing the total output by the number of workers employed. It is measured in terms of output per unit of input.
- Productivity is measured as $\frac{\text{Total output}}{\text{Total input}}$.
- Productivity is one measure of the degree of efficiency in the use of factors of production in the production process.
- It is important that students understand that productivity is an average, calculated by dividing total production by the quantity of the factor of production used to produce it. It is therefore a measure of the efficiency with which a factor of production is used to generate output.

Ask the students to consider why improving productivity would be important for a business.

EXPLORING

The exploring questions use a stimulus of photographs in the Student's Book to ask how might a government increase the *quantity* of each of the factors of production in an economy.

It would be useful to look at each picture and identify what the picture shows. Students could refer to skilled workers and suggest that the government could use education to improve both the quantity and quality of the workforce. Government could encourage investment in new machinery and the use of new technology by industry through lower interest rates which increases the quantity and quality of capital. Government could remove unnecessary regulation or lower taxes which would encourage more people to start their own businesses and entrepreneurs to invest. Government could invest in flooding barriers which could add more land available for use.

DEVELOPING

Teaching tips

- It would be useful to ask students to collect articles containing examples of supply-side policy measures from their country and from other countries. These could be used in the project work. Articles bring the subject alive and provide real life evidence.
- Opinion is divided between economists on almost every major policy issue. It would be useful to use this unit to show these different opinions. However you need to avoid showing your own viewpoint; rather you should be a neutral umpire. Students should be encouraged to have their own views as long as they back them up with economic processes and terminology. Having a class debate on some of these issues would aid understanding.
- Spend time explaining the aggregate supply diagrams in the Student's Book. Aggregate Supply is included in the Student's Book but is not on the syllabus. Students do not need to use the terminology, but can do so.

Additional activity – Quality or quantity?

Use Activity sheets 4.5a and 4.5b

The aim of this activity is to support students' understanding of supply-side policies.

Place students in groups of three. Provide each group with a copy of Activity sheets 4.5a and 4.5b. Ask the students to categorise the supply-side policies in Activity sheet 4.5b in terms of whether they improve the quality or quantity of land, labour, capital or enterprise. They should place the cards in Activity sheet 4.5b in the appropriate boxes in Activity sheet 4.5a.

The first column on Activity sheet 4.5a is an improvement in the QUANTITY of resources, the second column is an improvement in the QUALITY of resources.

As this is group work, it would be useful to prepare by cutting up Activity sheet 4.5b into cards. Students can then place the correct cards on the grid but also change them easily.

After allowing enough time for the groups to complete the activity, run a plenary session going through all the explanations and inviting groups to contribute. Each time ask if everyone agrees and respond to any misunderstanding.

Suggested answer to in-text question 1:

Improving the quality of labour means using policies to improve the skills of the workforce. These policies can range from subsidising apprenticeship schemes to retraining schemes so that workers have the skills that industry needs to be productive and competitive.

Improving the quantity of labour means using policies to expand the number of people able and willing to work and increase the numbers in the workforce. These policies could range from making benefits more difficult to obtain and so encouraging more people to work or subsidising childcare to encourage an early return to work. Some students might refer to governments reducing the power of trade unions or reducing taxes that employers must pay when employing workers (for example, payroll taxes such as National Insurance in the UK).

Suggested answer to in-text question 2:

The similarities may include upward sloping demand/AD curve, downward sloping supply/AS curve. Differences may include focus on the whole economy rather than a market, general price level in an economy instead of market price and output of the economy (Y) instead of output in a market (Q).

Suggested answer to in-text question 3:

The answer is provided above the question in the Student's Book.

Additional activity

The washing line

This additional activity is about supply-side measures. It is to encourage students that it is good practice to have an opinion on what they are learning.

Set up a 'washing line' (a simple piece of string attached with thumb tacks) along one wall of the classroom. At one end of the washing line, peg a card with 'strongly agree' written on it. The other end should have a 'strongly disagree' card. If desired, 'agree' and 'disagree' cards can also be pegged along the washing line in the relevant places. A 'neither agree nor disagree' card could be added, but responses often cluster around this middle card, so an even number of responses (for example, strongly agree, agree, disagree, strongly disagree) would be ideal, as it forces students to take sides.

Now get the students to write statements about supply-side measures on cards. These statements should all start with *'It is acceptable to....'*.

Possible examples are:

'It is acceptable to lower taxes because workers will have the incentive to work longer hours.'

'It is acceptable to reduce union power as less time will be lost to strikes and other industrial action.'

Students need to phrase their statements to support all areas of the washing line spectrum, in other words, statements they think people will agree with or disagree with.

Put all the cards in a box and draw out a card for each student to attach to the washing line. (If the chosen card was written by the student, choose another). Students need to decide whether they agree or disagree with the statement on the card, then peg it on the line in the appropriate position.

Once the card is in position, students need to explain why they have chosen that spot. Students should also write up the justification for their chosen position.

Case study

Investment in Education in Finland

Provide some background information on Finland for the students. After having lived for decades in the shadow of the Soviet Union, Finland is now well settled in the European Union (EU) and is the only Nordic EU member to use the euro as its national currency. The country spends heavily on education, training and research, which has helped to develop one of the best-qualified workforces in the world.

- Population: 5.4 million
- Area: 338,145 sq km (130,559 sq miles)
- Major languages: Finnish, Swedish
- Life expectancy: 77 years (men), 83 years (women)
- Currency: euro

Suggested answers:

1. Three ways include:
   - subsidised day care for babies and toddlers, preschool and nine years of comprehensive school education for every child
   - the government also provides school lunches and free healthcare for all students as well as subsidising parents with around 150 euros a month for every child until the age of 17
   - for those already in work, the Finnish government has programmes in place to help them develop skills in areas including ICT
   - a state-funded network of public libraries also supports reading and literacy development throughout the population.
2. It has created a high-wage, high-skill economy which has enabled it to remain competitive in the international market.

APPLYING

Project work

This project work is based on using a news article as a basis for exploring a supply-side policy measure being used by a government and the likely impact of the supply-side measure in the short and long run. The teaching tip above suggested how students could collect such articles; alternatively you could provide them yourself.

It is not necessary to limit this to your own country, although the advantage of doing so would be familiarity.

The Student's Book considers the following supply-side measures which could act as a checklist for students when looking for an appropriate article.

- Education and training to improve productivity of labour
- Labour market reform such as reducing trade union power
- Lowering income tax and business taxes as incentives
- Increasing competition through deregulation and privatisation
- Encouraging entrepreneurship through subsidies and grants leading to product innovation and process innovation
- Improving infrastructure such as transport, communication and power grids

You should ask students to check with you once they have found their article to establish that it does illustrate a supply-side measure.

The second and third questions need a review of what is meant by the short run and long run. The checklist above could be used to ask how quickly the measures could have an impact so that this provides a context for their chosen article.

Expected outcomes

- An explanation as to why their chosen article is an example of a supply-side measure
- An examination of the short- and long-run impact

Knowledge check questions

Ask students to complete the knowledge check questions at the end of Unit 4.5 in the Student's Book.

Checking progress

Ask students to complete the Check your progress section in the Student's Book.

4.6 Economic growth

Learning objectives

By the end of this unit, students should be able to:

- define economic growth
- explain real gross domestic product (GDP) and how it can be used to measure economic growth
- explain GDP per head and GDP per capita
- describe the different stages of the economic cycle
- define recession and explain how a recession moves the economy within its PPC
- explain how changes in aggregate (total) demand may increase the utilisation of resources and GDP – resulting in a movement from inside towards the PPC
- explain how economic growth shifts the economy's PPC to the right and is caused by changes in investment, technology, and the quantity and quality of the factors of production
- describe the costs and benefits of economic growth in the context of different economies
- analyse the range of policies available to promote economic growth and discuss how effective they might be.

Key terms

Gross domestic product (GDP); final goods; consumer goods; capital goods; intermediate goods; money GDP; real GDP; real GDP per head (Real GDP per capita); economic cycle, boom; recession; slump; recovery; consumer confidence; business confidence; quota.

STARTING POINT

Allocate students to pairs and ask them to complete the starting point questions. After allowing time for the students to answer the questions, invite selected pairs to present their responses. Write their points on the whiteboard.

1. Students are likely to point out that a capital good is any good used to help future production. Examples are factories and equipment. A consumer good is any good that is not a capital good, is used by consumers and has no future productive use. Examples include cars, furniture and household appliances.
2. Students should infer that a change to consumer spending is an important economic indicator. If consumer spending falls, this would affect businesses who will see their sales fall; there can be knock-on effects in the economy. Consumer spending is like a barometer for the economy. The impact of falling consumer sending will reduce demand for goods and services leading to a fall in production and reduced employment.
3. Students might find this question more demanding at this stage in the discussion of economic growth. However, previous units (for example, Unit 4.5) looked at supply-side measures to improve productivity. You could build on this knowledge. Improved capital goods and investment will raise the productive efficiency of labour. If businesses are investing in new machinery or building new factories, it means that more can be produced in the future and the economy will grow. This could also be linked to Production Possibility Curves and why they shift outwards.

EXPLORING

In Unit 4.2, economic growth was introduced and defined and there is a case study on China's model of export-led growth. Before starting these questions, it would be useful to review students' understanding of economic growth. The exploring questions will need more teacher input. You might need to give some background to China's and the UK's growth rates before the students tackle the question. China's economy grew by 6.7% in 2016; the growth rate in the UK that year was 1.6%. It might be more useful to have a whole class discussion on this to enable you to use question and answer to broaden understanding of the issues. Alternatively, you could set a short research task and get students to feed back.

1. A typical answer could state that there is more investment in China than the UK and China has more spare capacity than the UK. You could point out that an IMF report on China stated that it was productivity improvements rather than investment in capital that fuelled the growth and that productivity gains accounted for more than 42 percent of China's growth. A conclusion could be that productivity rates are higher in China than in the UK.
2. Students would need to consider whether high growth rates can be sustained over the long term. Over the last thirty years, China has experienced much higher growth rates than the UK and in the short term this seems set to continue. This could be because China has a large home market still to exploit, higher productivity and ready supply of raw materials. Are falling growth rates the norm in mature countries? IMF figures in 2017 show that India's growth rates in 2017 are now higher than China's but also that mature economies such as Ireland and Iceland have experienced growth rates more than double that of the UK. The conclusion is that one cannot say with certainty whether China's growth rate will always be higher than the UK's.
3. Students saw in Unit 4.5 how supply-side measures could have an impact on growth and so their responses are likely to focus on these.

DEVELOPING

Teaching tips

- In order to understand economic growth, it is useful to examine the characteristics of more economically developed countries and compare them to those of less economically developed countries.
- Students need to understand that improving a nation's standard of living comes about through economic growth. A market economy creates incentives for economic growth as it is the pursuit of profit that acts as an incentive to take risks and invest. Often, in the discussion of economic growth, students miss out on the dynamic nature of an economy.
- Stress that government's role is providing the conditions that will enable economic growth to take place.
- Point out that economists are divided as to how to achieve the conditions for economic growth to take place.
- Students need to be helped when looking at GDP data for the first time. Always ask 'what is it telling us?'

Suggested answers to in-text questions 1–8:

Note that in answering the following questions students do not have to use the term aggregate demand. They can instead refer to total spending in the economy.

1. Consumer spending contributes to aggregate demand and so if more people spend in coffee shops this will boost aggregate demand. Some students might also refer to the impact of the earnings of the baristas as well as investment by owners in new coffee shops.
2. Students could point out that real GDP is more accurate as the total value for goods and services has been adjusted to take inflation into account.
3. A recession is a sustained period of negative GDP in the economy over time, also defined as two consecutive quarters (three-monthly periods) of negative economic growth.

   Suggest to students that they use a circular diagram to show the characteristics of a recession.

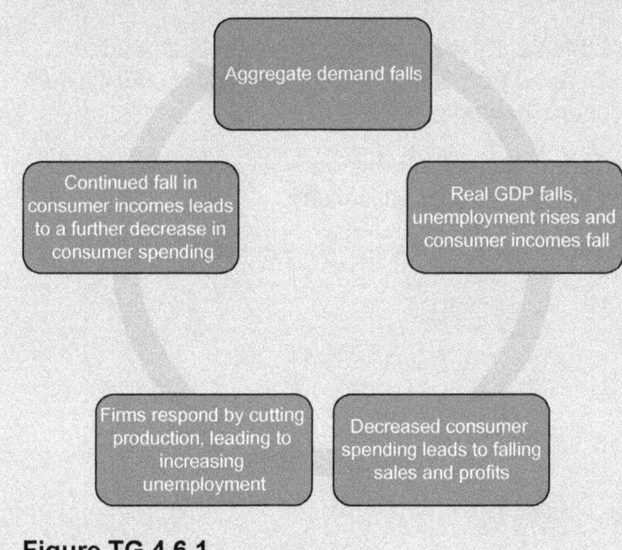

Figure TG 4.6.1

4. Unemployment can be shown on a PPC diagram using Figure 4.6.2 in the Student's Book to illustrate unemployed resources.

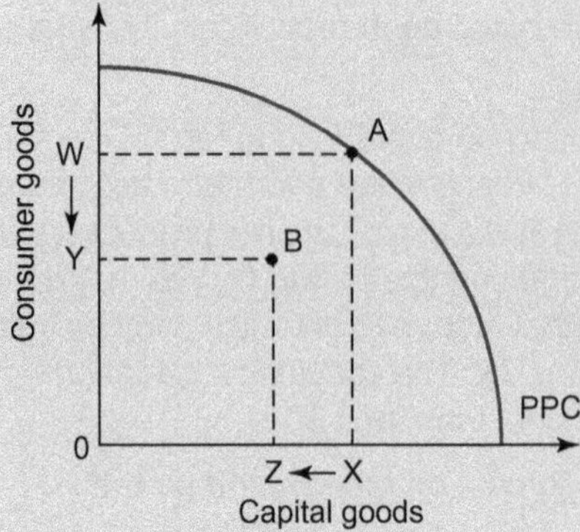

Figure TG 4.6.2

5. The following diagram was used in the Student's Book (Figure 4.6.3) to illustrate the effects on a factory being destroyed by fire on the country's economy.

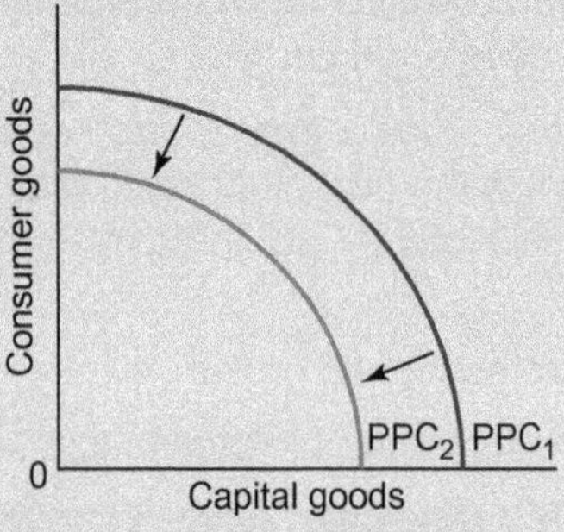

Figure TG 4.6.3

6. Students could refer to a rise in consumer spending fuelling growth as well as a rise in investment by building the shopping mall.
7. Underneath the question there is a table containing the benefits. After discussing the benefits of growth for households and businesses, you could ask students to close their books and set the in-text question as a test question.
8. Drawing out the problems is easier for the students as it shows depletion of non-renewable natural resources and pollution and environmental damage. Potential benefits could be that people have jobs in the factories that are polluting the air and that with the timber, firms are using the wood to meet construction industry demand.

Case study: Economic growth in Ethiopia

It would be useful to provide some background on Ethiopia. Ethiopia is Africa's oldest independent country and its second largest in terms of population. Apart from a five-year occupation by Mussolini's Italy, it has never been colonised. It has a unique cultural heritage.

It served as a symbol of African independence throughout the colonial period, was a founder member of the United Nations and is the African base for many international organisations.

Ethiopia has suffered periodic droughts and famines that led to a long civil conflict in the 20th century and a border war with Eritrea.

Population: 86.5 million

Area: 1.13 million sq km (437,794 sq miles)

Major languages: Amharic, Oromo, Tigrinya, Somali

Life expectancy: 58 years (men), 62 years (women)

Currency: Birr

Suggested answers:

1. One benefit of economic growth has been the rise in consumer spending as a result of rising incomes.
2. The Ethiopian government largely has invested in infrastructure which is likely to include transport and communication systems as well as developing industrial parks which will lead to the expansion of the secondary sector of the economy. Investing in infrastructure leads to the creation of jobs. This would lead to a rise in incomes and increased spending which will have knock-on effects in the economy.

Suggested answer to in-text question 9:

This should be familiar to students after their work in Unit 4.5. They need to mention that supply-side policy seeks to increase aggregate supply and the productive capacity of an economy by improving the quantity and/or quality of its resources. Examples are subsidies on research and development, privatisation and deregulation and lowering corporation tax.

APPLYING

Project work

Profile of a country

This activity is based on research carried out by the students to produce a profile on a country of their choice.

You need to prepare either a flip chart, a PowerPoint® slide or a handout showing the key topics relating to producing this profile:

- Country
- Population
- Real GDP over the past 3 years
- Real GDP per capita over the past 3 years

You must also have ready a list of suitable resource materials to support the students' research. You might prefer to give a list of ten countries for the students to choose from. Some students will need guidance on how to access the relevant information from the websites.

Resources could include websites such as the CIA World Fact Book website or the IMF website, textbook references and handouts.

Each student needs to use the resources to find out the answer to the two questions:

1. How has real GDP changed over the past three years?
2. What are some possible reasons for this change?

The student then needs to write a short report summarising their findings. The report should have a title page, a short introduction, clearly labelled diagrams and a short conclusion. The report must be completed and submitted by the deadline stated.

Expected outcomes

- A completed report with the required data
- Explanations for either a rise or fall in real GDP by referring to changes in consumer spending, resulting in higher or lower demand for goods and services. Changes in investment explaining that an increase in investment means that firms are investing in capital equipment and machinery as they seek to expand production or are not replacing machinery as they cut back on production. Some might refer to changes such as a rise in government spending or what is happening to net exports.

Additional activity

Brainwriting 6–3–5

Use Activity sheet 4.6

This activity is a form of brainstorming which will focus on how a recession can be avoided.

The name Brainwriting 6–3–5 comes from the process of having six students write three ideas in five minutes. Each student has a blank 6–3–5 worksheet (Activity sheet 4.6).

Divide the students into groups of six. Each student writes the topic for the brainwriting at the top of their worksheet. They then write three ideas on the top row of the worksheet in five minutes in a complete and concise sentence (6–10 words).

At the end of five minutes (or when everyone has finished writing), pass the worksheet to the student to the right. This student will then add three more **NEW** ideas. The process continues until the worksheet is completed.

There will now be a total of 108 ideas on the six worksheets.

Run a plenary session asking each group to present two ideas each. Write these on the whiteboard.

Go through the ideas and ask individual students to come up to the whiteboard and identify whether they are demand-side or supply-side ideas by writing DS or SS against each idea.

Support question

This support question asks students to write the features of the different parts of the cycle using the following phrases. They need to put each phrase in its correct box, for example, if low inflation is a feature of a recession it is written in the recovery box.

> low inflation, firms start to expand production again, more workers are taken on again, sales start to rise, unemployment is rising, consumer incomes are falling, increasing production of goods and services, unemployment is low, profits are rising, incomes are rising, firms cut production, very high unemployment, real GDP may be negative

Knowledge check questions

Ask students to complete the knowledge check questions at the end of Unit 4.6 in the Student's Book.

Checking progress

Ask students to complete the Check your progress section in the Student's Book.

4.7 Employment and unemployment

Learning objectives

By the end of this unit, students should be able to:

- define employment, unemployment and full employment
- describe the changing patterns and level of employment
- explain how unemployment is measured – claimant count and labour force survey
- state the formula for the unemployment rate
- describe the causes of unemployment
- describe the types of unemployment – frictional, structural and cyclical
- explain the consequences of unemployment for individuals, firms and the economy as a whole
- analyse the range of policies available to reduce unemployment and discuss how effective they might be.

Key terms

Employment; unemployment; labour force; natural rate of unemployment; formal economy; informal economy; claimant count; Labour Force Survey (LFS); frictional unemployment; seasonal unemployment; technological unemployment; structural unemployment; cyclical unemployment (also called demand deficient unemployment); voluntary unemployment; regional unemployment.

STARTING POINT

Divide the class into pairs or threes and ask students to answer the first two starting point questions. Invite selected pairs to present their responses and write key points on the whiteboard.

1. Students' answers could include: they have to as they need the income; job satisfaction from doing a job that they enjoy; take any job while they are looking for a job they really want; to support their families; to enable people to enjoy their leisure time.
2. Students are likely to point out that if the firm they work for is in difficulty, people might lose their jobs. Other points could be that jobs are too far away from home, or that people do not have the right skills or qualifications for the jobs that are on offer. The economy in the local area might have suffered and through closures there are very few vacancies. Others might point to personal circumstances such as illness or disability or having to look after young children or an elderly relative. It might be pertinent to point out that looking after people is hard work, however people are not paid to do it. The question is asking about paid work.

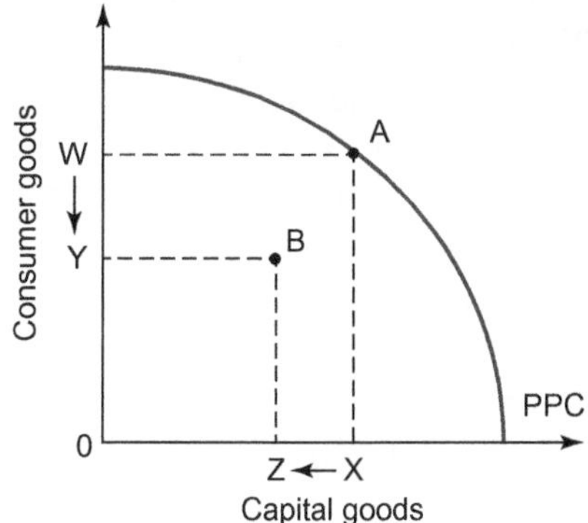

Figure TG 4.7.1

EXPLORING

The exploring questions look at the impact of unemployment on individuals, society and the economy. Put three sheets of flip chart paper on the board and title these 'Individual', 'Society' and 'Economy'. Hand out sticky notes and ask the students to write three effects on unemployment for each of individuals, society and the economy. Make sure they write their names at the bottom of the sticky notes.

Get students to put their sticky notes on the sheets that are on the whiteboard.

Select pairs to go through their points and use as a basis for discussion.

Answers could include:

Individual: Loss of income, decline in living standards, debt problems, psychological consequences (feeling of self-worth), impact on families, health problems (stress and depression), increase in divorce rates.

Economy: Higher payments for benefits, falls in tax revenues, increase in government borrowing, reduction in GDP, unemployed resources (country moves away from efficient allocation of resources), loss in business confidence, business profits fall leading to further job losses

Society: Tensions in a community when large numbers are unemployed, possibly leading to violence and other types of criminal behaviour; regional impact; knock-on effects.

DEVELOPING

Teaching tips

This unit is ideal to get students to have debates and so explore their own thinking about employment and unemployment. You could consider making some of the debate questions controversial depending on the confidence of the group. The following are possible debate questions/statements.

- There are always jobs for those willing and able to work.
- Should government do more to reduce unemployment?
- Do women face particular problems when seeking work?
- Why is youth unemployment so high in some countries?
- The smaller the country, the easier it is to solve unemployment.
- The answer to reducing unemployment is for everyone to take a pay cut.

Suggested answers to in-text questions

1. Students firstly need to explain the nature of the primary sector as the sector of an economy making direct use of natural resources or exploiting natural resources. This includes agriculture, forestry, fishing and mining. Students could point out that as countries develop, the primary sector takes up a smaller percentage of GDP and secondary and tertiary sectors take up a greater share. The difference is illustrated by countries such as the UK whose agricultural sector is 0.7% of GDP while in Pakistan it is 21.8%. Canada is unusual among developed countries in the importance of its primary sector, with logging and petroleum being two of Canada's most important industries.

   Another difference is that in developed countries the primary industry has become more technologically advanced, for instance the mechanisation of farming as opposed to hand picking and planting. In more developed economies, additional capital is invested in primary means of production.
2. You could set this as a small group-based research task. It is a complex issue which needs a discussion initially on the particular issues of youth unemployment. As many as 73 million young people are out of work worldwide. The average youth unemployment remains high. In Europe, for example, it is 23 per cent; in the United States, it is above 15 per cent.

   Solutions depend on causes. If it is lack of skills, then these can be addressed so that young job seekers' skills match employers' requirements. This could be by providing vocational training and courses while at school or college. More support for young people during vocational training could be provided to reduce high dropout rates from vocational programmes.
3. Ask students to find different measures used in the country such as those who are claiming benefits. Students could also be asked to investigate regional unemployment, breakdown by gender and breakdown by age.

4. Students should refer to structural unemployment and cyclical unemployment. Structural unemployment is a serious concern for most governments as it may result in a large number of job losses. It may also require retraining large numbers of workers so they have the necessary skills to re-enter the labour force, which can take many years. Cyclical unemployment is generally considered to be a serious concern as it affects the whole economy and can last for a long period of time if a recession is bad enough.
5. Students could provide this in the form of a table.

Reason for closure	Type of unemployment
Ice cream factory at a seaside resort closes in the winter	Seasonal
A labour intensive factory is closed to be replaced by a fully automated factory	Technological
The last washing machine factory closes because of foreign competition as competitors' wage costs are lower	Structural
Factory producing luxury processed foods closes due to fall in spending in a recession	Cyclical

6. Students could use a diagram to illustrate their answer:

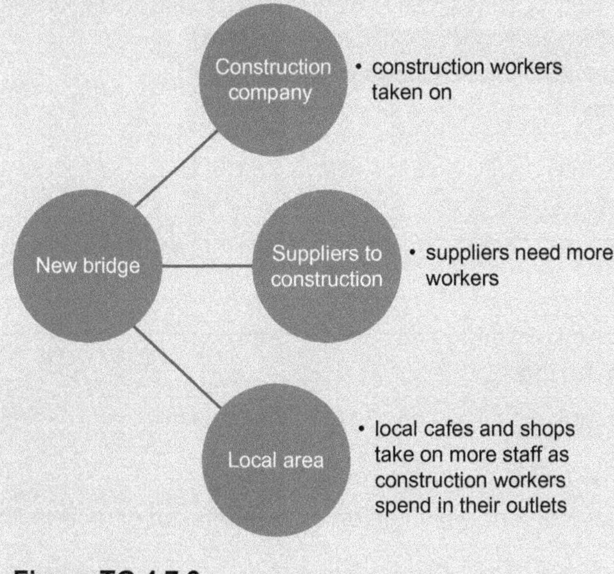

Figure TG 4.7.2

Additional activity

The diamond 9

Use Activity sheet 4.7

This activity is based on unemployment.

Use Activity sheet 4.7 to prepare nine diamond shaped cards displaying different scenarios.

Ask the students to arrange the diamond cards into a larger diamond shape with those scenarios they consider to be most important at the top of the diamond and the ones they consider least important at the bottom of the diamond.

When this has been completed individually, compare the responses of individual students. Use this to prompt discussion about the effects of unemployment. You can photograph the students' individual diamonds and print them. Ask students to write up notes of their explanations for their diamond shape, adding the printed photograph.

Support activity

Student quiz on types of unemployment

Students need to devise five quiz questions with answers based on types of unemployment.

Issue each student with five blank cards. Each student should number the cards and write their name on one side with a question about types of unemployment on the reverse of the card; they should write an appropriate answer to their question. Make sure students have their course notes or the Student's Book to support development of questions and answers.

For the quiz, arrange students in two equal teams. Ask one student to keep score using a suitable score-card. Player 1 for Team A asks one of their questions to Player 1 of Team B, who needs to answer the question. Discuss the answer with the group and ask the group to determine if the answer is correct. Player 1 of Team A then confirms the answer they had devised. (You need to correct answers if the student's answer was not wholly correct.)

The scorekeeper records 1 mark for a correct answer under the appropriate team's score column. Play then passes to Player 1 of Team B, who asks their question to Player 1 of Team A, and so on.

Total the scores at the end of the quiz to see which team won.

After the quiz, collect students question/answer cards and check that answers provided were correct. Return any incorrect answers to students and ask them to change their answer to the correct one.

Example score card:

Team A	Score	Team B	Score
Question 1		Question 1	
Question 2		Question 2	
Question 3…		Question 3…	

Case study: Youth unemployment in South Africa

Provide some background to South Africa, for example:

- South Africa has one of the continent's biggest and most developed economies.
- Up until 1994, it was ruled by a white minority government, which enforced a separation of races with its policy called apartheid.
- The apartheid government eventually negotiated itself out of power after decades of international isolation, armed opposition and mass protests.
- The democratically-elected leadership encouraged reconciliation and set about redressing social imbalances, but the economy has struggled.
- Population: 50.7 million
- Area: 1.22 million sq km (470,693 sq miles)
- Major languages: 11 official languages including English, Afrikaans, Sesotho, Setswana, Xhosa and Zulu
- Life expectancy: 53 years (men), 54 years (women)
- Currency: Rand

Lead a discussion before setting the case study on the impact of youth unemployment on the economy and young people themselves.

Suggested answers

1. Reasons include: lack of particular skills and experience required by employers; location issues, jobs might be away from home and the young person cannot afford accommodation and/or transport; employers prefer older workers who have relevant skills and/or experience so less time is spent in training new entrants; there might be poor job information and a lack of career guidance or support.
2. Unemployed youth miss out on a critical stage in their career development so they might lack confidence, self-discipline, have a poor work ethic and weak interpersonal communication skills. If South Africa's trend of high youth unemployment continues, it could lead to increased social inequality, an underperforming economy, emigration of educated youth and eventually falling tax revenues for the government in the future.

APPLYING

Project work

The project work asks that students use the internet to find evidence for one of the types of unemployment: frictional, seasonal, technological, structural or cyclical. Go over the main features of the types of unemployment. You could decide to limit this to your country or use examples from other countries in your region or further afield.

Students could use online newspaper articles or supporting data in the form of a chart or table. Additionally, students, when starting this unit, could start collecting hard copy articles on unemployment from newspapers and magazines.

One issue is that articles are likely to cover more than one type of unemployment. Also articles might not use economic terminology. One technique would be to get students to highlight the articles they find using different colours to refer to a different type of unemployment. It would help if you agreed on the colours to be used as this would help in checking student understanding quickly.

Students need to write a paragraph explaining the type of unemployment with reference to the information in the newspaper article or supporting data. It would be useful if students provided further background to the articles they are using and analyse the possible impact on individuals, the community and the economy.

Expected outcomes

- Students identify one type of unemployment from the article and write an explanation identifying the type of unemployment such as seasonal, frictional, technological, structural or cyclical.
- Students analyse the article describing the impact of the unemployment on individuals, the community and the economy.

Extension

Using the article they have selected, students should suggest what could be done by government to reduce the unemployment illustrated.

Students could refer to expansionary monetary and fiscal policy, job creation schemes, education and training, better information and communication about job opportunities

Knowledge check questions

Ask students to complete the knowledge check questions at the end of Unit 4.7 of the Student's Book.

Checking progress

Ask students to complete the Check your progress section in the Student's Book.

4.8 Inflation and deflation

Learning objectives

By the end of this unit, students should be able to:

- define inflation and deflation
- describe how inflation is measured using the consumer prices index (CPI)
- explain the causes of inflation: demand-pull and cost-push
- explain the causes of deflation: demand-side and supply-side
- describe the consequences of inflation and deflation for consumers, workers, savers, lenders, firms and the economy as a whole
- analyse the range of policies available to control inflation and deflation
- analyse policies to control inflation and deflation and discuss how effective they might be for different countries.

Key terms

deflation; consumer prices index (CPI); weighted price index; basket of goods; weighting; weighted average; base year; demand-pull inflation; cost-push inflation; positive supply shock; hyperinflation; purchasing power; cost of living; fixed income earners; pensioners; menu costs; shoe leather costs; wage–price spiral.

STARTING POINT

The starting point questions are suitable for a class discussion which will enable you to use question and answer to direct the discussion. List the key points on the whiteboard.

1. Consumers will normally buy more goods and services although some consumers will choose to save instead.
2. Firms, if they have spare capacity, would produce and supply more goods and services.
3. The consequence depends on what was the cause of consumers receiving more money.
   - Firms might respond to a rise in sales by offering overtime to workers. This increased income means that production keeps pace with changes in income. The consequence on the price level would be limited.
   - If not then demand might outstrip supply and the level of prices rises.

EXPLORING

Ask the students to list the goods and services they have bought in the last week.

Ask if they have observed any price changes for these products. Tell the students that sometimes a business can hide a price increase by making, for example, a chocolate ball smaller or putting less crisps in a packet. Students could use the internet to research news stories regarding this.

Explore the reasons why a business might increase or decrease prices. Draw two tables on the whiteboard headed 'Increase price' and 'Decrease price'. Invite students in turn to come up to the whiteboard and write one point. The first student would write in the 'Increase price' table and the second student would write in the 'Decrease price' table etc.

Increase price	Decrease price
Raw material costs have risen	Costs have fallen
Wages have increased	To attract more customers
Taxes have increased	Special offers
Want to make more profit	Response to competitor who lowers price
Increased demand results in the shop running out of stock and so can increase the price of the last remaining items	Increase market share
The only competitor has closed down so customers have no choice	

DEVELOPING

Teaching tips

- Encourage reinforcement by asking students to define and redefine inflation during the course of the unit. Often they understand inflation as price rises but miss the sustained rise in the general level of prices.
- Students need to grasp that with inflation a given face value of a currency will provide less purchasing power over time. This means that inflation is a sustained decline in the value of a currency.
- Changes in relative prices affect the pattern of demand more than absolute changes – if everything goes up in price by 10% and so does income then the 'real economy' is unaffected as households continue to buy the same quantities of all goods.
- Students find it difficult to understand that deflation might not be a good thing and so some time needs to be spent thinking this through. When the inflation rate is close to zero, there is more danger of deflation than high inflation. Deflation means that small businesses face real difficulties as debt obligations are harder to meet when the prices of the goods they sell are going down.

Additional activity – Demand-side policy board game

Use Activity sheets 4.8a and 4.8b

This activity is intended to give students practice at making extended chains of analysis when discussing the use of fiscal and monetary policies to achieve government objectives.

Make one copy of the game board (Activity sheet 4.8a) enlarged to A3 size. Photocopy Activity sheet 4.8b onto coloured card (enlarge cards, if possible). Prepare one set of cut up cards for each group of three students in the class. Each group will also need one six-sided dice and a counter for each player.

Procedure

1. Explain to students that they are going to play a board game that requires them to develop extended chains of analysis when talking about the effects of fiscal and monetary policies.
2. Divide students into groups of three or four and give each group a copy of the game board, a set of cards, a dice and a counter for each member of the group.
3. Each student takes five cards and places their counter on START. The remaining cards should be placed in a pile face down in the centre of the game board. Students should arrange their cards on the table in front of them. It does not matter if other students can see their cards.
4. Students take it in turns to roll the dice and move their counter.
5. If a student lands on *The government cuts spending* and they have the following cards in their hand: *inflation falls*, *aggregate demand decreases*, *unemployment rises*, *output (production) of economy rises*, *cost of borrowing falls*, they can form a chain of analysis linking the following cards to a fall in government spending – *aggregate demand decreases*, *unemployment rises* and *inflation falls*. As they do this, the student must explain how each card links to the fall in government spending by verbalising their reasoning to their group. Students may challenge each other's reasoning if they feel it is not accurate.

6. A player is awarded one point for each card they successfully link to the government policy. They should put these cards to one side and replace them with cards drawn from the top of the pile so that they always have at least five cards in their hand.
7. If a player lands on *swap cards*, they may swap any number of cards from their hand with cards drawn from the pile, placing their 'used' cards at the bottom of the pile. If a player lands on *Policy Decision* they may choose the government policy to link their cards to. If a student lands on *Pick up a card*, they may pick up one card from the pile and add it to their hand so they have more than five cards in their hand.
8. As students play the game, move around each group and check that they are playing correctly. Also be on hand to settle any disputes between players!
9. The game ends when there are no cards left in the centre of the board or when a predetermined time limit has been reached. The winner is the student who has accumulated the most cards/points.

Suggested answers to in-text questions:

1. The simple average is 7.5% and the weighted average is 9%. The weighted average provides a more accurate indication as it weights items according to their importance in a household's spending.
2. An increase in the price of oil can lead to inflation as it puts up costs to industry which will be passed on in higher prices.
3. The customer can buy more goods and services with their income because deflation means prices are lower which means with the same income someone can buy more. In terms of the causes of deflation, if the deflation was caused by a decrease in aggregate demand, fewer goods and services would be bought and sold. If deflation was caused by an increase in aggregate supply then more goods and services would be bought and sold. This is illustrated in the diagrams 4.8c and 4.8d in the Student's Book.
4. Prices will still be increasing, but by less than before.
5. The value of the money is likely to fall and so less would be bought.
6. It would be better to hold gold not cash. Inflation causes the real value of cash and savings to decrease over time. Some banks pay their customers interest which can help to maintain the value of savings. However, interest rates are unlikely to keep pace with rising prices during periods of high inflation. Individuals and businesses may respond by reducing savings during periods of high inflation, instead holding their money in other forms such as gold. Over time gold holds its value; as more people seek to buy gold, its value will rise.

Case study

Hyperinflation in Venezuela

Ask students to imagine a scenario in which a person in Venezuela carries money in a wheelbarrow. Why might this be?

Printing money has led to hyperinflation because the increase in the money supply from the printing of money caused the general level of prices in the economy to rise. The government continued printing money to finance its spending and this puts pressure on prices. Consumers start to expect prices to rise and so stockpile goods to avoid paying higher prices later. This leads to demand-pull inflation which spirals into hyperinflation.

Suggested answers

1. Consequences mentioned in the text include:
   - people lost their life savings as cash became worthless
   - banks and lenders went bankrupt as loans lost their value and bank customers did not make deposits
   - the value of the Bolivar fell which put importers out of business
   - unemployment rose
   - tax revenues fell.

Suggested answers to in-text questions:

7. If consumers expect the prices of cars to be cheaper in the future, they may choose to delay their purchase of a car until a future date. The effect of this would be a fall in consumer spending today which would result in a fall in aggregate demand in the economy.
8. Higher interest rates put up the cost of borrowing and so sales of houses might slow down.
9. Expansionary fiscal policy involves increasing government spending and/or lowering income tax rates to increase total spending in the economy (aggregate demand) and the general price level in the economy. If people receive a tax cut, their disposable income rises and they might decide to use this income by eating out more. A restaurant would benefit.

Additional activity

Chocolate bar inflation activity

Use Activity sheet 4.8c

This activity will help students explain the impact of inflation on purchasing power. The following materials are needed: mini chocolate bars, flip chart or marker board, markers, token money (use Activity sheet 4.8c).

Instructions:

1. On the flip chart, display a graph with the X and Y axes. Label the Y axis with 5, 10, and 15 to represent the money supply. Label the X axis with 1, 2, and 3 to represent the rounds of the auction.
2. Distribute the money and tell students to make sure they have the token $15 in their envelope (five one-dollar bills and two five-dollar bills).
3. Tell students that they will be participating in an auction. Discuss what an auction is (students are most often familiar with e-Bay) and how it works (that is, highest bidder wins etc.). Next, tell students that you will be auctioning off chocolate bars. Explain that there is no guarantee how many rounds of the auction there will be or what type of chocolate bar will be auctioned.
4. Tell students that in the first round, they have $5 to spend and have them take out the five one-dollar bills. Describe the items to be auctioned in the first round (three miniature chocolate bars and the flavour of the chocolate bars).
5. Begin the bidding at $1 and ask for bids. When you receive the final bid (up to $5), trade the chocolate bars for the money. Ask students how much money they had this round (money supply is $5) and how much was spent to purchase the chocolate bars. Mark the amount that was spent for the chocolate bar on the graph.
6. Tell students that in the second round, they have $10 to spend and have them take out one of the five-dollar bills. The student who made the purchase in the first round will have less to spend. Describe the item to be auctioned. Begin the bidding at the purchase price from the first round. When you receive the final bid (up to $10), trade the chocolate bars for the money. Ask students how much money they had this round (money supply is $10) and how much was spent to purchase the chocolate bar. Mark the amount that was spent for the chocolate bars on the graph.
7. Tell students that in the third round, they have $15 to spend and have them take out the other five-dollar bill. The students who made the purchases in the first and second rounds will have less to spend. Tell students this will be the last round of the auction. Describe the item to be auctioned. Begin the bidding at the purchase price from the second round. When the bid reaches $15 (it normally will because this is the final round), ask students if anybody will give you $16 (typical response is that they don't have that much money). Remind students that they can do with their money what they choose (that is, lend, borrow, save etc.). Students will generally begin collaborating (lending and borrowing) to purchase the chocolate bars. Continue the bidding to a high level then stop the bidding (normally around $30–$40). Trade the chocolate bars for the money. Ask students how much money they had this round (money supply is $15) and how much was spent to purchase the chocolate bar. Mark the amount that was spent for the chocolate bars on the graph.
8. Review each round of the auction. Ask students how much money they had in round one and how much was spent for the chocolate bars in round one. Review for the second and third rounds.

9. Discuss the increase in actual prices and whether having more money actually made them better off. Show on the graph what the relative price of the goods should have been based on the money supply (that is, if the chocolate bar sold for $3 in the first round, the relative prices in the second round would be $6 and $9 in the third round – this correlates with the available money supply). See the attached graph for a visual representation of this information.

10. Additional discussion questions:

    What determined if you were going to bid on the chocolate bars? (possible responses: the type of chocolate being auctioned, expectation of chocolate being auctioned in future rounds). If different chocolate was auctioned each round, discuss the concept of comparable goods.

    What supply and demand concepts were associated with auction? (possible responses: limited supply of chocolate bars, demand of students for the chocolate)

    Did anyone choose to save and not bid on the chocolate bars at any point? Why? (possible responses: didn't like the product offered, wanted to save money). For those that did not bid at all, you may want to reward them with a chocolate bar as 'interest' on the funds they chose to save and invest.

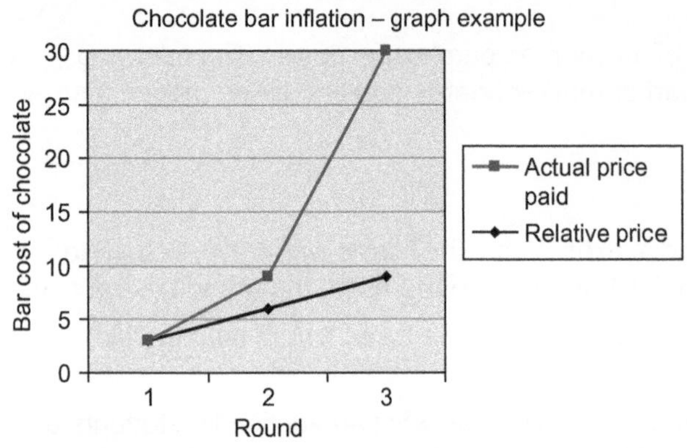

APPLYING

Project work

You need to undertake some initial research so that you can advise students accordingly. In 2017, there were only two countries experiencing deflation. The highest inflation rates in non-war-zone countries, were experienced by Venezuela, Nigeria, Argentina and Tanzania. However, you could check on the IMF World Economic Outlook Database which is a reliable source of information.

After choosing the country and finding its current inflation rate, some comparative data would be useful to see how the general price level is changing. The World Economic Forum has country profiles as does the World Bank.

When the students write their single sheet report, ask that they give the sources for their information.

Expected outcomes

- A one-page report with sources of information. The report will state a country's current inflation rate and the causes of changes.
- Students will identify the impact of the changes in the general price level. These can be based on their knowledge of economics if information on the impact on their chosen country is difficult to obtain.

It would be useful to run a plenary session inviting students to present their data. Write a summary table on the whiteboard and ask students to make a copy.

Knowledge check questions

Ask students to complete the knowledge check question at the end of Unit 4.8 of the Student's Book.

Checking progress

Ask students to complete the Check your progress section in the Student's Book.

Chapter review

Ask students to complete the Chapter Review questions at the end of Chapter 4 in the Student's Book.

5.1 Living standards

Learning objectives

By the end of this unit, students should be able to:

- identify indicators of living standards, including real GDP per head and the Human Development Index (HDI)
- describe the components of real GDP per head and HDI
- explain the advantages and disadvantages of real GDP per head and HDI
- analyse the reasons for differences in living standards and income distribution within and between countries.

Key terms

Real GDP; real GDP per head (or real GDP per capita), living standards, life expectancy, Human Development Index (HDI)

STARTING POINT

You may begin with revision of the concept of GDP before the students attempt the pairs questions. This could be in the context of the circular flow of income, so the point could be made that GDP and GNI are different ways of looking at the same thing. GDP measures the value of output in a country whereas GNI measures the incomes of those producing the output.

Suggested answers

1. Real GDP measures the value of output of a country produced in one year. The effect of any price changes is removed from the figures so they represent genuine changes in output rather changes that arise purely from changes in prices.
2. Real GDP per head is real GDP divided by the population of a country.
3. It would be expected that students could readily explain the differences between the different sectors of the economy. The point could be made that a thriving service sector is often seen as an indicator of economic development. To what extent is this happening in the students' country?

Support questions:

The following support questions may help some students with the 'real' concept.

- Imagine you had an allowance of $X (a reasonable figure in local currency). How would you feel if this allowance was doubled?
- How would feel if you then found the price of everything you wanted to buy had also doubled?
- What would have happened to your real income?

EXPLORING

Responses to question 1 could be summarised on the board in two columns: material and non-material. You may have to make some non-material suggestions, for example, political freedom and freedom from the fear of crime. This theme could be followed through in question 2. Hopefully students will suggest material factors like jobs, income and wealth and also non-material factors such as friendship groups, playing games/ sport and family life. Students could be asked to make connections between the two columns. For example, the pleasure of following a football team may be in the non-material column but a significant amount of income may be needed to participate in this activity, for example, to purchase television subscriptions, replica kit and match tickets. The learning point is that economic life affects happiness through a variety of routes, some of which are not immediately obvious.

For question 3, the students could work in pairs or small groups. Each group could be given at least two of the factors identified in question 2 and be asked to make suggestions as to how government could provide these factors. Suggestions to be summarised on the board. Do any patterns emerge?

Extension question

Should the government be responsible for making us happy? This question should be used to explore free market versus interventionist approaches to managing the economy. It may help if half the class argue in favour of 'happiness intervention' and half against.

DEVELOPING

Teaching tip

HDI is an index number. Some students find index numbers confusing, in particular the fact that they do not have any units attached to them. It is likely that price indices have already been covered in the course. If so, remind the students about CPI and RPI. Emphasise that index numbers are used to summarise change across a range of variables. In the case of CPI the variables are the well known 'basket of goods' but with HDI the 'basket' contains factors that affect living standards. Just because the index number is improving it does not mean that all the elements of the index are improving: HDI may be going up but healthcare may possibly be getting worse.

Additional activity

International comparisons

Using the table on page 284 of the Student's Book, ask the students to compare the real GDP per head in New Zealand with the real GDP per head in Bangladesh. Also compare Burundi and Norway. Both comparisons should involve a calculation. So, in Norway an average person is x times better off than in Burundi.

Now compare the same pairs of countries using the table on page 286 of the Student's Book.

Questions

1. Which method shows the more extreme differences in living standards?
2. Suggest reasons why the two forms of measurement give different views of inequality.

Extension questions

3. If you were an aid worker and wanted to encourage charitable donations, which table would you use? Why?
4. To what extent do the figures for real GDP per head and HDI explain the increase in international migration in recent years?

Answers

1. Real GDP per head figures.
2. Real GDP per head gives a narrow view. HDI takes into account more factors. HDI will be less affected by: differences in purchasing power of the dollar in each country; differences in the informal economy and the provision of some goods and services through aid.
3. Real GDP per head as it highlights inequality and may encourage more people in wealthy countries to donate.
4. You may have knowledge of local migration patterns that may inform answers to this question. The real GDP per head figures do seem to partly explain the drive to move out of Africa and parts of Asia. The differences shown by HDI figures are less extreme but still show significant differences.

Suggested approach to in-text question 1:

You are advised to check that updated figures are available when setting this task. Also, students whose country is not in the textbook table may well wish to check the progress of their country.

Suggested answer to in-text question 2:

The students in the left-hand picture are working in a better resourced environment. This could be because they are living in a more developed economy which has more resources to spend on its education system. Alternatively, the students in the left-hand picture could be from better off income groups in the same country as those in the right-hand group. The differences in the quality of the educational resourcing could become more extreme in the future if some students are denied access to higher incomes through having a limited education. The differences could reduce if there is more mobility between income groups in society.

Suggested approach to in-text question 3:

This question will need to be handled sensitively, especially in classes where students are from a wide range of backgrounds. Students may be uncomfortable if they self-identify as being low income, or indeed privileged, groups. An alternative approach would be to identify the factors affecting living standards in the country.

Suggested answer to in-text question 4:

Governments can improve living standards by implementing policies to promote sustainable economic growth with due regard to the environment. Such policies might include infrastructure development and spending on education. Policies that redistribute income can also be introduced, for example, ensuring that all members of the community have access to health and social care.

Case study

Sri Lanka's human development

You could read the first paragraph to the class. You could comment on the very high, high, medium and low categories for HDI. Students might interested in how their country and near neighbours compare with Sri Lanka.

You could ask the students to comment on the table. You could ask them to create a third column showing the percentage increase in each variable. This would highlight the outstanding growth in GNI per head. You could also explain that GNI and GDP are closely related.

The students could be asked to read the last paragraph and orally answer question 1 in class. The answers can readily be obtained from the last paragraph of the case study. The students could then write answers to question 2 which should cover such points as pollution, income distribution, working hours and availability of consumer goods.

Extension question

GNI per head in Sri Lanka has increased much faster than HDI. Suggest reasons for this difference.

Answers could include:

High inflation in Sri Lanka; move from informal to measured economic activity; exchange rate of Sri Lankan currency to the dollar. Also HDI may not indicate some improvements in living standards, for example, increased availability of cars and other consumer goods.

APPLYING

Project work

Research to be presented in tabular format. The extension question might be simplified for less able students; they might just compile a list of other factors that affect living standards.

Expected outcomes

Results to be presented in tabular format, possibly with a third column to highlight differences between the two countries. It may have to be accepted that data on some research criteria may not be readily available. An alternative approach to the extension task could be to ask the students to suggest modification to the HDI, rather than creating a new indicator.

Knowledge check questions

Ask students to complete the knowledge check questions at the end of Unit 5.1 in the Student's Book.

Checking progress

Ask students to complete the Check your progress section in the Student's Book.

5.2 Poverty

Learning objectives

By the end of this unit, students should be able to:

- define absolute poverty and relative poverty
- explain the difference between absolute poverty and relative poverty
- describe the main causes of poverty including unemployment, low wages, illness and age
- analyse the policies to alleviate poverty and redistribute income, including those promoting economic growth, improved education, more generous state benefits, progressive taxation, and national minimum wage.

Key terms

Absolute poverty; relative poverty

STARTING POINT

The disadvantages of a market economy could be summarised on the board, for example, ignoring demand for those without income; wasteful competition and ignoring external costs and benefits. All these points could be linked to the theme of poverty. Additionally, the disadvantages of a planned economy could be considered, particularly low output, poor quality output and the lack of incentives for innovation.

A table could be used to approach question 2

Annual income before tax ($)	Annual tax paid ($)	Percentage of annual income paid in tax
5000	500	
20000	3000	
100000	25000	

The students could complete the table and then be asked to comment as to whether this country has a progressive, regressive or proportional tax system. Hopefully they will establish that it is a progressive system – the implications for poverty can then be raised. The students could then be asked to produce a similar table showing a regressive system. Proportional taxation could then be revised through discussion, referring to the percentage columns of the tables already created.

Question 3 could be covered by creating a spider diagram on the board. Students could make suggestions such as: lowering taxes; increasing government spending; government subsidising industries; government taxing imports; government directly employing more people and encouraging inward investment.

Extension questions

1. A politician states that the taxation system is progressive because the rich are paying more than the poor. Use a numerical example to explain why this is not necessarily the case.
2. In most countries VAT (sales tax) is thought to be regressive. Explain why this is likely to be the case. In what circumstances might the statement not be true?

Suggested answers to extension questions:

1.

	Person A	Person B
Income per year	10000	50000
Tax paid per year	1000	4000

In the above example, Person A pays less tax than person B but the system is regressive because person A pays tax at a rate of 10% of income whereas person B pays at a rate of 8%

2. A sales tax is usually regressive because it is levied on items that poor people cannot avoid buying, such as food, clothing and household items. Rich people will also spend on these items but such spending is likely to be a smaller proportion of their income, so the tax is regressive. However, if the sales tax is only applied to luxury items, for example ocean going yachts, it would be progressive as only the rich would purchase such products.

EXPLORING

For question 1, students should readily be able to suggest points like unemployment, ill health and lack of skills. For question 2, it may help the students if they are asked to produce two lists: one for direct interventions and one for indirect interventions, that is, interventions that would improve the general condition of the economy. Question 3 may elicit a range of responses, depending on the differences involved. Extreme differences may lead to social unrest and absolute poverty will lead to part of the population being less productive than it otherwise would be. There is also the issue of equity or fairness. However, some differences may encourage ambition and aspiration. Some people may see differences in income as the just reward for achievement and may tolerate, or even support, extreme inequality, for example, footballers' salaries in the UK.

DEVELOPING

Teaching tips

Throughout this unit there may be opportunities to bring in the role of satellite television, social media, access to mobile data services and improved internet download speeds as determinants of perceived relative poverty. People are increasingly able to compare living standards internationally (at least superficially) so the benchmark for relative poverty will increasingly be influenced by the standards set by the most developed economies. This can create a tension with other macro economic objectives, for example, environmental goals relating to climate change. To what extent should developed economies *reduce* growth targets to allow less developed economies to catch up, without significant global environmental damage?

Additional activity

Exploring relative poverty

Ask the students to consider the following indicators of living standards:

1. Ready access to clean drinking water.
2. The ability to eat meat or fish every day.
3. Access to subscription satellite television services in the home.
4. Living in a house/flat with one bedroom for each family member.
5. The ability to take two or more overseas holidays every year.

The students can consider the statements individually, in pairs or small groups. Any statement that they consider to be part of a 'normal' lifestyle should be written on a sticky note. Those working in groups should only record statements that all group members are agreed upon. After, say ten minutes, the sticky notes should be placed on the whiteboard. The students should have a short period of time to review the whole board.

The follow up discussion will be influenced by the results. If the sticky notes differ then this can be used as an indicator of the difficulties of defining relative poverty. Students may be invited to defend some of the more extreme sticky notes or asked why they excluded or included certain statements. If working in groups, the students could be asked if selecting the statements led to any disagreements. You may choose to mention that there are official measurements of poverty, for example, the HPI indices for developed and developing countries.

You may vary the five statements, according to local conditions. The aim should be to have at least some statements that provoke debate.

Suggested answers to in-text questions:

1. Students should volunteer opinions as to the extent of absolute or relative poverty in their country. This would then determine which type was most applicable.
2. This is because the legal minimum wage may not be sufficient to enable the worker to purchase the goods and services normally consumed in that society. This problem would be made worse if the worker was trying to support other family members with the wage.
3. One problem of subsidising farmers could be that taxes may have to rise to fund the subsidy, increasing poverty for some taxpayers. It could also encourage inefficiency in the rice industry meaning that, for the country as a whole, rice would become more expensive. More information on this topic may be found in Unit 6.2.
4. Answers will obviously vary, according to the different circumstances of each country. Responses may be along the lines of: job creation would be the most effective policy as it would give people an income so they could provide for their families. Also, many people cannot afford basic foodstuffs, so it would help if the government subsidised food prices and also provided free school meals for children.

Case study

Child poverty

You could read through the first paragraph with the students. Also, there could be a brief question and answer session in class to revise the definitions of absolute and relative poverty.

Answers to question 1 could be elicited through question and answer with the class. The students could then give written responses to question 2.

Suggested answers:

1. Hunger, poor health, poor education and reduced opportunities in adult life.
2. The most effective policy, in the short term, would be to provide clean water and food, as otherwise the children could die or become seriously ill. In the longer term, education might the most effective way to reduce poverty as it could help people to increase their income by moving into better paid employment. A case could be made for all the policies in the extract.

Support question

The students could be asked to convert $1.90 into domestic currency and make suggestions as to what could be purchased with that amount. The responses could be linked back to the discussion of absolute and relative poverty.

Extension question

Would it be possible for a child (or adult) to live in absolute poverty in a developed economy?

This question could lead to a discussion. The following issues could be covered:

- Unequal income distribution could allow this to happen.
- Many developed economies have a state funded 'safety' net, particularly for children, so absolute child poverty would be very rare in those countries.

- Adults would be more likely to experience absolute poverty, for example, because of mental health issues or substance abuse.
- Relative poverty, including child poverty, is widespread in developed economies. The subjective nature of relative poverty could be explored (see additional activity).

APPLYING

Project work

Expected outcomes

The students should offer examples of the type(s) of poverty occurring in their country. The policies recommended should be supported by explanations as to why they are appropriate. The final choice should be supported by distinctive reasoning, rather than just re-stating earlier material.

Knowledge check questions

Ask students to complete the knowledge check questions at the end of Unit 5.2 in the Student's Book.

Checking progress

Ask students to complete the Check your progress section in the Student's Book.

5.3 Population

Learning objectives

By the end of this unit, students should be able to:

- describe the factors that affect population growth, including birth rate, death rate, net migration, immigration and emigration
- analyse the reasons for different rates of population growth in different countries
- analyse how and why birth rates, death rates and net migration vary between countries
- explain the concept of an optimum population
- analyse the effects of increases and decreases in population size and changes in the age and gender distribution of population
- describe a country's age and gender distribution from its population pyramid
- identify whether a country is developed or developing from its population pyramid.

Key terms

Birth rate; fertility rate; death rate; infant mortality rate; net migration; immigration; emigration; subsistance economy; ageing population; remittance; dependant population; over population; under population; optimum population; slums; overcrowding; human trafficking; age distribution; gender distribution; occupational mobility; geographical mobility; occupational distribution; geographical distribution; population density.

STARTING POINT

You may seek the answer to question 1 very quickly, for example by a show of hands. Some students cannot progress with the starting point questions if they do not know a migrant. Such students could be guided to relate questions 2 to 4 to their own qualities and prospects. Responses could be summarised on the board and are likely to relate to the financial benefits of migration, the need to migrate due to security issues and the social stress (and rewards) of migration.

EXPLORING

Students should readily be able to offer suggestions in response to stimulus materials. For questions 2 and 3, the students may need reminding to consider the positive and negative aspects. In many cases, a disadvantage for the country of origin will be an advantage for the destination country, for example a loss or gain of key workers. If the responses are summarised in the form of a grid on the board (country of origin advantages and disadvantages; destination country advantages and disadvantages) then this relationship can be emphasised.

DEVELOPING

Teaching tips

- As this topic is quite descriptive and 'content heavy', you may want to give the students notes, for example in the form of gapped hand-outs, so they can move through the descriptive material quickly. This will leave more time for exercises and diagram work, for example population pyramids.
- A 'gapped hand-out' is document where most of the notes on a topic are prepared by the teacher and given to the students. However, certain key points are left out for the students to fill in as the lesson progresses. Thus the students have more time to listen and contribute to discussion but they also concentrate as they know they will have to regularly record key information. For example, the hand-out may include definitions of immigration and emigration but the students may be asked to add a definition of net immigration. It is good practice to ensure that most of the gaps can be filled in by reference to the text book: this means that students who have missed lessons can use the hand-out to catch up.

- Although population growth and associated environmental destruction is a concern, you may wish to discuss the following, more positive, points with the students:
  - The world has coped with a doubling of its population several times throughout history.
  - Some experts believe that world population will never double again.
  - Despite the terrible warnings in the early 1970s of the effects of over-population, the world's population has continued to increase and living standards have never been higher for a larger proportion of the global population.

Additional activity

Concept mapping

Four key concepts (for example, from the key terms list) are written on the board in one colour. The challenge is to link any two concepts by creating sentences. The sentences should begin and end with a concept and the links can contain a maximum of three words. Each concept should be linked at least once. At least three links should be created but the more the better. The students should create the maps on rough paper (or a computer screen). This is an alternative to asking questions; the theory is that the students will not be able to link the concepts sensibly, unless they understand them.

The concepts could be slums; overcrowding; human trafficking; living standards.

The sentences could be:

Overcrowding may create slums.

Slum conditions encourage human trafficking.

Living standards are worsened by overcrowding

This activity may be resisted by the students at first but they become used to it. It can be adapted to any topic and is useful for creating display materials. If using computers, graphics can be imported to illustrate the concepts. A board demonstration, as in the example above, is essential. You may choose to allow students to use more than three words to link the concepts.

Support activity

Create the links for the students and ask the students to match the links to the concepts.

Extension activities

Allow students to select concepts and increase the number of concepts on the map.

The students could try to construct one sentence that uses as many of the concepts as possible.

Suggested answers to in-text questions:

1. You might want to have the answer to the first part of this question to hand, unless the class can use the internet to research the answer. A high figure may indicate that the students live in a developing country. It may indicate that subsistence farming is practised and/or family size is large enough to help look after people after retirement age.
2. You might want to have the answer to the first part of this question to hand, unless the class can use the internet to research the answer. A low death rate may indicate that the student lives in developed country with high standards of nutrition, health care and social care.

3. The emigration of skilled workers, ceteris paribus, will cause the production possibility cure to shift inwards towards the origin. See figure TG 5.3.1 below.

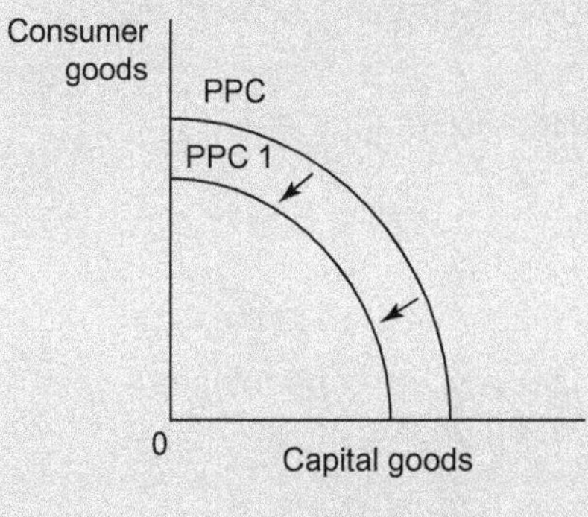

PPC - before emigration
PPC 1 - after emigration

Figure TG 5.3.1

4. A high dependant population will increase the dependency ratio, putting increased pressure on the working population. Taxes or borrowing may have to increase to pay for the health, social care and financial needs of the dependant population.
5. An increase in population is not considered to be a problem if a country is under-populated. An under-populated country would not have enough people to exploit existing natural resources, for example, fertile land. However this is a subjective 'growth focused' view based on the values of industrialised nations. Indigenous people might have a different view.
6. Immigration may allow gaps in the labour market to be filled, for example, in the hospitality and health care industries. This would increase the productive capacity of the economy and also increase demand.
7. Entrepreneurs and businesses which focus on products and services aimed at the ageing population would benefit the most. The nature of these products would depend on the affluence of the ageing group. Businesses and young people could also benefit from the skills and experience of older people, if they passed these on in the form of training.
8. Students might suggest that the low number of females in Middle Eastern countries is surprising. Is this because they have high numbers of migrant male workers?

Case study

Population growth in Malawi

You could read through the case study with the class. The answers to the first two questions are readily available from the text and so may be answered by the students as the reading progresses (preview the questions before starting the reading). The class can then discuss the extension questions in pairs/groups before moving to writing individual responses.

Suggested answers:

1. The population is rising because of the high birth rate and low death rate.
2. As the population of Malawi rises, the land and natural resources available, per head of population, will reduce. This may well lead to food shortages and may make the impact of climate change more severe.

Extension questions

1. Discuss methods that could be used to solve Malawi's economic problems.
2. Has Malawi exceeded its optimum population?

Suggested answers:

1. You may summarise some key approaches/ideas on the board before students attempt the question. These could include:
   - increasing the efficiency of agriculture – using a more capital intensive approach
   - industrialising – the path chosen by most nations
   - campaigns to reduce birth rates – as in China.
2. Students should be encouraged to revisit and paraphrase the definition offered in the textbook.

Students may explore and challenge the 'optimum' concept. Would Malawi really benefit from maximising output? Is output per head more important? Should more emphasis be given to short- or long-term issues?

APPLYING

Project work

The students may explore differences in the absolute size of populations, age distribution and gender distribution. Alternatively students might consider change as key factor, for example, is the country's population rising, stable or falling? GDP per head would be a good starting point for assessing the impact of population on the economy of a country.

Expected outcomes

- Identification of **three** differences between the populations of the two countries.
- Explanation of the reason for each difference.
- Explanation of **one** way in which each difference might affect the economy of the country.
- Written report and presentation of findings to the class.

Knowledge check questions

Ask students to complete the knowledge check questions at the end of Unit 5.3 in the Student's Book.

Checking progress

Ask students to complete the Check your progress section in the Student's Book.

5.4 Differences in economic development between countries

Learning objectives

By the end of this unit, students should be able to:

- define economic development
- explain the characteristics of developed and developing countries
- analyse the causes of differences in income; productivity; population growth; size of primary, secondary and tertiary sectors; saving and investment; education; and healthcare between developed and developing countries
- analyse the impact of these differences on the economic performance of developed and developing countries.

Key terms

Economic development; developing country; developed country; poverty cycle; intergenerational poverty.

STARTING POINT

The pairs discussion should be used to revise earlier learning about economic growth. You could sketch a production possibility curve on the board and the students could be asked to amend it to demonstrate growth. For question 2, the factors could be listed on the board, for example climate, access to common land, the ability to obtain food and shelter and the position of any given person in the social hierarchy. It would help to clarify the term 'living standards' before the students work on their answers. The government may influence living standards through welfare and taxation policies. For example, using tax revenues to provide an infrastructure that supplies clean water.

EXPLORING

The students may identify temporary 'home-made' housing, outdoor cooking and makeshift furniture as differences. The workers in one picture are engaged in primary sector work (likely to be low paid) whereas in the second picture the workers look more affluent and are likely to be commuting to tertiary sector employment. These differences may be caused by: lack of income to provide alternatives; a government that cannot afford to develop social housing; a government that lacks the will to develop social housing; displacement through war/social unrest/economic migration; absence of laws to prevent the creation of informal settlements, for example, shanty towns and favelas. The impacts will be mainly negative in terms of health, physical comfort and psychological well-being. However, there is the possibility that this lifestyle is better than some alternatives, depending on the previous situation of the inhabitants.

DEVELOPING

Teaching tips

- The knowledge check questions can be used to focus on question-answering techniques. Questions 2 and 3 use the command word 'identify' so there is no need to go beyond a brief statement of the relevant points. Also, there are several characteristics that could be selected for identification but students should not mention more than three, as the maximum mark has been achieved. One characteristic may be described and explained in detail but this part will still only be given one mark.
- Before attempting questions 2 and 3, advise the students not to simply 'reverse' the points made in question 2 when answering question 3, for example, developed nations meet the basic needs of the people, developing nations do not meet the basic needs of the people. This will prepare the students for how to approach discussion questions. For example, students may be asked to compare a developing and a developed country. An answer which only compared using the 'reversal' approach would be seen as one-sided.

Suggested answer to in-text question 1:

A country with a low level of economic development may fail to meet the basic needs of significant numbers of the population, for example, access to clean water and health care. The availability of consumer goods may be restricted and the nation may be experiencing political instability and corruption.

Suggested answer to in-text question 2:

The standard to achieved developed status is very high (see Unit 5.4 in the Student's Book). Therefore the students may quickly reason that their country is either developed or developing – even if only one of the required criteria has not been met the country will be classified as developing. This simple approach can be extended using the 'National Assessment' activity below.

Additional activity – National Assessment

This additional activity is linked to in-text question 2. It is designed to help the students think more about the criteria used for describing development and explore perceptions of their country's state of development. Before attempting the activity it would be best to reflect on the answers that the students produced for the question. The following points may emerge.

- The standard required for achieving developed status is set very high in that all the development criteria have to be met.
- Given the above, most countries will be classed as developing; this will cover a range of countries, varying from those that are one criterion away from developed status to those with widespread absolute poverty.
- Therefore, using some kind of grading system for development might help. The HDI grading system already exists. Students might be more engaged by sport-related grading, for example, the top tiers of UK football are: Premier League, Championship, League One and League Two. You could use any sporting context, appropriate to their country. Examination grades would be another option.

Support activity

Use Activity sheet 5.4a

The students could work in groups or pairs when completing the 'my perception' column. This should be done before any research is undertaken. You could vary the living standards column on the left to allow more accessibility for the students in any given context. The responses in the boxes are likely to be, yes/no, high/low, top 10 etc. but could be a little more detailed. After completing the boxes, the students should then grade their country according to the grading system you have chosen, for example, grade C or League One.

Research could then be undertaken individually or in groups. If the internet is not available (or time available is short) you could give their view on the research column as a basis for comparison. At the end of the research period the country's grade should be reassessed in light of the information gathered.

At the end of the activity the students should reflect upon any differences between their original perceptions and the research outcomes. Hopefully students may have different views and reasons for these differences can be explored. A key point to be drawn out is that there are many several facets of development and any two 'developing' nations may be experiencing quite different living conditions. The students may then attempt questions like:

How close is x (country) to being considered developed? Can x justify its developed status?

Suggested answer to in-text question 3:

It would be expected that developed countries would have over 50% of their employment in the tertiary sector. The other countries would therefore be classified as developing. However, other criteria would have to be achieved to confirm developed status. Another indicator could be the levels for employment in the primary sector. This would be high for developing countries. Thailand is an interesting case. The percentage of tertiary employment indicates that it may be developed but the high percentage of employment in the primary sector is more typical of developing status.

Case study

South Korea's economic development

The picture could be used for an introductory discussion about the nature of growth. Why is a picture of a city centre used to symbolise growth? Could there be alternative models for growth?

As you or the students are reading the case, the answers to question 1 could be obtained by questioning the class. Responses could be summarised on the board. For the second question, advise the students that the answer is not contained within the case study. The students will have to think back to their learning earlier in the unit. Ideas for development could be summarise on the board using a spider diagram (also known as a mind map or concept diagram), before the students write individual responses.

Suggested answers:

1. South Korea may be considered to be developed as it has modern infrastructure and improved public services. There is a high level of spending on education. The low death and birth rates have resulted in an ageing population.
2. The ageing population will increase the dependency ratio in South Korea. If taxes have to rise to fund more care for the elderly, then funds available for investment may fall, leading to lower economic growth. Also, family members may become involved in the care process, reducing the labour force available. However, it may be that the ageing population can contribute to growth. Improved health and technology mean that people can continue work into old age. The old will continue to generate demand by spending wealth accumulated in their lifetime. Industries will be developed around the care of the elderly. Therefore an ageing population is more likely to change the nature of output, rather than the level of economic growth.

Additional activity – Matching activity

Use Activity sheet 5.4b

Ask students to match the key terms with the descriptions in Activity sheet 5.4b.

APPLYING

Project work

The students could be directed to look at countries that are at different stages of development. This could lead to different features being discussed when the class shares results. Students could also 'grade' the country they have researched (see Additional activity – National Assessment).

Expected outcomes

The five criteria may include education, healthcare, economic data, employment sectors and population data. The students should identify key information and make brief evaluative comments. For each criteria, an assessment should be made as to whether that criteria meets the required standard to be considered 'developed'. Presumably one or more of the criteria will not reach this status, given that developing countries are being researched.

Knowledge check questions

Ask students to complete the knowledge check questions at the end of Unit 5.4 in the Student's Book.

Checking progress

Ask students to complete the Check your progress section in the Student's Book.

Chapter review

Ask students to complete the Chapter Review questions at the end of Chapter 5 in the Student's Book.

6.1 International specialisation

Learning objectives

By the end of this unit, students should be able to:

- understand why specialisation at a national level is important
- discuss the advantages and disadvantages of specialisation at a national level.

Key terms

Specialisation; factor endowments; overdependence

STARTING POINT

These questions may take longer than usual because productivity is a technical term that students may confuse with production. Hopefully one student will mistakenly suggest an explanation which relates to production. You can then give a correct explanation (simple board work example using output per worker to define the term). It is worth emphasising that the students would be expected to know the difference between production and productivity. This can then lead into the responses to question three. The students should be identifying issues like: practising/getting better at something (advantages) and boredom/repetition (disadvantages). In relation to businesses, students may suggest problems that arise if a business specialises but then loses its market.

EXPLORING

Use the same approach as in the starting point questions. It is assumed that the students will be familiar with the term 'factors of production' from a previous lesson. If you are uncertain on this point, some form of formative assessment could be undertaken. Once students have answered the questions, emphasise the fact that land refers to all natural resources. Many students assume that the word only refers to the land itself and would not recognize coal deposits and fish stocks as being part of the factors of production land.

Factors of production are combined to produce output which increases the GDP of a country. A simple example is the combination of land and labour to produce agricultural crops. In a modern economy most production involves the combination of all four factors. For example, car production requires raw materials (land) to be processed by machinery (capital) that is designed and operated by humans (labour). Risk-taking and management (entrepreneurship) is needed to organise the other factors of production.

In question two, students should explain that land, labour and possibly water are being used to grow crops. The value of these crops would then add to the GDP of the country when they were sold. Better students (or if necessary you) might raise the point that if subsistence agriculture is being practised then there may not be an impact on GDP. Students may also point out that capital and enterprise could be involved (see below).

Extension questions

Can you identify any capital items in the pictures? (Yes, the worker's basket and the fact that the fields have been terraced). Why is the basket an item of capital?

How would you answer the question if you were told that the worker ran her own farm? (Students should bring in entrepreneurship/enterprise). It is worth reminding the students that labour and enterprise are sometimes referred to as human capital.

DEVELOPING

Teaching tips

Take some time to explain the word **endowment** as it is not a word that the students will come across in everyday speech. All countries will have some of the four factors of production but some countries will be well known for one or two particular factors. Some examples are given in the text. Ask the students to think of 'three word links'. Start with the examples in the text: Maldives; land; tourism. How many can they think of in one minute? Jot down and then share with the class. Some students may attribute different factors to the same country and from this it may emerge that some countries, for example the US, are fortunate enough to have strong factor endowments in all areas.

The table on 'advantages and disadvantages of specialisation at a national level' is important: students who understand and can apply the contents of the table should be successful when responding to questions. One point to draw out from the table is that a lot of the benefits of specialisation come through international trade. Students may need detailed explanation of the impact of exchange rates on import and export prices. The table could be explored by asking the students (working in pairs) to identify examples of each advantage/ disadvantage that apply to the country they are living in.

Suggested answer to in-text question 1:

Before the students start this question, ask them to think about the country they are in. What would it have been like in prehistoric times (lots of land, a few people, not much else)? This gives the students the start to their answer – they can then develop it by moving through time. Remind the students to project into the future – this may bring up such issues as resource depletion. The students should also comment on such issues as population growth, skills development and capital formation.

More able students might repeat the exercise for another country (you to specify).

Suggested answer to in-text question 2:

Answers could include the point that less developed countries would be dominated by primary and possibly secondary industry with good factor endowments in land and cheap labour. Therefore they specialise in agricultural products or low-tech manufactured products. Developed economies would have strengths in highly skilled labour and high technology capital investment. Therefore they would produce complex manufactured goods, financial services and IT-related products and services.

Additional activity – Being clear on factors of production

Use Activity sheet 6.1

Activity sheet 6.1 provides a passage that has been written by a student who has not been paying attention in class. Put the students into small groups (max 4) and ask them to find points that would improve the passage. Be clear as to which group member is going to record each group's suggestions. After five minutes find out which group has the most suggestions. Ask one member of the group to read them out. Other groups can challenge the points made (you rule as to whether a challenge is valid). The number of valid points made are recorded on the board. Once all the suggestions have been reviewed another group could challenge if they feel they have more valid points.

Alternatively, the passage could be used as the basis for an individual homework. Students should make at least five justified suggestions that would improve the passage.

Case study

Sri Lanka's tea industry

When reading through the case study (it is suggested that you read it out) , attention could be drawn to the difference between the employment and GDP figures (without explicitly giving the answer to the extension question).

Suggested answers:

1. Answers should refer to favourable climatic and geographical conditions. Also the plentiful supply of labour.
2. The market is open to competition from other countries, especially African nations, who may have cheaper labour than Sri Lanka.

Extension question

Assess the possible impact of a decline in the tea industry on the Sri Lankan economy.
A strong student would notice that the main impact would be on employment (with the economic and social consequences that go with that). The impact on GDP would be relatively small, indicating that tea is a low value added but labour-intensive product.

APPLYING

Project work

Some of the preceding work has focused on the student's native country; weaker students could use that information as the basis for their poster. More able students could pick a new country to research. The poster could well be in the form of a PowerPoint presentation.

Expected outcomes

Emphasise the need for clear examples in the project work. The research should be applied to the country in question, rather than being a restatement of the material in the text book.

Knowledge check questions

Ask students to complete the knowledge check questions at the end of Unit 6.1 in the Student's Book.

Checking progress

Ask students to complete the Check your progress section in the Student's Book.

6.2 Free trade and protection

Learning objectives

By the end of this unit, students should be able to:

- define globalisation
- define multinational company (MNC)
- describe the costs and benefits of MNCs to their host countries and home countries
- describe the benefits and drawbacks of free trade for consumers, producers and the economy in a variety of countries
- describe methods of protection, including tariffs, import quotas, subsidies and embargoes
- explain the reasons for protection, including infant industry, declining industry, strategic industry and avoidance of dumping
- analyse the consequences and effectiveness of protection for the home country and its trading partners.

Key terms

Globalisation; multinational company (MNC); home country; free trade; free trade agreement (FTA); barriers to trade; protectionism; tariff; import quota; subsidy; export subsidy; embargo; infant industry (or sunrise industry); declining industry (or sunset industry); strategic industry; dumping; retaliation

STARTING POINT

Indirect taxes are usually taxes on expenditure that can to some extent be avoided or passed on by the tax payer. Such taxes are likely to have been covered as part of earlier work on supply and demand. If so, this is an excellent opportunity to revise this topic. A key learning point is that indirect taxes work through the supply curve: weaker students will want to shift the demand curve to the left. Point out that this approach fails the 'common sense test'. Would higher taxes on products really lead to lower product prices? A comparison can then be made with changes in direct tax, for example, income tax, which would operate through the demand curve. The conclusion will be that indirect taxes raise prices and lower output.

Internal economies of scale can be approached by asking students why businesses may become more efficient as they grow larger. Students should make points like 'buying in bulk', better use of machinery/ technology and marketing economies.

Support questions

Look at the first four pictures in the unit:

1. How many companies can be identified that are possibly MNCs?
2. What product(s) are the MNCs well known for?
3. Use research or class discussion to find at least two places in the world where each MNC produces.

EXPLORING

1. This can be answered quickly either by direct questioning or pairs being given time to make suggestions. Results to be summarised on the board.

2 and 3. The class could be divided into small groups to consider these questions (some groups to look at question 2 and others question 3). One person to feed back from each group. Students could refer to the following points:

- People feel safe with brands – they know what to expect (link to consistent quality).
- Consuming some brands may confer status on the consumer.
- Businesses may benefit from being able to move production to countries where the costs of production are low.

- If sales in one country are falling, businesses may be able to compensate by increasing sales in countries where the market is stronger.
- Operating in more than one country helps businesses to grow and gives them more opportunities to achieve internal economies of scale.

All the above points are positive. In the interests of balance (an important aspect of evaluation), some groups might be asked to consider the drawbacks of multinational operations.

DEVELOPING

Teaching tips

International economics may seem complex to some students. Reassure them that much of their prior learning, for example, supply and demand, economies of scale and opportunity cost, can be applied to the international sector. The main difference is that the international sector involves the exchange of currency to facilitate trade, so it is important that the role of exchange rates is made clear at an early stage.

An interesting issue to raise, possibly in a feedback session, is whether free trade should be restricted within a country, that is regional protectionism. Most students are instinctively against this and yet the same students may favour international protectionism. You may wish to use the example of China and its policy of Special Economic Zones to explore this issue.

Additional activity

'No person is an island'

Use Activity sheet 6.2

This could be an in-class or homework activity. The aim is to help students realise that international economics can be related to everyday economics. It should also reinforce any learning on protectionist measures.

Answers to question 1: a) labour, b) goods and services, c) any savings or debt

Answers to question 2: a) subsidy, b) embargo, c) quota, d) tariff

It may be enough just to answer the questions as given. Extension work could involve the issue of fairness or winners and losers from protectionism, for example, some domestic workers being protected but all consumers having to pay more for possibly inferior products.

Suggested answer to in-text question 1:

The key point here is that a multinational company produces in more than one country; an exporter may be based in one country. References to being active or selling in more than one country may be seen as being too vague. It should be acknowledged that there is a good deal of overlap between the two terms. Nearly all multinationals are exporters but some exporters may not be multinationals. You may be able to provide local examples of businesses that export but are not multinationals.

Suggested answer to in-text question 2:

Students should be directed to the 'benefits and costs of MNCs to the host country' table in the Student's Book which describes the various problems caused by MNCs. This should be the starting point for their answers. If working in groups, each group could be given two costs to consider. Expected answers would include the use of a legal framework, for example, anti-pollution laws, and the use of the taxation system.

Case study

Food retail in India

Read the first paragraph to the class. Lots of issues can be explored through class discussion. The situation in India could be compared to the situation in the local economy. Are multinationals allowed to operate food supermarkets in the local economy? How do the students feel about this (whatever the situation that prevails). What if Indian consumers want to eat food that is processed overseas? The students could read the second paragraph to themselves.

Suggested answers

1. To help the students to focus, the question could be divided into: advantages to consumers; advantages to workers; advantages to producers (suppliers) and advantages to the government. The students could be asked to focus on one aspect and then share their responses with the rest of the class.

   Examples of advantages: Consumers – more choice, better quality, cheaper prices. Workers – more work, better pay. Suppliers – more potential customers and possibly higher prices. Government – inward investment, improved balance of payments, increased tax revenue.

   You may wish to point out to the students that the question asks them to focus on advantages. Therefore it is acceptable, indeed important, to focus on the possible positive outcomes. The possible downside of introducing multinational competition may well be considered in feedback or class discussion but would not be part of a formal answer to the question.

2. Establish the answer to the first part through class discussion (otherwise students cannot progress to the second part). Answers to the second part should include the practical difficulties involved in monitoring the new businesses and the danger of creating an expensive bureaucracy that removes any benefit arising from increased competition. Presumably the Indian suppliers would help the government as it would be in the suppliers' interest to point out breaches in the agreement.

Suggested answer to in-text question 3:

Students may legitimately suggest protectionist measures as suitable actions by government, for example, introducing tariffs to protect domestic employment. The government may also use planning laws to prevent or reduce environmental damage. Governments may also encourage 'fair trade' agreements with multinational companies. When feeding back to the class on the responses to this question you could raise some more advanced points, for example, protectionism may protect a small group in society but at the expense of many others (in this case consumers). Problems attributed to free trade may mask more fundamental problems in the economy such as the unequal distribution of income or lack of investment in industry.

Suggested answer to in-text question 4:

This question may best be introduced by whole class identification of at least one benefit and one drawback of each reason stated in the 'reasons for protection' table in the Student's Book. Guidance may be needed regarding drawbacks as they are not stated in the table. Students should then be asked to write about one reason, stressing its benefits. Some comparison with other reasons may be made but this would not be essential. Students should be advised that a case could be made for most of the reasons and any plausible justification would be credited, for example, protecting sunrise industries would have the potential for future benefits in terms of growth and employment. There is no definitive answer.

APPLYING

Project work

It may be easier for the students if they are allowed to research articles from any source, rather than just newspaper articles. Information could be presented in a table. It may well be that a source does not give information on all the questions, so encourage the students to make sensible suggestions to complete any gaps.

Expected outcomes

Clear presentation of relevant data. The important feature of the work would be that it applies the knowledge and theory learned in class to a 'real world' situation.

Knowledge check questions

Ask students to complete the knowledge check questions at the end of Unit 6.2 in the Student's Book.

Checking progress

Ask students to complete the Check your progress section in the Student's Book.

6.3 Foreign exchange rates

Learning objectives

- define foreign exchange rate
- identify the equilibrium foreign exchange rate
- explain the factors affecting the demand for and the supply of a currency in the foreign exchange market
- explain the effects of foreign exchange rate fluctuations on export and import prices
- analyse how price elasticity of demand (PED) of exports and imports affects the export revenue and import expenditure
- distinguish between floating and fixed exchange rate systems
- describe the advantages and disadvantages of a floating and a fixed exchange rate system.

Key terms

Foreign exchange rate; floating system; fixed system; foreign exchange market; appreciation; depreciation; short term capital flows (hot money); foreign direct investment (FDI); floating exchange rate; fixed exchange rate; revaluation; devaluation.

STARTING POINT

In the opening questions emphasise that a market is not a physical location. If the class are aware that the new topic is foreign exchange rates then they might try to relate their answers to this topic. This would make question three difficult, so it may be necessary to reassure the students that they can refer to any product or service.

A market is any 'place' where the price and quantity of a good (or service) to be traded is decided. It may not be a physical location: some markets are conducted in cyberspace, for example foreign exchange markets.

Price elasticity of demand is a measurement of the sensitivity of the demand for a good or service when the price of that good or service is changed. It is assumed that all other factors that might affect demand, for example incomes, are held constant.

Factors affecting price elasticity of demand include: the price and availability of substitute goods; the price and availability of complementary goods; whether the good is an essential or luxury; the proportion of income spent on the good.

EXPLORING

These questions may be covered quickly. Students may point out that currency can now be ordered online and delivered to an address (in some countries). Some students may find question three difficult. Remind them to use a model where the answer is obvious, for example, £1 = $2 so $1 costs 50p. This will help the students to establish a method. They can check their answers by 'multiplying back'. Looking ahead to the development section, the students could be asked to calculate the value of 1CNY in US dollars.

DEVELOPING

Teaching tips

It is sometimes difficult to explain the need for foreign exchange markets to students. They may take the following view, 'I would accept any currency because I know I can get it changed by a foreign exchange dealer, for example, a bank/bureau de change.' These views can be challenged by using the support questions below:

Support questions

Why would the bank/bureau de change want to buy the foreign currency from you? (because they will have customers who want to buy the foreign currency)

Would the student accept a currency that they had never heard of or from a country that was known to be experiencing economic difficulties? (no, because they would not be confident that the currency could be exchanged)

The important point to emphasise is that for one party to sell a currency, another party must be prepared to buy it. The currency dealers will not want to buy a currency that they cannot resell.

The potentially serious nature of shortages of foreign exchange may be discussed. There is enough food in the world for everyone to be fed. The problem for some nations is that they cannot generate enough foreign exchange to buy the food from producer nations.

Additional activity – Fill in the gaps

Use Activity sheet 6.3

The textbook refers to currencies strengthening and weakening. These terms are commonly used but carry the danger of being 'value-loaded'. Students may perceive that a currency depreciation is an exclusively negative event. It may be better to encourage the students to use terms such as appreciate/depreciate or rise/fall. The 'fill in the gaps activity' (also known as a cloze passage) in Activity Sheet 6.3 can be used to encourage a balanced view of exchange rate movements.

Suggested answer to in-text question 1:

Foreign exchange is needed to pay overseas suppliers for their goods and services. It is also needed to purchase investment goods, for example machinery, when foreign direct investment takes place. Transfers may also need to be made, for example, migrant workers may wish to send money home to their families.

Suggested answer to in-text question 2:

The main similarities are that a quantity to be bought and sold will be decided, together with a price. The main differences are that the foreign exchange market operates mainly in cyberspace (transactions made by computers) and that the market approaches the conditions needed for perfect competition (under a floating exchange rate system). Perfect competition exists when there is an identical product available from many suppliers, bought by many buyers, all with perfect knowledge of the product and the various prices being quoted by each supplier with near cost-free switching of supplier possible. Compared to most product markets, the price of foreign exchange is more volatile. Prices change every second and move both up and down.

Suggested answer to in-text question 3:

An exchange rate appreciation means that an overseas customer will need more of their currency to buy a unit of the domestic currency. Therefore, if the domestic price is constant, the product will become more expensive for the overseas customer in terms of their currency. For example, a British consumer is purchasing olives from an Italian supplier. The exchange rate is £1 = €1.50 and price of the olives is €12 per kilo. The olives will cost the British consumer £8. If the exchange rate changes to £1 = €1.25 then the same olives will cost the British consumer £9.60, an increase in price of £1.60 per kilo.

Suggested answer to in-text question 4:

An exporter will want an exchange rate that helps to make them internationally competitive on price. They will like a floating rate if the currency 'floats' to a low exchange rate but not if it rises to a rate that makes the business uncompetitive. Similarly, exporters would like a low fixed rate but not a high one. Other factors will also be important to exporters: they may accept a higher exchange rate if they are experiencing cost reductions in the domestic market. For example, technological innovation may allow domestic production costs to fall and so domestic prices may be reduced, keeping export prices low even if exchange rates rise. Also, exporters may like the predictability of a fixed rate to enable them to plan but not if the rate is fixed at a level that makes them uncompetitive.

Case study

Hong Kong's linked exchange rate system

You may wish to read the case study with the class and explore some issues before the class attempt the questions. Emphasise that although the Hong Kong dollar is linked to the US dollar it will still float against all other currencies. Also some international commodities are traded and priced in dollars, so this would be another advantage of linking Hong Kong's currency to the US dollar.

Suggested answers

1. The main benefit is the stability of import and export prices when trading with the US and some internationally traded commodities.
2. Low inflation rates assist the US in maintaining low interest rates which, in turn, make it easier to have relatively stable exchange rates.

   In feeding back, you might explore the downside of Hong Kong's approach: an exchange rate that is appropriate for the US economy may not be appropriate to Hong Kong. Although both economies favour a free market approach, they are different in other respects, for example, factor endowment.

APPLYING

Project work

You may encourage/direct the students to research different currencies, for example, some that have experienced rising exchange rates and others that have experienced falls. It may also be interesting to research currencies that are 'in the news' at the time, for example, Venezuela at present. It may help students if they are directed to find data on GDP per head and inflation (see task 3 of the project work).

Expected outcomes

The students should produce comparative data for several countries. These can be reviewed to see if any patterns emerge. One issue should be cause and effect. Are exchange rate movements the cause of changes in the economy or the result of other changes, for example, inflationary pressures?

Knowledge check questions

Ask students to complete the knowledge check questions at the end of Unit 6.3 in the Student's Book.

Checking progress

Ask students to complete the Check your progress section in the Student's Book.

6.4 Current account of balance of payments

Learning objectives

- identify and describe the components of the current account of balance of payments – trade in goods, trade in services, primary income and secondary income
- calculate deficits and surpluses on the current account of the balance of payments and its component sections
- explain the reasons for current account deficits and surpluses
- analyse the consequences of a current account deficit and surplus – impact on GDP, employment, inflation and foreign exchange rate
- analyse the range of policies available to achieve balance of payments stability
- discuss the effectiveness of policies to achieve balance of payments stability.

Key terms

Visibles; trade in goods; trade surplus; trade deficit; invisibles; trade in services; primary income; wages; interest; profits; dividends; current transfer; secondary income; foreign currency reserves; creditor; debt; debt repayments; principal; interest; payment defaults; assets; bail out loan; consumer goods; capital goods; expenditure switching policies; expenditure reducing policies.

STARTING POINT

Reassure the students that much of their prior learning on supply and demand will now be applicable to this topic. Questions 2 and 3 could be answered using a table.

When introducing the table, you could check understanding of the term revenue (question 1) and contrast this with expenditure. In this case, revenue will be linked to exports and expenditure to imports. It is also a good opportunity to remind students of the difference between revenue and profit, a common point of confusion.

Export/ import	Price elasticity of demand	Price up or down	Revenue change	Local example
Export	Less than one			
Export	More than one			
Import	Less than one			
Import	More than one			

When feeding back on the table results you could raise the issue of PED being exactly one.

EXPLORING

Begin with the pairs discussion of questions 1 and 2. Students should raise points such as 'so the business knows how it is doing' and 'running out of money'.

When answering question 3 the students may repeat material from questions 1 and 2 but in a national context. A key learning point is the government collects import and export data for the economy to help with economic management. Weaker students need to be guided away from the idea that governments themselves are significant importers and exporters.

DEVELOPING

Teaching tips

Although the capital account is not in the IGCSE Economics specification, it may help the students if it is introduced at an early stage. It can then be used to explain why some countries can run persistent current account deficits and also how countries like Germany (see later case study) can recycle surpluses back into the international economy. The example of Greece and 'bail-outs' might be used.

Students sometimes develop the misconception that governments buy all the imports for the country, receive the revenue from exports (see Developing section) and hold reserves of foreign currency to facilitate such trade. Remind the students that international trade flows arise mainly from the actions of individuals and businesses; international trade could take place without any government intervention. Foreign exchange reserves may be used to manage the exchange rate but are not essential for international trade.

Additional activity – Live now, pay later

Use Activity sheet 6.4

The exercise below gives the students practice in using the terminology of international trade and can be used to explore the positive and negative aspects of running a current account deficit. Half the class could be asked to defend Rana's position and half the class could support her parents. You could devise similar passage (based on a saver) that could be used to analyse the issue of running a budget surplus.

Rana has always enjoyed spending money. She has a large overdraft, a bank loan to purchase a car and has financed several foreign holidays through the use of credit cards. She eats out most of the time. Rana has now reached the credit limit on her credit cards. Fortunately, she has a well-paid job and a pleasant rented flat to live in. Rana's parents, who have always managed to save money, are concerned about Rana's spending patterns but Rana says she can pay her bills and wants to enjoy life. She thinks that her parents worry too much.

Provide students with Activity Sheet 6.4 and ask them to write a short passage describing Rana's position and what may happen in future. They should use the following words/phrases in their answer: standard of living, current account deficit, borrowing, expenditure reducing, unemployment and interest rates.

Example response

Rana is running a current account deficit. This is because to maintain her standard of living she is spending more than she is earning. She is financing this through borrowing. In the future she may face problems if she becomes unemployed or if interest rates rise. She needs to stop eating out (expenditure switching) and spend less in general (expenditure reducing) as she will not be able to sustain this lifestyle in the long run.

Support question

Some students may be given the example response above. Key words could be deleted and the student could fill in the blanks.

Suggested answer to in-text question 1:

Visibles include wheat and furniture; invisibles include legal services and entertainment.

Suggested answer to in-text question 2:

Two key indicators that country A is a developed country are that there is a significant surplus of trade in services and a net outflow of secondary income. These figures could be associated with a country that has a well developed tertiary sector and can afford to make significant foreign aid donations and/or have a significant population of migrant workers.

Application Task

Question 1

	Component section	Inflow of money into Country B ($m)		Outflow money from Country B ($m)		Net balance ($m)
1.	**Trade in goods**	Visible exports	76	Visible imports	40	36 surplus
2.	**Trade in services**	Invisible exports	28	Invisible imports	38	(10) deficit
3.	**Primary income**	Inflow	30	Outflow	35	(5) deficit
4.	**Secondary income**	Inflow	16	Outflow	5	9 surplus
Current account balance						30 surplus

Question 2

2. The country has a current account surplus of $30m

Question 3

3. The country's balance of payments is dominated by visible trade and the healthy surplus in this sector ensures that the current account overall is in surplus. The service sector is relatively under-developed. This is possibly a developing country that is exporting a large quantity of a raw material, for example oil.

Suggested answer to in-text question 3:

If the demand for imports is price inelastic then introducing an import tariff would increase a current account deficit or reduce a current account surplus. This is because total spending on imports, including the tariff, would increase; this is because the percentage fall in demand would be less than the percentage increase in price. The tariff would, however, be an effective means of raising tax revenue.

Suggested answer to in-text question 4:

Expenditure reducing policies could have the beneficial effect of reducing inflation through a fall in aggregate demand (total spending). However, the fall in aggregate demand could also increase unemployment and lead to lower household incomes and living standards. If the expenditure reduction was caused by higher interest rates then the cost of borrowing would increase, which would adversely affect households with debts, particularly mortgages.

Case study

Germany's record current account surplus

You could preview question 1 with the class and ask them to read the first two paragraphs.

The final paragraph requires you to give careful guidance. It is a 'classic error' that students confuse a budget surplus/deficit with a current account surplus/ deficit. This is a good opportunity to revise the difference between the two (question and answer with class and summarise responses on the board).

Suggested answers:

1. The students could offer answers to question 1 as they come across them (the weak euro and low demand for imports arising from increased saving by the ageing population).
2. The measures in paragraph three have a direct relevance to spending a budget surplus but this is not the question and students should be warned not to answer the question in this context. Once this guidance has been given, the students will hopefully produce answers along the following lines: All the measures proposed by the German government should increase domestic demand and therefore the demand for some imported goods and services. An increase in imports should reduce the balance of payments surplus.

APPLYING

Project work

You may allocate countries to the students to ensure that different types of economy are covered. If the students cannot find secondary evidence that explains the reasons for a deficit/surplus they should be allowed to make suggestions based on general knowledge or material covered in the lessons. It may also be useful to collect data on the GDP of the countries concerned.

Expected outcomes

The data collected (deficits/surpluses, GDP and brief reason) could be summarised on the board in the form of a table (or the students could use ICT to create a table once the results had been pooled). Surplus/deficits could be expressed as a percentage of GDP and the students could be asked to compare this new column with the original figures for deficits/surpluses.

Knowledge check questions

Ask students to complete the knowledge check questions at the end of Unit 6.4 the Student's Book.

Checking progress

Ask students to complete the Check your progress section in the Student's Book.

Chapter review

Ask students to complete the Chapter Review questions at the end of Chapter 6 in the Student's Book.

Activity sheet 1.1a My economic problem

Instructions

In this activity, you are to keep a record (diary) of your spending as well as your income over two weeks. This information will be private between you and your teacher. Some categories have been included in Activity Sheet 1.1b and there is room for you to add categories. After listing and totalling your spending there are two scenarios for you to consider.

Scenario 1: You face a 20% fall in your income. Note down how this would change your spending. Explain how you made your decisions.

Scenario 2: You face a 20% increase in your income. Note down how this would change your spending. Explain how you made your decisions.

Income for the two weeks: Write here what money you have available to spend and what the source of this money is.

My explanation for my decisions in Scenario 1 is

My explanation for my decisions in Scenario 2 is

Activity sheet 1.1b

Spending diary				
Category	**List spending in Weeks 1 and 2**	**Total for category**	**Scenario 1**	**Scenario 2**
Transport				
Meals out, fast food etc. and takeaways				
Sweets and snacks				
Books, magazines				
Video games etc.				
Cosmetics, toiletries				
Entertainment				
Gifts				
Savings				

Activity sheet 1.3 Making choices

Scenario

Local government has announced that they have been given money to invest in the local community. They invited groups to suggest how this should be spent. Three groups have suggested three very different projects.

Project 1: A youth centre

There is a problem in the town in that there are very few facilities for young people. In the evenings and at weekends young people are meeting in the town centre and have caused problems with their anti-social behaviour. There has been minor vandalism and late-night disturbances. Staying out late is harming school work as well as causing difficulties in their homes. A youth centre would provide sports facilities and run sports clubs, and would have experienced staff who would run a range of activities in the evenings, weekends and school holidays.

Project 2: A day centre for old people

The town also faces an ageing population as people are living longer. A lot of these old people do not have the support of families who have moved away to seek jobs in other towns and many live alone as their partners have died. Many of these old people have little support and have limited resources available to them. A day centre would mean that they have somewhere to go and meet people and ensure they have at least one good meal a day. There would be activities provided as well as advisors and medical staff.

Project 3: A nursery

Many young families are on the edge of poverty. They need both parents to be earning to survive. They cannot afford to pay for someone to look after the children to go to work. Their children are also suffering because their diet is poor and so the children have health problems. A nursery would allow parents to drop off their young children before going to work. They will pay a small contribution which would be taken out of their earnings. In return, their children would be looked after by experienced staff who would carry out educational activities. The children would be fed as well as there being rest facilities. The nursery would also hold regular child clinics with health professionals.

Activity sheet 2.4 Market stall

You own a market stall selling fresh fruit and vegetables in a busy market. It is important that perishables such as soft fruit are sold out each day. Look through the following scenarios and decide what action you would take as the owner.

Name:

Scenario	Action in response
You have noticed that customers are buying far more mangoes than usual and you estimate that you will sell out by mid-morning. You find out that this is because the previous night a TV chef went through a delicious mango recipe.	
You estimated from previous days the amount of cauliflowers you need to buy in the market and advertise these for $1 each. Nobody is buying any but the next stall is selling out charging 75 cents for each cauliflower.	
There has been torrential rain in the town and nobody is visiting the market.	
A market stall nearby has bought a juicer and is offering fresh fruit juices. The price of the juice is 40% higher than if customers had just bought the fruit.	
When you went to buy your fruit and vegetables, there were not very many lettuces available and their price had gone up from 25c yesterday to 50c today.	

Activity sheet 2.5a Price survey

This activity asks you to survey prices of products in different outlets in your area. For each product, you should stick to one brand to compare prices. Note down the shop and the price.

Name:

Date of Survey:

	Shop	Price
Soft drinks		
Chocolate bar		
Fruit juice		
Peanuts		

Present this information in a short report. It might be appropriate to use tables and diagrams.

Are there any price differences?

If there are differences

- how great are the differences? (Use percentages)
- why might there be differences

What explanation can you provide if there are no or little differences?

Activity sheet 2.6a Shifts in supply and demand

In small groups, discuss each of the changes in Activity sheet 2.6b and place them in the appropriate quadrant of the table below.

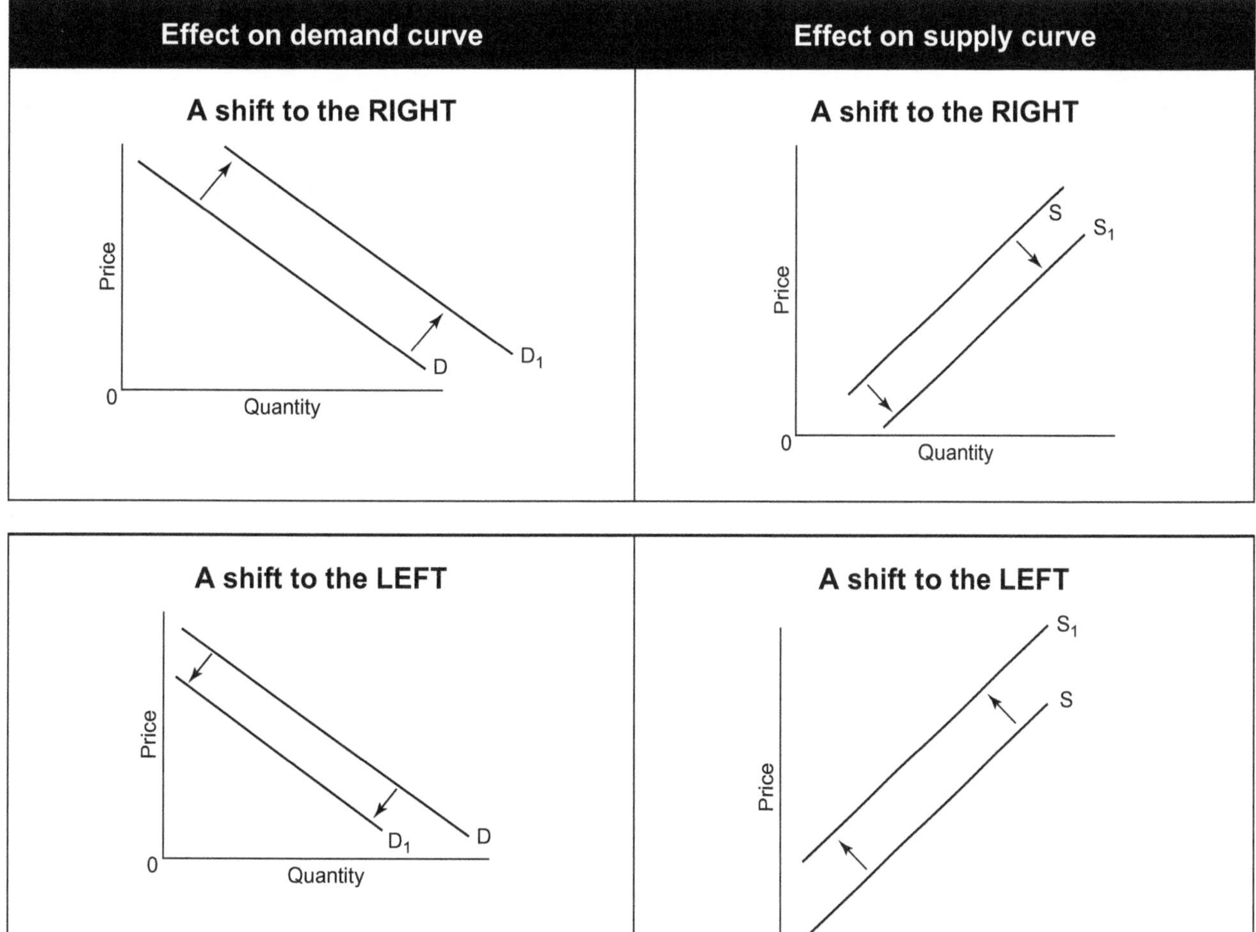

Activity sheet 2.6b Shifts in supply and demand

A movie star is seen wearing a traditional dress from a particular country.	New technology improves the efficiency of wine production.
A clothing brand launches an aggressive marketing campaign to promote their products.	The effect of a fall in the price of oil on air travel.
The effect of an increase in the price of air travel on overseas holidays.	Robots replace some types of labour in the vehicle manufacturing industry.
A video game maker reduces the price of its game console in order to gain a higher share of the market over its competitors.	The effect of an increase in petrol prices on car sales.
A shoe manufacturer introduces division of labour into their production process.	Consumers' incomes rise.
A cosmetics producer employs pop stars to advertise their products.	The effect of an increase in the size of the population on the housing market.
Good weather conditions result in high yields of kiwi fruit.	Rice producers expect that the price for their product will be much higher in the future.
People expect house prices to continue rising in the future.	An economic downturn means that people are eating out less frequently.
An article is published in a national newspaper linking fast food consumption with an increased risk of heart disease.	An invasion of locusts (a type of insect) wipes out crops of corn.

Activity sheet 2.6b (continued)

The government launches an educational campaign aimed at raising the public's awareness of the dangers of smoking.	The effect on supply of an increase in the price of apples relative to the prices of other types of fruit.
The shortage of skilled labour in the IT industry leads to rising salaries for employees.	A hurricane devastates banana crops in the Caribbean.
A high rate of inflation reduces households' real disposable income.	Research shows that consumption of eggs increases cholesterol and blood pressure.
The government increases the value added tax (VAT) on all goods and services from 7% to 10%.	The government tightens laws on the piracy of DVDs and computer software.

Activity sheet 2.6c What will happen?

In the table below there are a series of statements. You have to explain what will happen next.

This could mean price changes, demand increases, supply increases, conditions change which could cause a demand curve to shift or a supply curve to shift with the knock-on effects shifts could cause. You might decide that there would be no change or that you have insufficient information to decide. If this is the case, you would need to state what other information you would need. Use your knowledge of demand and supply but also use your common sense.

Statement	**What will happen?**
A shop selling sweets decides to drop the price of all its chocolate bars.	
There has been a very wet winter and the strawberry harvest is very poor.	
Incomes of 18–25-year-olds have risen over the past year. What would this mean for the demand for salt?	
A new type of chip for use in mobile phones has reduced the costs of manufacture.	

Activity sheet 2.6c (continued)

Incomes of people over 60 have risen.	
In the town there are two fast food restaurants. One of these has distributed 20% off meals vouchers.	
The government increases the tax on petrol.	
A fall in the birth rate means that the number of children under 12 has fallen substantially.	
As a result of increased paper costs, all newspapers produced in a country have raised their prices by 10%.	
Coffee shops are having to pay more for top quality coffee because of a world shortage of quality beans.	

Activity Sheet 2.7: Charlie's

Charlie's is a garage with a café which is situated on a main road. It is the only petrol station within 30 km. The café concentrates mainly on selling pizzas. There is no other pizza outlet but there is a fast food restaurant nearby that sells burgers.

Charlie wants to know whether he can increase prices at the garage and the café.

1. From the initial information above, what advice could you give Charlie?

Charlie has historical records which link prices to his sales.

For petrol, his data show:

Price of petrol	Sales of petrol/day
$2.50	3000 litres
$1.90	4000 litres
$1.10	5000 litres

For pizzas, his data show:

Price of pizzas	Sales of pizzas/day
$3.00	10
$2.75	20
$2.50	30
$2.25	40
$2.00	50

2. Charlie is currently charging $1.90 a litre for petrol and $2.75 for a pizza.

Should he change his prices to $2.50 a litre for petrol and $2.50 for a pizza? Show your workings.

Activity sheet 2.9 Group discussion using T-charts

The public sector should provide most products and services in an economy.	
We agree because:	*We disagree because:*

The private sector should provide most products and services within an economy.	
We agree because:	*We disagree because:*

Private sector firms can be trusted to act fairly and do not need supervising.	
We agree because:	*We disagree because:*

Large inequalities do not matter.	
We agree because:	*We disagree because:*

Activity sheet 2.10a Types of market failure

Work in groups of three to categorise cards under the headings on the grid below.

Type of market failure	Explanation	Example	Ways government can correct the market failure
Negative externalities			
Positive externalities			
Merit goods			
Demerit goods			
Public goods			
Lack of competition			
Immobility of resources			

Activity sheet 2.10b Types of market failure

Private producers may ignore the harmful effects of their production on **third parties** because they want to maximise their profit. If firms only consider private costs and ignore the external costs of production, their products will be over-provided by the market.	A firm producing chemicals dumps toxic waste into a river killing the fish and making the water unsafe for locals to drink.	• Indirect taxes can be imposed on the product. • Laws and regulations could be used to protect the environment and people's health. • Firms can be made to pay large fines.
Consumers may ignore the benefits to others when they consume a product. If consumers only consider the private benefits and ignore the external benefits of their consumption, certain products will be under-provided by the market.	Vaccinations against contagious diseases, education	• Subsidies can be placed on products with external benefits in order to make them cheaper. • The government could provide the product for free (direct provision).
Consumers may not fully realise how beneficial some products are for them which may lead to under-consumption and under-production of these products in a market system.	Education, health care, dental visits, motorcycle helmets, insurance	• Subsidies can be placed on merit goods in order to make them cheaper to increase their consumption. • The government could provide the product for free (direct provision).
In a free market, harmful goods may be produced and available to consumers who want to buy them. Consumers may not fully understand the harmful effects of these goods which may lead to over-consumption and over-production of the goods in a market system.	Consumption of cigarettes, fatty food	• Laws and regulations which prohibit the consumption and production of certain goods • High indirect taxes can be imposed to reduce consumption
Some goods will not be provided by private firms because they are **non-excludable** and **non-rival**, even though they are beneficial for society.	Street lighting, national defence, flood defences, lighthouses	• The government can provide these goods itself or pay private firms to provide them.
If some firms dominate the market for a particular good or service (they have monopoly power), they may restrict output and charge consumers very high prices.	A single supplier of electricity charges households unreasonably high prices making it unaffordable for some consumers	• The government can regulate firms so that they keep their prices low. • The government could encourage competition in the market in order to bring prices down.
Workers may not be able to move from producing products that are decreasing in demand to products that are increasing in demand due to **occupational immobility** (they lack the necessary skills) or **geographical immobility** (they are not able to relocate).	If the demand for a country's financial services is increasing while demand for steel is decreasing, there may be a shortage of financial services and unemployment of workers and capital equipment in the steel industry.	• Government can invest money in improving education and provide training in areas where new skills are needed. • Government can provide investment grants to make it easier for firms to change the use of land and buildings.

Activity sheet 2.10c: The debates!

Prepare for a debate on the scenario below. Each team needs to prepare to put forward their arguments using their knowledge of economics.

Group A Scenario

A new airport has been proposed because the existing airport in the area is working at capacity and cannot be expanded. A new airport means that 200 houses will have to be pulled down. Additionally, the area is the only habitat for a very rare butterfly and the end of the runway is close to another housing estate of 300 houses which are to remain. The airport is needed to enable the tourist industry to be expanded and plans are also in place to build new hotels and restaurants.

Team 1 will argue for the building of the airport.

Team 2 will argue against the building of the airport.

Group B Scenario

The city officials want to ban cars from using the city centre. They want to force people to use car parks on the edge of the city and use public transport to the city. They think that this will ease congestion and improve the air quality substantially. Opponents think that the city will lose out to nearby towns and say that shoppers will choose to go elsewhere. They also think that it will harm the business community and cause problems for people getting to work. The opponents have suggested that the number of city buses would have to expand from the current 500 to 4000 to cope with the extra commuters. They suggest instead that tolls are introduced to enter the city centres.

Team 3 will argue for the ban.

Team 4 will argue against the ban.

Activity sheet 3.1a: Functions of money game

Currency cards

Notes and coins 	Rice 
Cowrie shells 	Salt 
Tea leaves 	Whale teeth 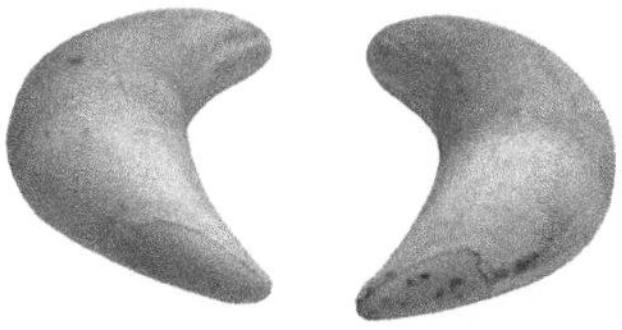
Cows 	Gold coins 
Fish 	Diamonds 
Sand	Rocks 

Activity sheet 3.1b: Functions of money game

Random selection spin wheel

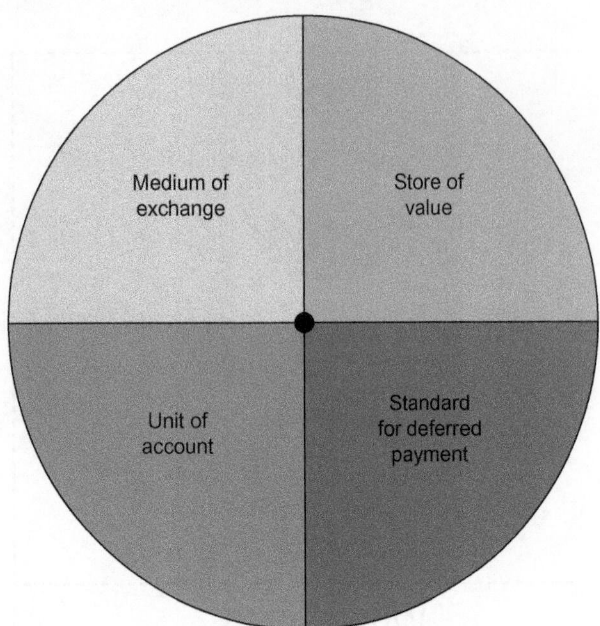

Activity sheet 3.2 Survey of household expenditure

Add the categories that you have agreed with your classmates. Collect information on what your household has spent money on in the previous week.

Survey of household expenditure From .... To			
Category	**Specific items**	**Estimated expenditure**	**% of total expenditure**
Example: *Clothes*	*2 shirts*	*$60*	*20*
Food			
Clothes			

Activity sheet 3.3 Falal's and Antonio's pay

You should read the short passage below relating to the pay of Falal and Antonio and then answer the questions.

Falal is paid a salary of $42 000 a year.

Antonio is paid a basic wage of $20 per hour for a 35-hour week. Some weeks, however, he does 5 hours overtime and is paid for those 5 hours at $25 an hour.

Questions:

1. How much is Falal paid every month?

2 a) How much is Antonio paid a year if he does no overtime?

b) Assuming that a month has 4 weeks, how much is Antonio paid every month?

3 Is Falal or Antonio paid the most?

4 One year Antonio has completed 120 hours overtime. How much was he paid that year?

Activity sheet 3.4a Score sheets for the blue and red game

Score sheet for teams					
Round	Card played	Opponent's card	Score	Total score	Comments
In rounds 1-4: Both teams play blue: score +5. Both teams play red: -5. If one team plays blue and one team plays red: blue -5, red +5.					
1					
2					
3					
4					
You may now send one of your team to negotiate with your opponents. In rounds 5 and 6 the scores will be doubled [x2].					
5					
6					
You may now send one of your team to negotiate with your opponents. In rounds 7 and 8 the scores will be quadrupled [x4].					
7					
8					

Activity sheet 3.4b Referee's score sheet for the blue and red game

<table>
<tr><td colspan="4">Referee's score sheet</td></tr>
<tr><td>Round</td><td>Both teams play blue</td><td>Both teams play red</td><td>One team plays blue and the other red</td></tr>
<tr><td>1-4</td><td>+ 5 for both teams</td><td>-5 for both teams</td><td>Blue scores -5
Red scores +5</td></tr>
<tr><td colspan="4">Teams may now send one person to negotiate with the representative of the other team.
In rounds 5 and 6 the scores will be doubled – see below.</td></tr>
<tr><td>5-6</td><td>+10 for both teams</td><td>-10 for both teams</td><td>Blue scores -10
Red scores +10</td></tr>
<tr><td colspan="4">Teams may now send one person to negotiate with the representative of the other team.
In rounds 7 and 8 the scores will be quadrupled – see below.</td></tr>
<tr><td>7-8</td><td>+40 for both teams</td><td>-40 for both teams</td><td>Blue scores -40
Red scores +40</td></tr>
</table>

Activity sheet 3.7 Calculating costs and revenue

1. Complete the table below. [6]

Output	FC	AFC	VC	AVC	TC	AC
0	200	----	0	----		----
10			200			
20						28
30					750	
40				20		
50			1200			

2. Explain what is happening to AFC, AVC and AC. [6]

3. Using the values for AFC, AVC and AC, plot the information on a diagram. [8]

Activity sheet 3.8 Product differentiation

Choose four completely different products, for example: cars; mobile phones; ice creams; and newspapers and complete the table below.

Product	Method/s of product differentiation	Explain why you think it is/is not effective
1.		
2.		
3.		
4.		

Activity sheet 4.1 Group categorising

Public sector
Private sector
Both

Activity sheet 4.2 Jigsaw reading activity

A	Country A has enjoyed rapid economic growth over the past ten years, most of which has come from the sale of its exports abroad. As a result, it has a very large trade surplus on its balance of payments. Inflation is above the target set by the central bank and is continuing to rise due to high demand for exports. The economy is close to full employment as large numbers of workers are employed in the secondary sector to produce manufactured goods for export. As a result, wages are rising leading to higher costs of production for producers. Many producers are passing this higher cost onto consumers in the form of higher prices.	**Explain what the primary aim of this government should be. Justify your opinion.** ....
B	Country B is a developed economy which has enjoyed sustainable economic growth over recent years. Unemployment is relatively low, with most workers employed in the tertiary sector of the economy. As incomes have risen, spending on imported consumer goods has increased resulting in a large and increasing trade deficit on the balance of payments. As a result of this, consumers, firms and the government have had to borrow large sums of money from abroad to finance their spending on imports. Interest rates on these borrowed funds are high.	**Explain what the primary aim of this government should be. Justify your opinion.** ....
C	Country C is facing negative economic growth. As a result of falling production in the economy, firms are making workers redundant contributing to increasing unemployment and falling incomes. Inflation is low due to the falling consumer spending and low demand in the economy. As a result of high levels of unemployment, an increasing number of people are living in poverty and are in need of financial assistance from the government. Spending on imports is low because of falling incomes.	**Explain what the primary aim of this government should be. Justify your opinion.** ....
D	Country D is a developing country and has enjoyed strong, sustained economic growth over recent years. While prices are rising due to high aggregate demand, inflation in the economy remains at an acceptable level. However, some members of the population have benefited from the increased economic growth more than others and the gap between rich and poor is increasing. Wages for unskilled workers are still relatively low and working conditions can be poor. As the economy continues to develop, unskilled workers are gradually being replaced by machinery and require retraining to find new jobs.	**Explain what the primary aim of this government should be. Justify your opinion.** ....

Activity sheet 4.3a Where to spend

Scenario handout 1

You have a $100m budget. You cannot borrow to increase the spending budget.

In Year 2 you face the following events. You need to decide how you will respond to these events and decide on your budget.

- Investment is needed in healthcare with a new maternity wing needed that will cost $2m.
- Police believe that a $2m investment is needed to improve security at airports.
- There is an ageing population which will mean greater demands on healthcare and will mean more will have to be spent on pensions. The estimated impact on government spending is an additional $4m in Year 2.
- Industry pressure groups are asking for government to invest in improved railway infrastructure which would help growth. This would cost an estimated $5m.

Decision sheet

Country...

You have an available budget of $100m

Area of spending	Year 1 $m	Year 2	Year 3
Welfare	16		
Defence	8		
Education	14		
Healthcare	18		
Police and fire	6		
Transport	5		
Pensions	20		
Flood defences	3		
Industry support	5		
Agriculture support	5		
Total	100		

Scenario handout 2

The money that the Government raises in taxation has fallen by $10m in Year 3.

In addition, a recent storm destroyed flood defences in a tourist area and to restore them would cost $3m.

Make your decisions based on these new developments.

Activity sheet 4.3b Where to spend

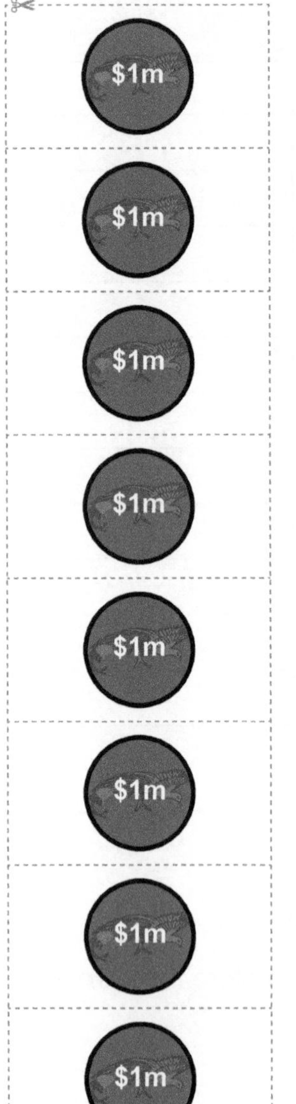

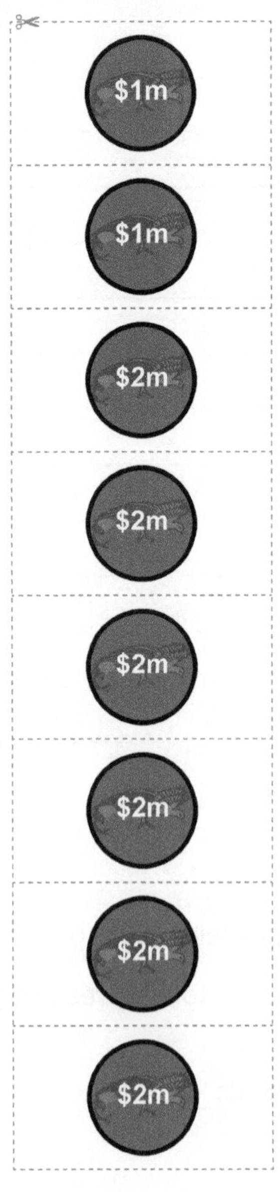

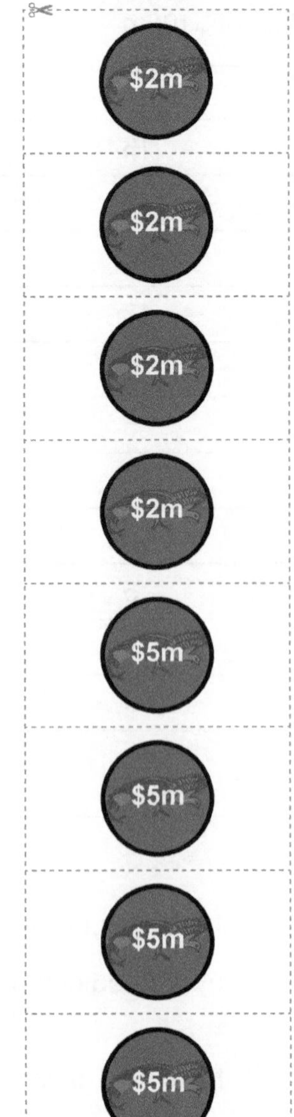

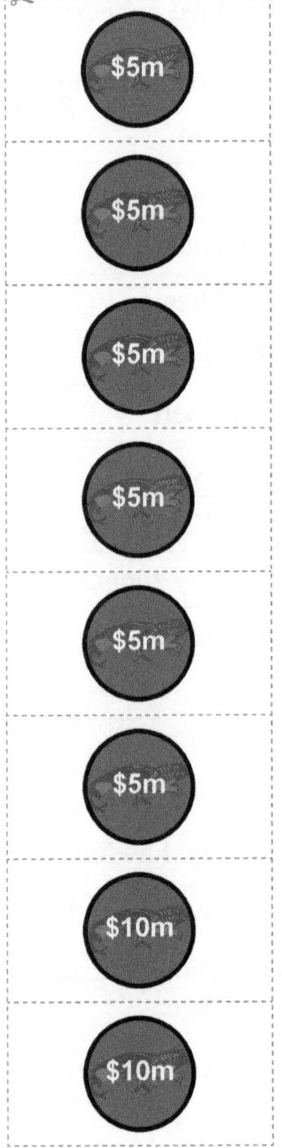

Activity sheet 4.3c Classification of taxes

Key terms:

- **Indirect taxation** – a tax on expenditure
- **Direct taxation** – a tax on the income of an individual or business
- **Progressive taxation** – a tax system which takes a higher proportion of income from the rich than the poor
- **Regressive taxation** – a tax system which takes a higher proportion of income from the poor than the rich
- **Proportional taxation** – a tax system which takes an equal proportion of income from all income earners (rich and poor)

Questions:

1. Country A has the following income tax rates.

Income per year ($)	Marginal tax rate
0–10,000	10%
10,001–100,000	20%
100,001–200,000	30%

   a) Mr Rich earns $200,000 per year. How much does he pay in tax?

   b) Mr Poor earns $20,000 per year? How much does he pay in tax?

   c) Is Country A's income tax system classified as progressive, regressive or proportional? Why?

2. The government of Country A imposes an indirect tax on food of 20%.

   a) Mr Rich spends $10,000 on food each year. How much would the new tax cost him?

   b) Mr Poor spends $2,500 on food each year. How much would the new tax cost him?

   c) Is Country A's indirect tax on food classified as progressive, regressive or proportional? Why?

3. The government of Country A changes the income tax system so that all individuals pay a flat rate of 20% tax on their income regardless of how much they earn.

   a) How much does Mr Rich now pay in income tax?

   b) How much does Mr Poor now pay in income tax?

   c) Is Country A's income tax system progressive, regressive or proportional? Why?

Activity sheet 4.5a Quantity or quality?

Work in groups of three to categorise the supply-side policies in Activity Sheet 4.5b in terms of whether they improve the quality or quantity of land, labour, capital or enterprise.

	An improvement in the QUANTITY of resources	An improvement in the QUALITY of resources
LAND		
LABOUR		
CAPITAL		
ENTERPRISE		

Activity sheet 4.5b Quantity or quality?

The government invests in improving school education.	The government provides training in ICT for adults.
The government lowers the income tax rate.	The government provides training for small business owners on how to run a successful business.
The government subsidises the purchase of machinery by firms.	The government makes it easier for foreign firms to set up in the country.
The government subsidises research into new production techniques and processes.	The government invests in developing roads, ports and transport systems.
The government subsidises the exploitation of the country's oil and coal reserves.	The government subsidises the cost of fertilisers for farmers.
The government lowers the corporate tax rate for small and medium-sized enterprises (SMEs).	The government increases the retirement age from 60 to 65 years old.
The government passes a law making it more difficult for trade unions to take strike action.	The government provides grants to people to start up their own businesses.
The government makes it easier for people with certain skills to immigrate.	The government makes university education free to its citizens.
The government lowers welfare benefits to the unemployed.	The government sells the state-owned postal service to the private sector.

Activity sheet 4.6 Brain writing 6–3–5

Topic: How can a recession be avoided and economic growth encouraged?			
Learner	**Idea 1**	**Idea 2**	**Idea 3**
1			
2			
3			
4			
5			
6			

Activity Sheet 4.7 The diamond 9

Diamond card sets

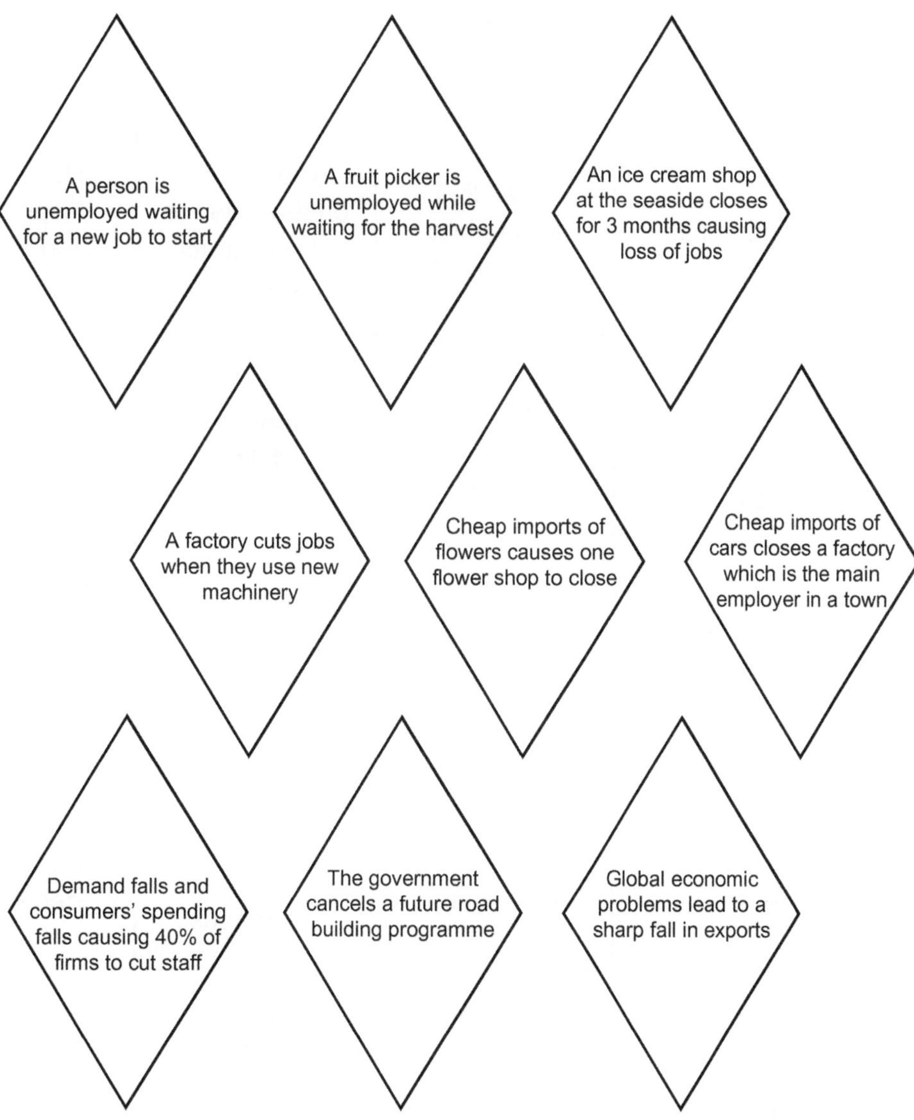

A person is unemployed waiting for a new job to start
A fruit picker is unemployed while waiting for the harvest
An ice cream shop at the seaside closes for 3 months causing loss of jobs
A factory cuts jobs when they use new machinery
Cheap imports of flowers causes one flower shop to close
Cheap imports of cars closes a factory which is the main employer in a town
Demand falls and consumers' spending falls causing 40% of firms to cut staff
The government cancels a future road building programme
Global economic problems lead to a sharp fall in exports

Activity sheet 4.8a Demand-side policy board game

Unemployment falls	Incomes rise	Consumer spending increases	Aggregate demand increases	Output (production) of the economy increases
Economic growth	Inflation rises	Spending on imports increases	Trade deficit on the balance of payments worsens	Household disposable income increases
Aggregate demand increased	Output (production) of the economy increases	Business investment increases	Unemployment falls	Incomes rise
Aggregate demand increases	Economic growth	Inflation rises	Spending on imports increases	Trade deficit on the balance of payments worsens
Incomes fall	Consumer spending decreases	Aggregate demand decreases	Output (production) of the economy decreases	Business investment decreases
Inflation falls	Spending on imports decreases	Trade deficit on balance of payments improves	Household disposable income decreases	Consumer spending decreases
Output (production) of the economy decreases	Business investment decreases	Unemployment rises	Incomes fall	Consumer spending decreases
Economic growth slows	Inflation falls	Spending on imports decreases	Trade deficit on the balance of payments improves	Cost of borrowing falls

Activity sheet 4.8a (continued)

Business investment increases	Consumer spending increases	Unemployment rises	Economic growth slows	Aggregate demand decreases
Consumer spending increases	Business investment increases	Aggregate demand increases	Output (production) of the economy increases	Business investment increases
Inflation rises	Spending on imports increases	Trade deficit on the balance of payments worsens	Cost of borrowing rises	Cost of borrowing rises
Business investment decreases	Aggregate demand decreases	Output (production) of the economy decreases	Business investment decreases	Economic growth slows
Aggregate demand decreases	Cost of borrowing falls	Economic growth	Consumer spending decreases	Inflation falls

Activity sheet 4.8b Demand-side policy board game

START

Policy decision

Strong economic growth – **move forward five spaces**

The central bank raises interest rates

Business confidence is low – **move back four spaces**

Swap cards

The government spends on building new hospitals and schools

The government cuts spending

Policy decision

The government cuts the income tax rate

Pick up card

The central bank cuts interest rates

Policy decision

Business confidence is high – **move forward three spaces**

The government reduces spending

Swap cards

The central bank increases interest rates

The government increases income tax

Global economic recession – **move back six spaces**

Policy decision

The central bank lowers interest rates

Pick up card

The government raises the income tax rate

Cards

Activity sheet 4.8c Chocolate bar inflation activity

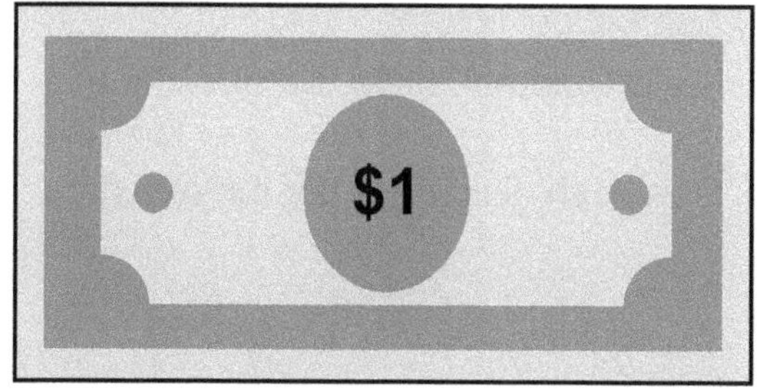

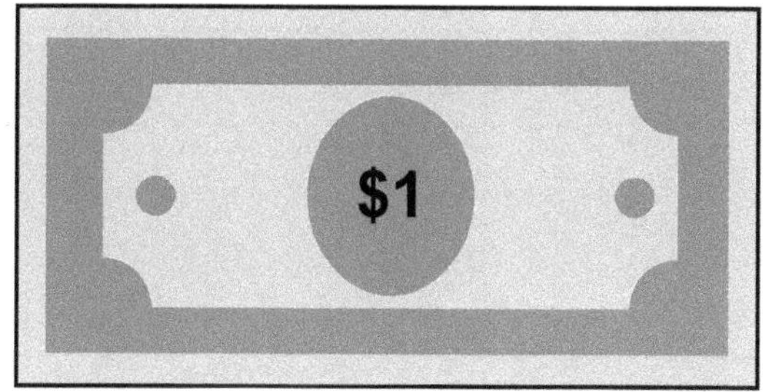

Activity sheet 5.4a National assessment

Instructions

1. Look at the different criteria that are used to measure living standards. How well does your country meet these criteria? Record your views in the 'My perception' column.
2. Grade your country, based on your perceptions. Your teacher will already have discussed the grading system to be used.
3. Now research each criteria and record your results in the 'Research' column. After the research has been completed, grade your country again.

Points for review/discussion

Did your class all come to similar views about your country or were there differences?

What has the activity taught you about relative poverty?

Living standards	My perception	Research
Clean water readily available		
Healthcare available to all		
Education available to all		
Consumer goods widely available and affordable		
GNP per head – world ranking		
HDI – world ranking		
Widespread absolute poverty		
High life expectancy		

Activity sheet 5.4b Matching activity

Match the key term with the description. The key terms are:

- Balance of trade
- Visibles
- Dividends
- Primary income
- Default
- Capital goods
- Balance of trade
- Current transfer

Key term	Description
	A gift of money
	Goods in tangible form
	Inflows of primary income minus outflows of primary income
	Value of visible exports minus value of visible imports
	Goods used to expand output
	Value of visible imports minus value of visible exports
	Failing to repay a loan
	Proportion of profit paid to shareholders

Activity sheet 6.1 Being clear on factors of production

The passage below has been written by a student who has not been paying attention in class.

Make at least five justified suggestions that would improve the passage.

All countries have three factors of production: land, labour and capital. Labourers work in fields and factories. Land is available to build on and capital is the money used to pay for things. It is not a good idea for countries to specialise because then they would only be able to produce a few products and they would soon run out of the resources needed to produce these products. It would be better if countries produced a little bit of everything because then consumers would have more choice and the nation would have more productivity.

Suggestions for improvement:

1.

2.

3.

4.

5.

6.

Activity sheet 6.2 'No person is an island'

1. As a young worker (in the near future) what would be:
   (a) your 'exports' to the rest of society
   (b) your 'imports' from the rest of society
   (c) your 'balance of payments'.

2. Which form of protectionism (subsidy, embargo, tariff or quota) would best match the following situations?
   (a) A friend's parents give her money so she is able to work for lower wages than you.
   (b) A firm in the next town will not allow you to work for them because they want to employ workers in their local area.
   (c) A local business will only employ you for ten hours per week. The owner says this is so he can employ other young workers as well.
   (d) There are jobs available in a nearby city but you have to pay a daily tax if you want to enter the city limits. People who live within the city limits do not have to pay the tax.

Activity sheet 6.3 Fill in the gaps

Complete the paragraph below. Fill in the gaps using the following words:

- *imports*
- *inelastic*
- *costs*
- *elastic*
- *inflation*
- *employment*
- *rise*

When the value for a country's currency falls there will be winners and losers. Exporters may be pleased if the demand for their product is price ______ and the market can respond quickly. ______ may increase in export industries. Businesses that have to compete against foreign imports may also benefit because ______ will now cost more. However consumers may suffer because ______ may rise due to the ______ in the price of imports, particularly if the demand for imports is price ______. Businesses with products that have a high import content will find their______ increasing.

Activity sheet 6.4 Live now, pay later

Read the following passage:

Rana has always enjoyed spending money. She has a large overdraft, a bank loan to purchase a car and has financed several foreign holidays through the use of credit cards. She eats out most of the time. Rana has now reached the credit limit on her credit cards. Fortunately, she has a well-paid job and a pleasant rented flat to live in. Rana's parents, who have always managed to save money, are concerned about Rana's spending patterns but Rana says she can pay her bills and wants to enjoy life. She thinks that her parents worry too much.

Using the language of international trade, write a short passage describing Rana's position and what may happen in future.

Use the following words/phrases in your answer:

standard of living

current account deficit

borrowing

expenditure increasing

expenditure reducing

unemployment

interest rates

Answer:

____

____

____

____

____

____

____

____

____

____

Suggested answers to knowledge check questions

Unit 1.1

1. All societies have to face the economic problem which exists because although the needs and wants of people are endless [1], the resources available to satisfy needs and wants are scarce or limited. [1]
2. A need is something a person has to have to survive, such as food, water and shelter. [1] A want in economics is something that people desire to have, that they may or may not be able to obtain such as a computer or a car. [1]
3. Finite resources are non-renewable resources. They are resources that do not renew themselves. [1] An example is carbon-based, organically-derived fuel. The original organic material, with the aid of heat and pressure, becomes a fuel such as oil or gas. Earth minerals and metal ores, fossil fuels (coal, petroleum, natural gas) are all considered finite resources. [1] A renewable resource is a resource which can be used repeatedly and replaced naturally. [1] Examples include oxygen, fresh water, solar energy, timber, and biomass. Renewable resources may include goods or commodities such as wood, paper and leather. [1]
4. An example of the economic problem to producers is how they answer the question of how they should produce. Should they invest in more machinery so that they can produce more goods in the future or should they spend more on a current marketing campaign to sell more goods now? Should they hire more workers or should they invest in more labour-saving machinery? Which investment project should they invest in as they cannot invest in all the projects that they would like. Award one mark for the definition and one mark for an example. [2]
5. An economic good is a good or service that has a benefit to consumers and producers. Economic goods are scarce and people are willing to pay for them. Economic goods have a value placed on the good and so it can be traded in the market place and valued by the use of money. An economic good has some degree of scarcity in relation to demand and it is this that creates a value which people are willing to pay for. [2] This is in contrast to a free good (like air, sea water) where there is no opportunity cost and they are in abundance. Free goods cannot be traded – nobody living by the sea would buy seawater as there is no point. There are very few free goods as even water delivered to households has a price. [2]
6. Extension question: This builds on question 5. Students need to provide a reason for purchasing sand and why it is an economic good.

   Sand is used to provide bulk, strength, and other properties to construction materials like asphalt and concrete. It is also used as a decorative material in landscaping. Specific types of sand are used in the manufacture of glass and as a moulding material for metal casting. Other sand is used as an abrasive in sandblasting and to make sandpaper. [Award one mark for each example up to a maximum of two marks]. This sand has to be mined and treated.

   In these cases, sand is useful to consumers and producers. Sand used in construction is an economic good as it has a value and can be traded. [1]

   If you are on a beach using sand to construct sand castles, then an individual will not have to pay. [1] There is no opportunity cost for using the sand and there is an abundance of material. It is a free good in this case. [1] However if you wanted to build sand castles in a sand pit at home then the sand will have to be purchased. [1]

Unit 1.2

1. Land includes all natural physical resources. [1] Labour is the effort that people contribute to the production of goods and services. [1] Capital is the machinery, tools and buildings humans use to produce goods and services. [1] Enterprise brings all the other factors of production together to produce goods and services. [1]
2. Examples of land: fertile farm land, the benefits from the harnessing of wind power and solar power and other forms of renewable energy. [1] Labour: the supply of workers available and the physical or mental effort of human beings in the process of production. [1] Capital: machines, tools, buildings, roads, bridges, raw material, trucks, factories, etc. [1] Enterprise: an entrepreneur is a person who organises the other factors and undertakes the risks and uncertainties involved in production. He hires the other three factors, brings them together, organises and coordinates them so as to earn maximum profit. [1]

3. Factor mobility refers to the ability to move factors of production – enterprise labour, capital or land – out of one production process into another. Mobility may involve the movement of factors across industries within a country, as when a worker leaves employment at a textile firm and begins work at an automobile factory. [3]
4. New technology could improve the quality of capital resulting in increased efficiency. [1] Training courses could improve the productivity of staff and lead to improvements in human capital. [1] Renewable resources would improve the use of land, such as solar energy. [1]
5. Extension question: The student could go through each factor of production. [Award two marks for each explanation.] Land: the government could ease planning permission to make it easier for firms to develop buildings. Land might have been designated for rural use only but government could increase the amount of land for building factories by changing the designation. Labour: the government could subsidise crèche and nursery provision to make it easier for partners with children to work. Capital: government could give grants to firms to invest in new factories. Enterprise: government could provide training and advice for people to set up their own businesses. Up to 6 marks for a discussion of how the factors of production can be increased. Up to two marks for a discussion of the extent to which this is possible [e.g.: for Labour: "But this could be difficult to achieve if both parents are already in full-time work."]

Unit 1.3

1. Opportunity cost refers to a benefit that a person could have received, but gave up, to take another course of action. Stated differently, an opportunity cost represents the next best alternative given up when a decision is made. To award two marks, the student must include the idea of next best alternative in their answer. [2]
2. There are many examples that a student can give. For both marks, the student must give what the consumer decided on and what they have given up as well as stating as in this example what the opportunity cost is. Note that the answer does not have to have a monetary value. An example answer is 'Someone gives up going to see a film to study for a test in order to get a good grade. The opportunity cost is the cost of the film and the enjoyment of seeing it'.
3. In the above suggested answer, it is because the value they placed on getting a good grade was greater than the enjoyment from watching the film. [Award two marks for a full explanation of the answer they gave in Question 2.]
4. An example is 'A worker gives up leisure time when they go to work or work overtime'. [2]
5. There are many possibilities instead of going to work. Someone could sleep in or take their dogs for a walk. They give up all of these things if they choose to go to work. What they get from working is a greater benefit than the cost of giving up these things, such as the money they earn and the job satisfaction they receive. [2]
6. Producers have to decide what to make. [1] If a farmer uses a field to grow corn, he cannot keep cattle on that field. If a DVD player producer uses his factory space and workers to produce one model, he cannot use the same space and workers to make another model or another electronic good at the same time. [2]
7. In deciding what to produce, private sector firms will tend to choose the option which will give them the maximum profit. They will also take into account the demand for different products and the cost of producing those products. [2]
8. If the government decides to spend more on education, the opportunity cost involved may be a reduced expenditure on health care. [2]
9. Government has to decide where to prioritise. This may be because they see the benefit of a skilled and educated workforce as essential. [2]
10. There are not enough economic resources to produce all the goods and services we want. Capital, enterprise, land and labour are scarce and so decisions have to be made about the method and purpose of their use. When we decide to do one thing, we are deciding not to do something else. To ensure that we make the right decisions, it is important that we consider the alternatives, particularly the best alternative. Opportunity Cost is the cost of a decision in terms of the best alternative given up to achieve it. [2]
11. Extension question: Students should explain the two terms [award one mark for each term fully explained]. Students should then discuss the implication of there being no economic problem in that scarcity does not exist. [Award two marks]. Students could discuss the theory that if there was no scarcity the price of everything would be free, so there would be no necessity for supply and demand. Some could use an example of a desert island where a Robinson Crusoe has everything they need on the island. However there is still one scarce resource, and that is time. Robinson Crusoe would have to decide between building a shelter or finding food or swimming. Students could conclude that opportunity cost will still arise even if resources are unlimited. It is the cost of choosing the next best alternative and there is always a next best alternative. [Award two marks for the implications of no scarcity and two marks for the conclusion.]

Unit 1.4

1. The production possibility curve is a curve illustrating all maximum output possibilities for two goods, given a set of inputs consisting of resources and other factors. [2]
2. Students should produce a relevant PPC diagram. [Allow one mark for the curve and one for labelling each axis.] [3]
3. From a starting point on the curve, increasing production of a first good means decreasing production of a second, because resources must be transferred to the first and away from the second. Points along the curve show the trade-off between the goods. [2] The sacrifice in the production of the second good is called the opportunity cost (because increasing production of the first good entails losing the opportunity to produce some amount of the second). Opportunity cost is measured in the number of units of the second good forgone for one or more units of the first good [2].
4. Investment is likely to lead to economic growth with the PPC shifting outwards. [1] Investment could be in new technology. For example, if someone developed a faster computer, or a more efficient way of making cars, there would be a shift to the right in the PPC. [1] This means that if everything else is held constant more goods can be produced after the technological change. [1] [3] Allow two marks for the shift outwards and one mark for a correctly labelled PPC.

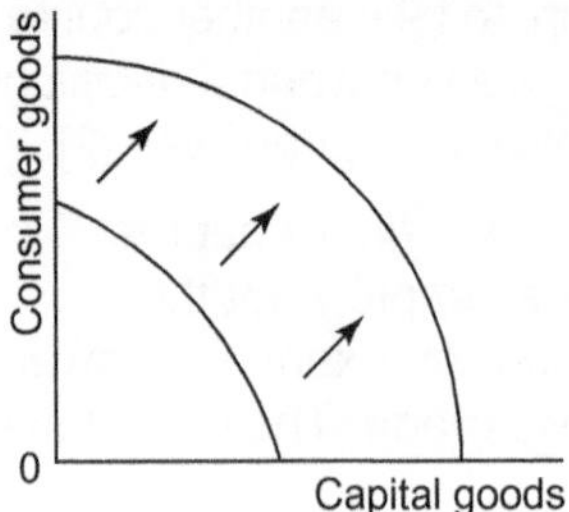

5. Extension question: To achieve economic growth there has to be an increased ability to produce capital goods such as factory equipment. [1] This means that there will be fewer consumer goods and there is a movement along the PPC. [1] The opportunity cost of producing more capital goods is that consumers will forego consumption. [1] However by producing more capital goods it is then able to produce more consumer goods in the future. [1] The economy would have an increased ability to produce both more consumer goods and more capital goods. [1] This would mean the PPC curve will move outwards. [1]
6. Extension question: This asks for the impact on the PPC when an economy suffering from unemployment is affected by an increase in labour productivity. They will draw a PPF similar to the one below. There would be a movement towards the curve. Whether it will be will depend on whether the improvement in labour productivity is in both industries or in just one. [Allow 4 marks for a diagram and two marks for an explanation.]

Unit 2.1

1. Micro economics is the study of individuals', households' and firms' behaviour in decision making and allocation of resources. It generally applies to markets of goods and services and deals with individual and economic issues. [1] microeconomic study deals with what choices people make, what factors influence their choices and how their decisions affect the goods markets by affecting the price, the supply and demand. [1]
2. Macro economics is the branch of economics that studies the behaviour and performance of an economy as a whole. It focuses on the aggregate changes in the economy such as unemployment, growth rate, gross domestic product and inflation. [1] Macro economics analyses all aggregate indicators. [1]
3. One example of decision makers who are involved in micro economics are consumers. Consumers respond to rising prices, for example, by buying less. Micro economics predicts what will happen to individuals' demand when price rises or fall [2]. A second example is the senior manager of a business who will decide whether they should reduce price or increase production. [2]
4. One example of decision makers who are involved in macro economics are governments who will make economic policy to achieve government economic aims and objectives such as economic growth. [2] Another could be the central bank which will decide whether to raise interest rates to try to reduce the inflation rate. [2]
5. Extension question: This question asks students to discuss whether there is always a clear distinction between micro economics and macro economics when studying particular issues in economics. This is a demanding question and needs a good understanding of both micro economics and macro economics. Students should consider the key characteristics of both. Macro economics is the study of the economy as a whole and examines the cyclical movements and trends in an economy such as unemployment, inflation, economic growth, money supply, budget deficits and exchange rates.

Microeconomics focuses on the individual parts of the economy. It studies decision making by households and firms and the interaction among households and firms in the marketplace. It considers households both as suppliers of factors of production (labour, land, capital, enterprise) and as ultimate consumers of final goods and services. It also analyses firms both as suppliers of goods and services and as demanders of factors of production. [Award two marks for describing macro economics and micro economics].

Because the economy-wide events studied in macro economics arise from the interaction of many households and firms, macro economics is rooted in micro economics so the distinction becomes more blurred. When economists study the economy as a whole (macro) they consider the decisions of individuals (micro). To understand what determines savings (macro), economists must think about the choices facing an individual in response to a change in interest rates and whether to increase or decrease saving by decreasing or increasing consumption (micro). [Award two marks for a discussion on the distinction and two marks for the examples given].

Unit 2.2

1. A market is an actual or nominal place where buyers and sellers interact to trade goods or services. [Allow one mark for stating it is an actual place.] [2]
2. [Allow one mark for each key question.] What goods or services should be produced? How should goods or services be produced, i.e. which method of production should be used? Who consumes the goods or services produced?
3. Students can use the What and How questions to explain how the price mechanism moves resource. [Allow two marks for each developed point.]

   What? Businesses produce the goods or services that earn them the highest profit. If consumers want more of a product they pay higher prices leading to increase in profit, so more is produced.

   How? Firms use the most efficient ways of making products; and by keeping down unit costs it helps their prices to stay competitive and leads to increased demand.
4. Extension question: The extension question asks how the price mechanism results in some people earning high incomes and some people earning low incomes. This can be answered as follows:

   High incomes can be earned because professional sports people have unique skills [1] and are highly marketable. [1] The transfer fees paid for footballers indicate how much football clubs are in need of star players. [1]

   Although playing an important role in a community, the street cleaner does not possess unique skills. [1] This means the amount of people who could do this job is high. [1] Wages are likely to be lower than professional sports people. [1]

Unit 2.3

1. Effective demand is the level of demand that represents a real intention to purchase by people who have the means to pay. [2]
2. Students need to provide a diagram showing an extension and a contraction in demand. Extension in demand is shown as a movement from Y to X in response to a fall in price from P_1 to P. Contraction in demand is shown as a movement from X to Y in response to an increase in price from P to P_1. [Award one mark for the demand curve, one mark for showing extension and one mark for showing contraction.]

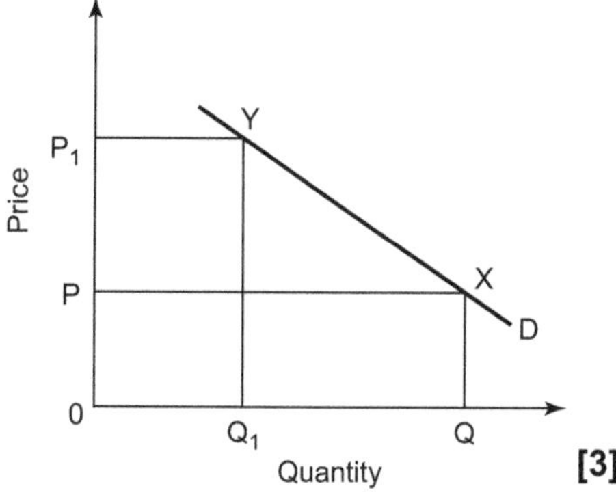

[3]

3. Answers could include an increase in incomes, a rise in price of a substitute good, a fall in price of a complementary good, an advertising campaign, a rise in population. [Award one mark for identification of each factor and one mark for each explanation.] [4]

4. 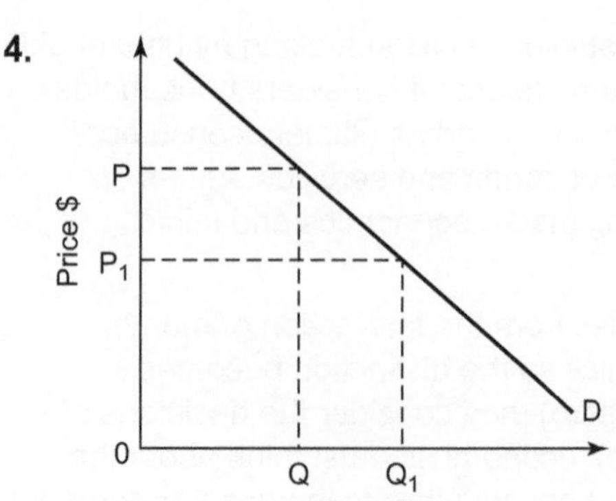

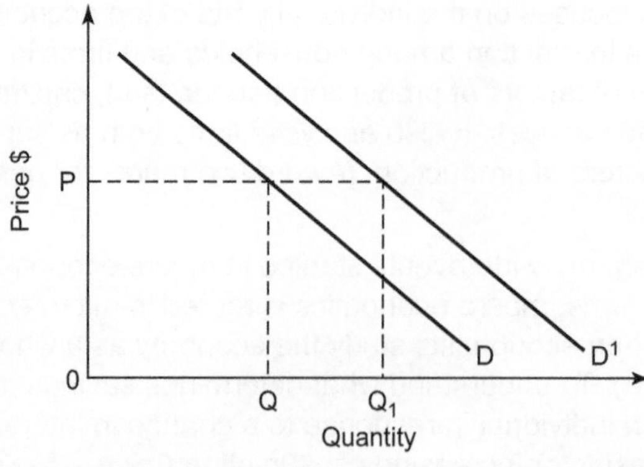

Award one mark for the extension diagram and one mark for the shift in demand diagram. Award two marks for an explanation of each diagram. In the first diagram, up to two marks for explaining that an increase in price resulting in a fall in quantity demanded is known as a contraction in demand. In the second diagram, up to two marks for explaining that factors that may lead to a shift in the position of the demand curve are referred to as the conditions of demand. These are non-price factors, which are any factors that affect demand for a good or service that do not include changes in the price itself. Any change in these factors would shift the demand curve [2].

5. Extension question: This question is similar to question 4 but gives a real life scenario. An increase in price of ice cream would lead to a movement along the demand curve [1] as the demand curve shows the relationship between price of ice cream and quantity demanded at every price, other things being equal. [1] There is a movement along the curve if no other determinant of demand changes. [1] However, an increase in income is a non-price factor. [1] Changes in income will cause the demand curve to shift to the right. [1] This means that at every price more is demanded. [1]

Unit 2.4

1. Supply is the total amount of a good or service available for purchase at any specified price. [2]
2. Students should draw a supply curve with correctly labelled axes [1] showing an extension in supply [1] and a contraction in supply. [1]
3. Students could refer to cost of inputs [1] where a lower input price means more profit and more of the good or service will be offered at that price. [1] Another condition leading to an increase in supply would be favourable weather conditions for agricultural products. [1] These favourable weather conditions could lead to a good harvest and an increase in supply. [1]
4. An increase or an imposition of an indirect tax will lead to a decrease in supply. The supply curve would shift from S to S_1. [2] [Award two marks for a correctly labelled diagram showing a shift in the supply curve.]

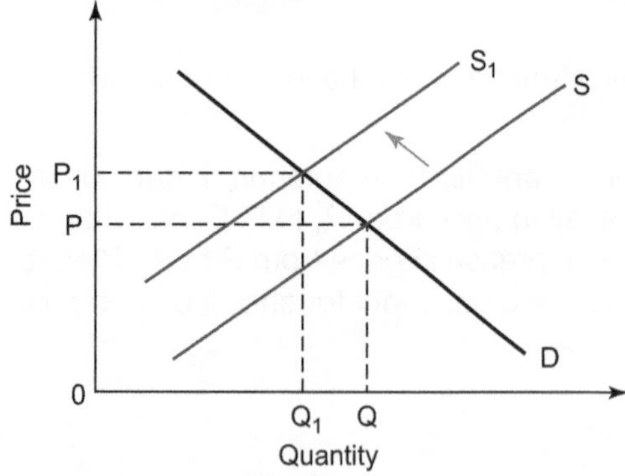

5. Extension question: The students could use the following diagrams.

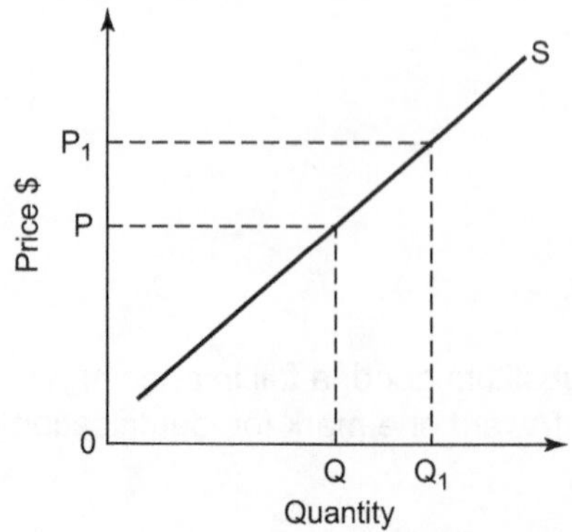

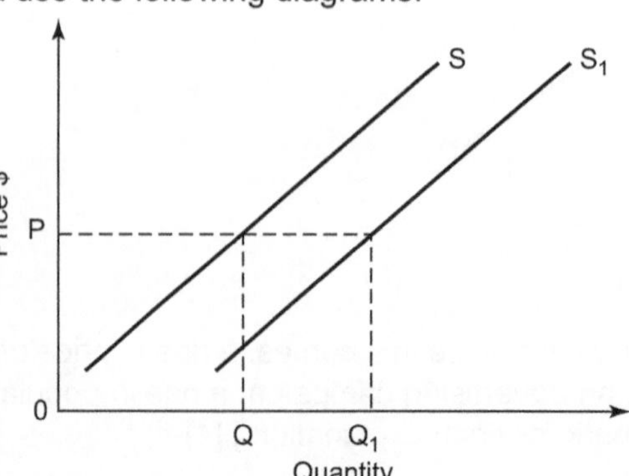

The rise in the price of phones would cause quantity supplied to increase from Q to Q_1 and there is the movement along the curve. [For each diagram: award two marks for an accurate diagram plus one mark for a supporting explanation.] An improvement in technology used to manufacture mobile phones will cause the whole supply curve to shift to the right from S to S_1 as more can be supplied at every price. The curve shifts because a determinant other than price has changed.

Unit 2.5

1. Economic equilibrium is a condition or state in which economic forces are balanced. Economic equilibrium may also be defined as the point at which supply equals demand for a product, with the equilibrium price existing where the supply and demand curves intersect. [2]
2. Students would base their diagram on Figure 2.5.2 in Unit 2.5 of the Student's Book. [Allow two marks for the diagram and one mark for a brief explanation.]
3. Students would base their diagram on the excess demand diagram (Figure 2.5.5) in Unit 2.5 of the Student's Book. [Allow two marks for the diagram and 1 for a brief explanation.]
4. Extension question: Students might need direction with this question. Equilibrium is where demand equals supply. Government intervention will disrupt this equilibrium. They might intervene because market forces might not produce the economic conditions government wants. Students could consider a price ceiling such as a price control that limits the maximum price that could be charged for a product or service. The purpose of a price ceiling is to protect consumers of a certain good. By establishing a maximum price, a government wants to ensure that the good is affordable.

   Students can also consider that in some cases equilibrium for some products is undesirable. Governments might want to reduce consumption of products such as tobacco through indirect taxation. In this case the supply curve would shift to the left. This intervention results in a new equilibrium.

   [Award up to 5 marks for why government intervention can reduce disequilibrium and up to 5 marks for why government policy may not have the desired effect.]

Unit 2.6

1. Students could identify changes in demand and supply such as an increase in income [1] or a fall in costs of production. [1]
2. Students would use a diagram similar to that used in Unit 2.6 in the Student's Book.

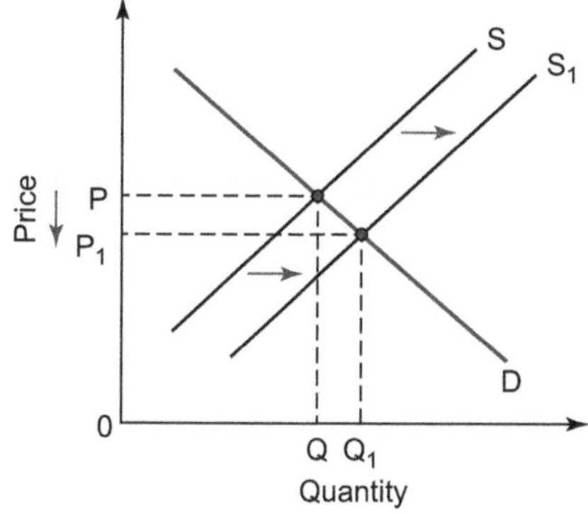

   [Award two marks for a correctly labelled diagram and one mark for a brief explanation of why the supply curve has shifted to the right and a fall in the equilibrium price has increased sales.] [3]
3. Students would use a diagram similar to that used in Unit 2.6 of the Student's Book.

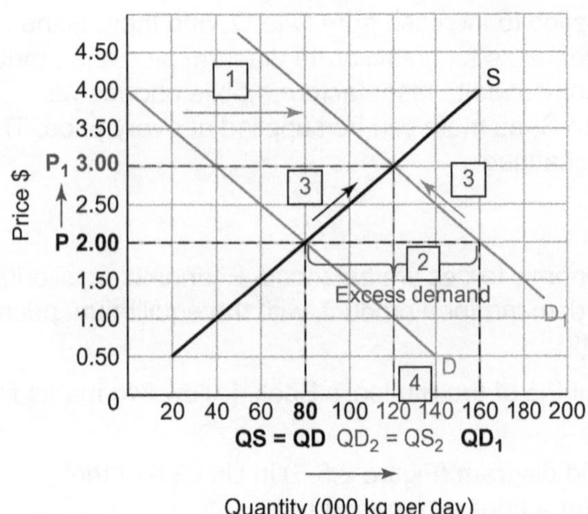

[Award two marks for a correctly labelled diagram and one mark for a brief explanation of why the demand curve has shifted to the right and the rise in the equilibrium price has increased sales.] [3]

4. Students could use a diagram showing the impact of a good harvest which shifts the supply curve to the right leading to a fall in price or a fall in price of substitutes causing the demand curve to shift to the left. [Award two marks for a correctly drawn diagram and one mark for a brief explanation.]

The questions below involve drawing diagrams to illustrate different scenarios. [For each question allow up to 4 marks for the drawing of each diagram: one mark for each curve drawn, one mark for correct labels and two marks for a brief explanation].

5. Extension question:

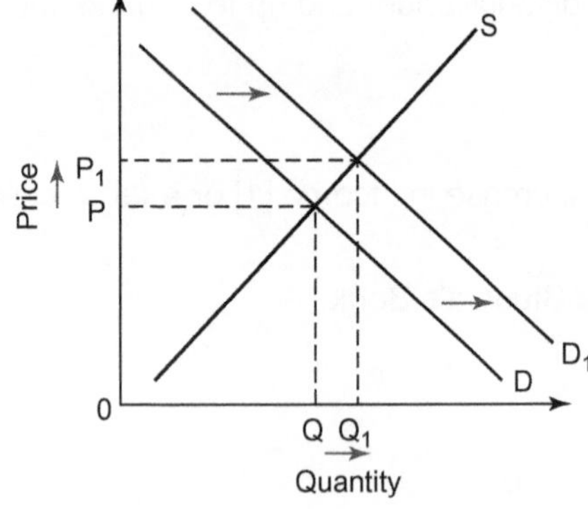

A successful advertising campaign would shift the demand for breakfast cereals to the right leading price to rise from P to P1 and quantity bought and sold from Q to Q1.

6. Extension question:

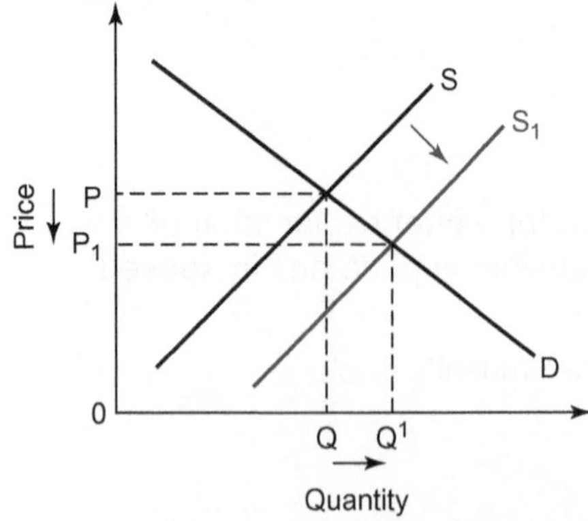

Improvements in technology will reduce the costs of production of television sets and cause the supply curve to shift to the right which leads to a fall in price and an increase in the quantity bought and sold.

7. Extension question:

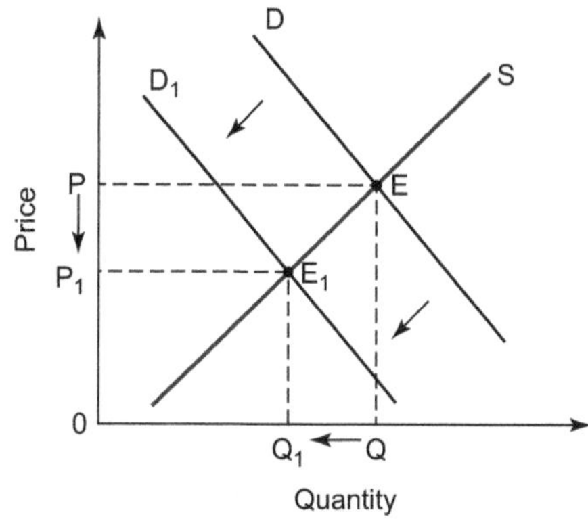

Downloading films and music are a substitute for using DVD players. If there is a growing demand for downloading, this would lead to a fall in demand for DVD players. The demand curve would shift to the left for DVD players, price would fall and fewer would be bought and sold.

8. Extension question:

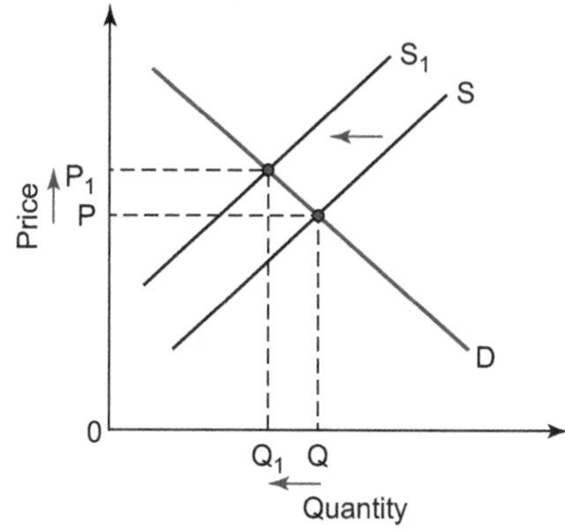

The tax would cause a shift in the supply curve of the sugar products to the left. This would lead to a rise in price and a fall in the quantity bought and sold.

Unit 2.7

1. PED = $\frac{\text{percentage change in quantity demanded [2]}}{\text{percentage change in price}}$
2. An inelastic PED for a good or service means that the percentage change in demand is smaller than the percentage change in price [2]
3. A PED of 2 means that the product is price elastic. [1] This means if price fell the percentage change in demand would be greater than the percentage decrease in price. [1]
4. Demand might be price inelastic because there are few substitutes. [1] When prices rise, consumers have no alternative but to pay the higher price or go without the product. [1] If a good or service has a very low price and is a small proportion of the income of the consumer, then PED tends to be inelastic. [1] This is because if the price increases it is not taking up much of a consumer's income and therefore they are likely to still buy the good. [1]
5. If the PED is -0.5, this means that the product is price inelastic. [1] This means that the percentage change in demand is smaller than the percentage change in price. [1] The firm should increase price as revenue would rise. [2]
6. Extension question: Government would want to tax products which are price inelastic. [1] The student should discuss what makes a good inelastic such as the availability of substitutes and the issue of necessity, luxury, and habit formation. [Award one mark for each determinant and one mark for an explanation up to a maximum of two determinants]. The tax puts up price but the percentage change in demand (fall in demand) would be smaller than the percentage change in price (rise in price). [1]

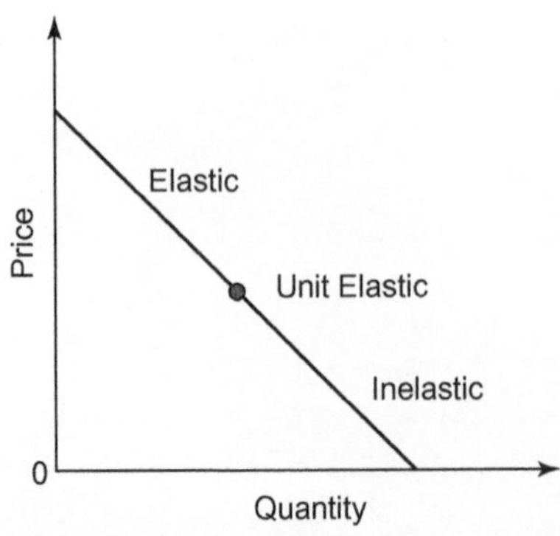

7. Extension question: Price elasticity will vary along a demand curve as shown in the diagram. However, if price falls below P demand is price inelastic and if price rises above P demand is price elastic. [Award two marks for a diagram and two marks for an explanation.] Students could conclude that as elasticity would vary along the curve then a decision as to whether price should be changed becomes more complex. If at a certain price demand becomes inelastic then it is not worth lowering price for example. [Award two marks for a conclusion].
8. Extension question: After Question 7, the student knows the PED is different on different parts of a straight-line demand curve. However, a straight-line demand curve has a constant gradient so the gradient of a straight-line demand curve cannot be the same as the PED along the curve. This is because the rates of change of price and quantity are not constant. As price increases, the % change in price diminishes while the % change in quantity demanded increases. So the slope, which is constant, cannot represent the formula:

$$\text{PED} = \frac{\text{percentage change in quantity demanded}}{\text{percentage change in price}}$$

[Award three marks for stating that the gradient of the straight-line curve cannot be the same as PED.] [Award two marks for the explanation. Award three marks for stating that the rate of change is not constant.]

Unit 2.8

1. $$\frac{\text{percentage change in quantity supplied}}{\text{percentage change in price}}$$

   [Award two marks for a correct formula. Award one mark if student states change rather than percentage change.]
2. Price elastic supply is when the percentage change in quantity supplied is greater than the percentage change in price. [Award one mark if student does not refer to percentage.]
3. As this is a two-mark question, asking for more than one factor, students can get two marks for stating two relevant factors – the student does not need to explain either of them. Answers include: the amount of stock, spare capacity, mobility of factors of production.
4. Students should show their workings. [If they enter 5% and 20% correctly, but make an arithmetic error, allow one mark.]

   $$\frac{\text{percentage change in quantity supplied}}{\text{percentage change in price}}$$

   Quantity supplied from 100 to 105 is 5%

   $$\frac{5\%}{20\%} = 0.25$$

   So, it is price inelastic.
5. The students should draw a supply curve linking the two points obtained from the data in Q4. [2]
6. [Allow one mark for mentioning three factors and one mark for an explanation of each factor.]
   - If the amount of stock or ability to store the stock is low, PES is inelastic.
   - Level of spare capacity. If all the machines in a factory are being used then supply will be inelastic as the firm is at full capacity and cannot quickly increase supply of the products.
   - The less mobile the factors of production and the higher the cost to move them to alternative production, the more inelastic supply will be.

7. It is important to know the PES if the government wants to know the impact of a subsidy.

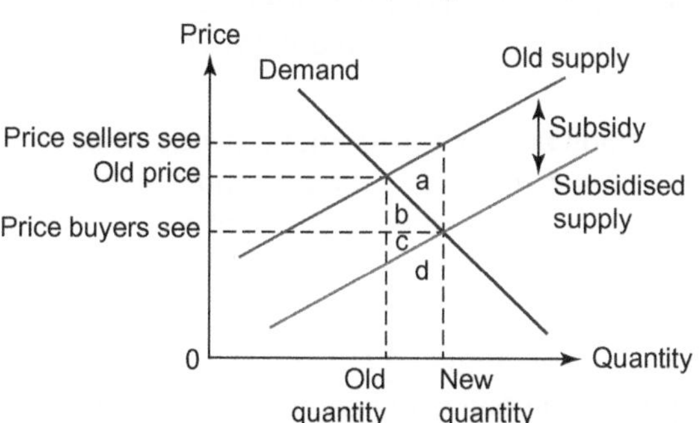

[Award one mark for a diagram showing that a subsidy would shift the supply curve to the right.] [1]

A subsidy is any form of government support provided to producers financed from taxation. [1]

A subsidy will shift the supply curve to the right. [1] The amount of subsidy is 'a' in the diagram. [1] The impact of the subsidy is shown by 'd' in the diagram. [1] If supply is more elastic, producers will be able to respond more quickly. [1]

8. Extension question: Any explanation about affecting price elasticity of supply needs to refer to the factors determining elasticity of supply:

Spare production capacity

Stocks of finished products and components – high level of stocks (inventories) means that supply can quickly be adjusted to meet changes in demand – this is important in commodity markets

The ease and cost of hiring additional factors of production

The time period involved in the production. In some agricultural markets, momentary supply is fixed and is determined mainly by planting decisions made months before, and climatic conditions that affect production yield. One way would be to operate a buffer stock system.

Award one mark for referring to factors that determine elasticity, two marks for mentioning stocks and time period with relevance to agriculture and one mark for identifying buffer stock schemes as a way of affecting PES. [4]

9. Extension question: A buffer stock scheme seeks to stabilise the market price of agricultural products by buying up supplies of the products when harvests are plentiful and selling stocks of the product when supplies are low.

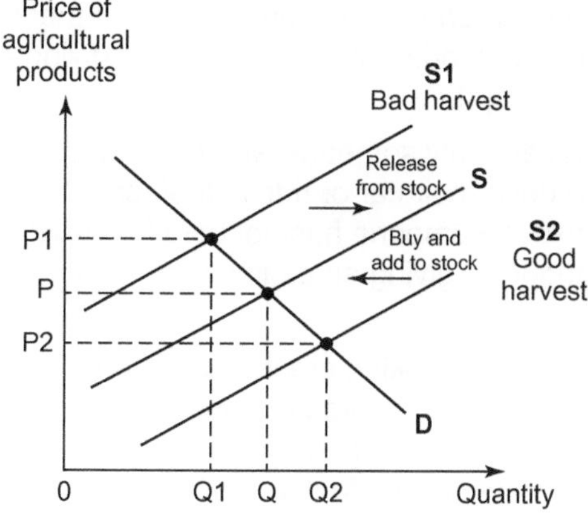

Use of diagram to show a buffer stock scheme [two marks showing releasing stock and two marks for adding to stock]. Two marks for a commentary of the diagram.

10. Extension question: Advantages: Stable prices help maintain farmers' incomes. Stability enables investment in agriculture and sustains rural communities [award one mark for each advantage]. Problems: costs of buying excess supply; a minimum price might cause over production; high administrative and social costs. [Award one mark for each problem.] [6]

Unit 2.9

1. This is a system in which the prices for goods and services are determined by the free market. [1] This is where the laws of demand and supply are free from any intervention by government. [1] There has to be an explanation to get the second mark.
2. One difference between them is that private sector organisations are not government-owned while public sector organisations are owned and managed by the government. [2] Students could also refer to objectives, with the objective for public sector organisations being to serve the citizens of a country while the objective for the private sector is to earn profit. [Award one mark if they refer only to 'not government owned'.]
3. [For each advantage, give a mark with a further mark for a brief explanation.] One advantage is increased efficiency [1] because firms need to ensure that they are price competitive to keep costs down and increase productivity by for example investing in labour saving machinery. [1] Another advantage is that it increases innovation [1] with firms investing in new ideas for products and services. [1]
4. [For each disadvantage give a mark with a further mark for a brief explanation.] Disparity in wealth as wealth tends to generate wealth. [1] It is easier for wealthy individuals to become wealthier than it is for poor people to become wealthy. [1] Environmental damage [1] as there is no government regulation and as it is more expensive to produce in an environmentally sound manner which reduces profits. [1]
5. Extension question: It is important to stress that the question asks WHY a government might wish to increase the share of the private sector and not HOW. [Allow one mark for each point plus one mark for development.]
   - Motivates people as they keep more of their income and pay less tax as the government provides fewer products and services. Individuals work harder and there are efficiency gains.
   - Any efficiency gains will make firms more competitive and this could lead to economic growth.
   - Entrepreneurs are prepared to risk more so that their innovation acts as a stimulus to the economy.
   - Governments borrow less as they provide fewer goods and services. This means there are more funds available to private sector firms to borrow to invest in new technology and new products and services. This stimulates growth and reduces unemployment.

Unit 2.10

1. It is when in any given market the quantity of a product demanded by consumers does not equal the quantity supplied by suppliers. [A full definition is required in order to gain the two marks.] [2]
2. Merit goods are goods such as education which consumers may undervalue but which the government believes are 'good' for consumers because they have positive externalities. Demerit goods, such as tobacco, have negative externalities resulting from their consumption and so the consumption of these goods will impose a cost on people other than those consuming the goods. Allow one mark for giving an example of each part and one mark for an explanation for each part [4].
3. A private good is one that is rivalrous and excludable such as a car. Only someone who has bought a car can use it and the owner does not have to allow anyone else to drive their car or ride in their car. A public good is defined as one which is non-rivalrous and non-excludable. If someone has not paid for street lighting, they cannot be prevented from benefitting. Allow one mark for giving an example of each part and one mark for an explanation for each part. [4]
4. Driving a car creates an external cost such as greater congestion. [1] Smoking creates an external cost to non-smokers through passive smoking and carries the danger of smoking related illnesses. [1] Cycling to work is an example of an external benefit as it helps to reduce pollution and congestion. [1] A beekeeper produces honey but as an external benefit their bees help to pollinate nearby fruit trees. [1] Students need to explain their example to gain the one mark, however award a maximum of two marks if a brief list of examples is provided without explanations.
5. The existence of external costs can lead to market failure. This is because the free market generally ignores the existence of external costs. Driving a car imposes a private cost on the driver (cost of petrol, tax and buying the car). However, driving a car creates costs to other people in society. These can include greater congestion and slower journey times for other drivers as well as pollution and health-related problems.

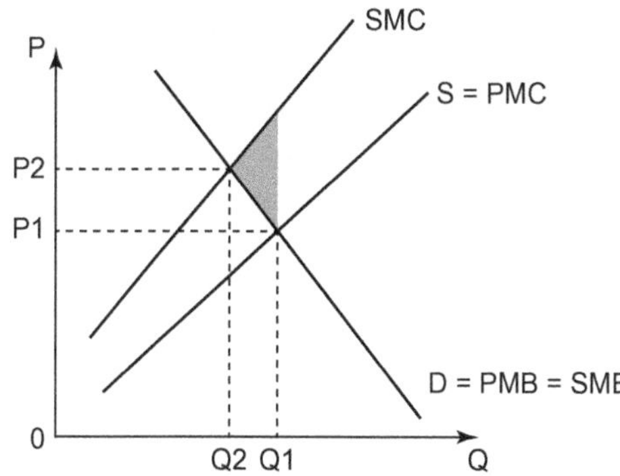

This diagram shows how the existence of external costs will cause the social marginal cost to be greater than the private marginal cost. Therefore, in a free market there will be over-consumption of the good [Q1]. Social efficiency will occur at Q2 where SMC = SMB.

[Allow one mark for an example, one mark for an explanation, three marks for their diagram showing how external costs will cause the social marginal cost to be greater than the private marginal cost and one mark for an explanation.] [6]

6. Students could state that the private benefits of electric cars are that they are quiet, can be charged at home and are cheaper to operate. They will point out that there are considerable personal benefits to the owner. [2] However the social benefits are also considerable. Electric cars are cleaner and so non-users would benefit. If more people used electric cars, this would have a significant impact on air quality and global warming. [2] This means that the social benefits would be higher than private benefits.

   [Award two further marks for explaining the economic terms used such as social benefits are business activities that have a beneficial or favourable impact on people or places.]

7. Monopolies can abuse their power through their dominance.

   - They can use their position to remove competition which could mean that consumers are paying higher prices than if there was a free market. The quantity supplied to the market may be restricted so that the price is higher and the monopolist gains a high profit. [1] This is market failure because consumers pay a much higher price for a lower quantity of the good or service than if the market is competitive. [1]
   - A monopolist has less incentive to innovate (create new products or means of production) than a competitive firm because there is no competitive pressure to be more efficient or to have a better product than other firms. [1] This is market failure because if a firm has no competitors then there is very little incentive to exert effort to become more efficient, meaning that the firm may end up spending more resources on production than necessary. [1]

8. Factor immobility is a cause of market failure because the factors of production do not move easily and quickly between different industries when consumer demand changes. [2] Factors of production in agriculture cannot be switched easily to car manufacture. [1]

   As demand changes, some industries will reduce in size as firms produce less of that good. Other industries may increase in size as demand increases. [2] The factors of production need to move from the industries that are decreasing supply to those that are increasing supply. Factor immobility does not allow this to happen. [1]

9. Extension question: Market failure occurs when the prices paid for the goods that are consumed do not reflect the true value of the costs of production or the benefits from consumption. This leads to the misallocation of resources. [1] Demerit goods are goods which have a negative impact on the consumer although these negative effects may be unknown or ignored by the consumer and lead to over consumption. [1]

   Over consumption causes negative externalities. These are costs to third parties. [1] Many consider cigarettes to be a demerit good because they have a negative impact on the consumers but also on the community. [1] These costs include odour, pollution, the process of passive smoking and the cost to the healthcare system caused by the cigarette ingredients. [1]

   Demerit goods result in a welfare loss because of the external costs they cause. [1]

10. Extension question: An external benefit is the positive effect an activity has on an unrelated third party. [1] Entrepreneurs do not capture all the benefits that result from them producing the goods. [1] If they received all these benefits then their revenue would be higher [1], and this would make producing the goods more profitable. [1] So, in response, they would supply more products [1] (and so allocate more factors of production to the supply of these products). [1]

Unit 2.11

1. A mixed market system consists of both private companies and government/state-owned entities. Both have control of owning, making, selling and exchanging goods in the country. [2]

2. 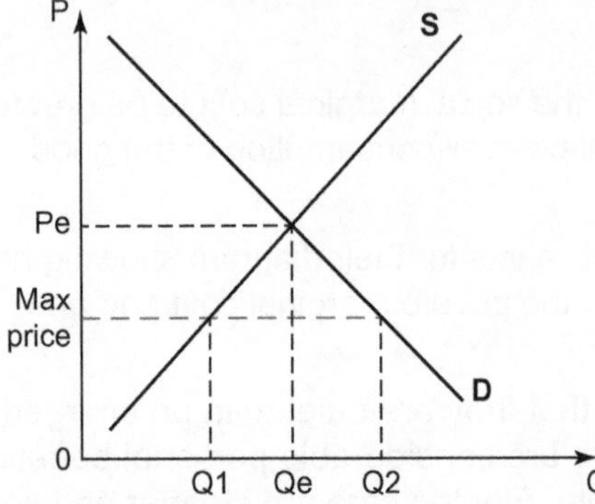

If the maximum price is set below the equilibrium price of Pe, the quantity supplied at this maximum price is Q1 and the quantity demanded at this maximum price is Q2.

This leads to an excess demand of Q1 to Q2. The market cannot reach an equilibrium and therefore price and quantity will remain at a disequilibrium. [Allow two marks for the diagram and one mark for the explanation.] [3]

3. 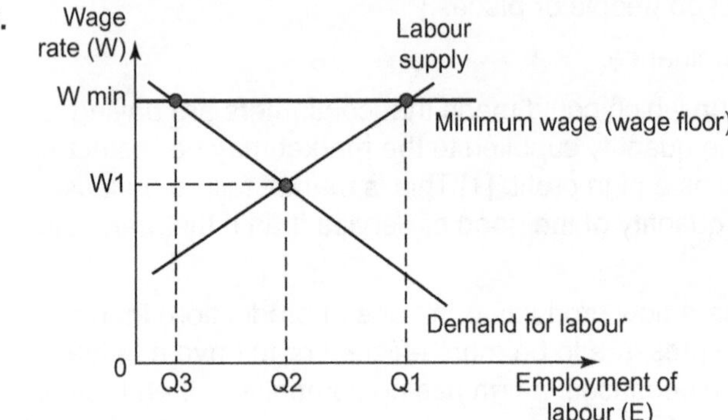

The minimum wage in the diagram means that the quantity of labour demanded is Q3 while the quantity of workers willing to supply their services to the market at this minimum wage is Q1. There is an excess supply of labour to this market of Q1 to Q3. This means workers will be offering to work but there will be too few jobs available. [Allow two marks for the diagram and one mark for the explanation.] [3].

4. Indirect tax provides an opportunity to charge for the external costs that have been imposed on third parties. [2] For example, indirect taxes make polluters pay. [1] An indirect tax increases the price of the product and so discourages use of products that generate negative externalities and demerit goods. [2] Problems are estimating a monetary value. [1] The price elasticity of demand has to be taken into account as a significant tax rise might be needed. [1]

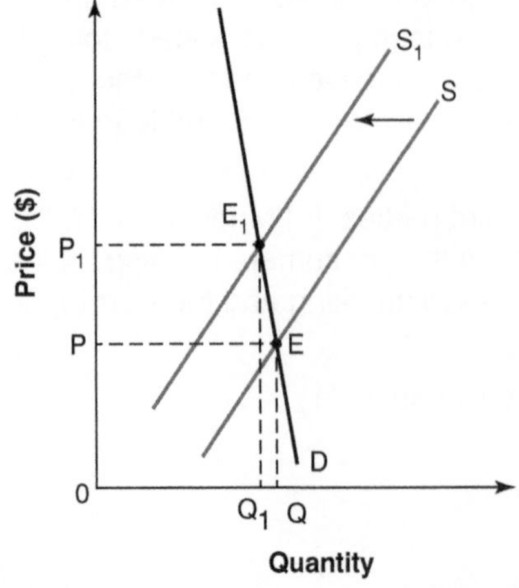

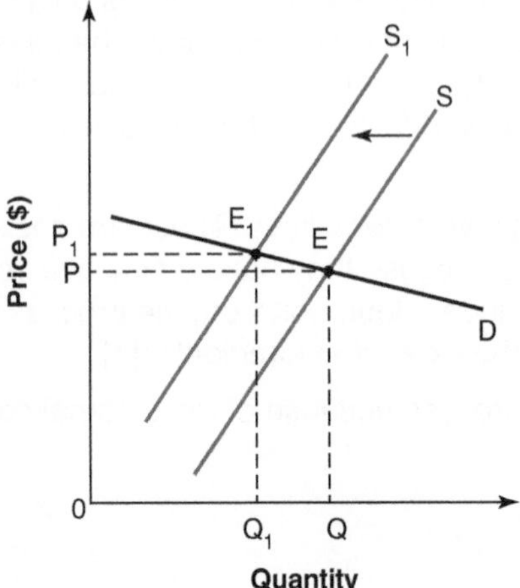

5. A subsidy shifts the supply curve down vertically by the amount of the subsidy, S to S1. This was mentioned in Unit 2.4. The diagram shows the effect of a subsidy given to firms. The effect is to lower the price from P1 to P2 and increase the equilibrium quantity from Q1 to Q2. [Allow 4 marks for the diagram, one mark each for the curves and one mark for P1, P2 Q1 and Q2. Allow two marks for an explanation.]
6. Demerit goods can be restricted and merit goods can be made compulsory to reduce the market failure. Individuals and firms can be made to take into account external costs and benefits by them when they are producing and consuming goods. A disadvantage is that the regulations may not be followed and it costs the government money to investigate and prosecute individuals or firms that do not follow the regulations. [Allow two marks each for explaining an advantage and a disadvantage] [4]
7. Privatisation is when the government sells off a state-owned enterprise. Nationalisation is when the state takes over a private sector business or sector. [Allow one mark for explaining each term.] [2]
8. The government must provide public goods or they will not be provided at all such as street lights or defence of the country by the armed forces. Also, goods and services that are directly provided by the government are often merit goods. The government may want to increase the production and consumption of these goods and so provides them itself. Examples of these goods are healthcare and education. Without the state providing them it could mean that a country has an uneducated and unhealthy workforce. [Award one mark each for two reasons and one mark for each point explained.] [4]
9. Price elasticity of demand affects the price and quantity demand after an indirect tax is imposed. [1] An inelastic PED will result in a much higher percentage rise in price than the percentage fall in sales. [1] An elastic PED will result in a much smaller percentage rise in price than the percentage fall in sales. [Allow one mark for each diagram used] [1]
10. Extension question: The main reasons for policy intervention by the government are: to correct for market failures, to ensure distribution of income and wealth is more equal and to manage the economy so as to reduce inflation or reduce unemployment. [Award one mark for each reason to a maximum of two marks.]

    Students could mention examples of market failure and examples of market intervention. [Award one mark for each example of market failure and one mark for describing the intervention to a maximum of 4 marks.] Examples include:

    - structural unemployment: investment in education and training, apprenticeship schemes
    - overconsumption of demerit goods with negative externalities: health education, age restrictions
    - failure of market to provide public goods because of the free rider problem: government provides and funds public goods
    - poverty causing low income groups, pensioners to suffer: use of taxation and benefits to redistribute income and wealth.

    [Award other examples of market failure given and descriptions of intervention.]

    Conclusion [award one mark for each point up to a maximum of two marks]:

    - One single intervention might not solve the market failure. It might take significant resources to make an impact.
    - Interventions in one area might cause problems in another. Redistributing income through taxing the wealthy might demotivate the entrepreneur who becomes less willing to invest or leaves the country.
    - Intervention does not always work in the way government intended or the way economic theory suggests.

Unit 3.1

1. Anything which is generally accepted [1] as a means of payment for goods and services [1].
2. The act of trading goods or services between two or more parties without the use of money [2]. The double coincidence of wants is worth one mark without development.
3. Medium of exchange [1] is anything which sets the standard of value of goods and services acceptable to all parties involved in a transaction [1]. Measure of value or unit of account [1] is the idea that money allows the value of different goods and services to be compared [1]. Standard for deferred payment [1] enables people to borrow money and pay it back at a later date [1]. Store of value [1] allows wealth to be stored in the form of money [1]. [Allow one mark for each function and one mark for each explanation.]
4. Acceptable answers: divisible; durable; scarce; recognisable; stability of supply; stability of value; and uniformity. [Allow one mark for each characteristic up to a maximum of 6 marks.]
5. Divisible: money in an economy needs to be able to be divided into smaller units [1] so that a range of prices can be offered for goods and services [1]. Scarce: money needs to be relatively scarce [1] if it is not to become worthless [1]. [Allow up to two marks for each.]

6. A central bank is the organisation that is responsible to its government for controlling the country's money supply as the issuer of notes and coins [1] and the level of reserves a commercial bank must hold. It also sets the rate of interest [1]. [Allow one mark for an idea and two marks for a full idea.]
7. It keeps the revenue raised by the government and makes payments on its behalf [1]. It also issues short-term and long-term government debt in order to raise extra funds for the government [1].
8. A commercial bank is a financial institution in which individuals and firms can save their money [1] and also obtain loans [1].
9. Making loans to firms so they can grow [1] by either building new office/factory space or by buying better/ newer machinery/technology [1]. Finance trade [1] by providing foreign exchange facilities to exporters and importers [1]. Help entrepreneurs start up [1] by lending money and giving advice [1]. [Award one mark for each benefit [maximum 2] and one mark for each explanation.]
10. Extension question: Benefits include: safe place to save their money; source of loans; provision of means such as mobile apps and debit cards to access accounts and pay for items without having to carry actual money; provision of credit cards; safe deposit boxes; and provision of foreign currencies. Problems include: credit cards can lead to debt; loans if not repaid can lead to the bank taking your possessions; rate of interest on savings may be much lower than elsewhere. [Maximum 5 marks for a one-sided answer.]

Unit 3.2

1. Income is the reward for the services provided [1] by a factor of production [1].
2. Real income is income taking the effects of inflation into account [1] so it is the purchasing power of income [1].
3. To enable them to have sufficient money [1] in the future to purchase an expensive item [1]. To enable them to have enough money [1] to put a deposit down, or obtain a mortgage on a house [1]. To guard against the future in terms of unexpected events [1] such as unemployment or illness [1]. To provide money [1] to support themselves in retirement [1].
4. Insufficient current income [1] so money is borrowed to enable them to survive [1]. To buy expensive items, such as a car, for which they do not have enough savings [1], but can afford to pay for in monthly instalments [1].
5. Disposable income is the income available to spend and save after direct taxes have been deducted [1] and any state benefits added [1].
6. A rise in direct tax would reduce a household's disposable income [1]. This means that there would be less money to both spend and save [1]. Households could either maintain spending, but reduce savings by the whole amount of their loss of income [1] or they could reduce spending on less important/ necessary items and reduce savings if this was not enough [1].
7. An increase in consumer confidence means that consumers think the economy and their situation is improving [1]. They expect to earn more [1] and could therefore increase spending [1]. They might also be more willing to borrow money [1] as they expect to be able to pay it back out of their higher income [1]. This again could be used to purchase more expensive items and could cause an increase in spending [1].
8. Extension question: Effects could include: falling into poverty [1] as they do not have enough money to buy essentials [1]; burden on children and/or relatives [1] who have to provide for them, such as housing, food [1]; need for the government to provide greater support/state pensions [1] so taxes have to rise to pay for this [1]; increase in demand for charities and charitable giving [1]. [Maximum of 5 marks for a one-sided discussion.]

Unit 3.3

1. Wages are payments to labour [1] for units of time or units of product [1].
2. Salary is an annual sum of money [1] usually paid in twelve equal monthly amounts [1].
3. Answers could include: Job security [1] is where a job which does not carry fears of being made unemployed [1]. Travelling distance [1] as some workers prefer a short journey to work so they do not have to lose time travelling [1]. Other non-wage factors include: job satisfaction; career prospects; job security; fringe benefits; working conditions; and travelling distance. [Award one mark for a factor and one mark for an explanation.]

4. The demand for labour is a derived demand so if demand for a product fell so would the demand for labour.

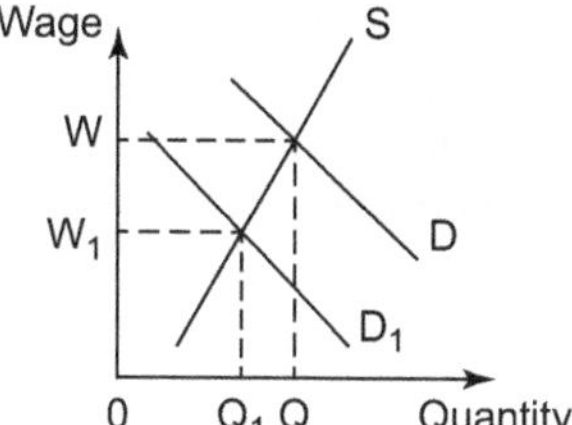

Figure TG 3.3.5

[Award two marks for an accurately drawn diagram: one mark for the axes labelled and one mark for the lines being correctly shown and labelled. Award two marks for the explanation: if demand for workers fell from D to D_1 then pay would fall from W to W_1 [1] and the number employed from Q to Q_1] [1].

5. Earnings are the total amount received [1] including additional payments [1].

6. Specialisation is the process by which individuals, firms, regions and whole economies concentrate [1] on producing those products in which they have an advantage [1].

7. Answers could include: By dividing the job into smaller parts the worker becomes more skilled [1] as they have become specialised [1]. It also allows them to do what they are good at [1] thus increasing their job satisfaction [1]. Other advantages include: increased skill; doing what they are best at; making the job easier to do; increasing job satisfaction. [Award one mark for an advantage and one mark for the explanation.]

8. Extension question: Benefits to the worker include: increased skill [1] so they are able to go on to higher paid jobs [1]; doing what they are best at [1] so they are not so frustrated with work [1]; increased job satisfaction [1]; increasing their overall happiness [1]; increased standard of living [1]; higher pay [1]. Costs include: boredom [1] as they repeat tasks hundreds of times [1]; deskilling [1] as they do not use some of their skills doing the job [1]; and lack of job security [1]. [Award up to 5 marks for a one-sided answer. To gain more than 5 marks there should be a balanced answer with both sides considered.]

Unit 3.4

1. A trade union is an organisation of workers which actively supports its members [1] through a variety of ways such as increasing wages and improving working conditions [1].

2. Collective bargaining is a process of negotiation over pay and conditions [1] between a trade union, representing a group of workers, and employers [1].

3. Trade unions protect their members [1] and seek to ensure that they are fairly paid and have good working conditions [1]. They also seek to protect jobs [1] both in individual firms/industries and in the case of individuals and unfair dismissal [1]. Other roles include: ensuring that laws on areas such as working conditions and equal pay are obeyed; improving quality of public services; engaging in political issues. [Award one mark for a role and one mark for an explanation.]

4. Industrial action is any measure taken by a trade union to try to enforce their demands or to address their complaints [1]. This may take the form of strikes, overtime bans, go slows, work to rule or sit-ins [1].

5. This will depend on your country or on which other countries they have studied. They could refer to the teachers' strike in Argentina or the general unrest of some unions in Indonesia. [Award one mark for each example up to a maximum of two marks.]

6. Unions will negotiate with employers for higher pay [1]. In general, unionised workers are better paid than non-unionised workers [1]. Trade union members often get more fringe benefits [1] because unions may be willing to accept these when employers will not agree to higher pay [1]. Other advantages include: better working conditions/ensure legislation is adhered to; increased job security; protection against unfair employer action. [Award one mark for the advantage and one mark for the explanation.]

7. Trade unions may restrict the number of people in work [1] which can cause the government to pay more benefits to the unemployed [1]. Unions force up wages which can increase the costs of production [1] leading to exports being less competitive [1]. Unions can be in opposition to the government [1] which can lead them to try to disrupt government plans [1].

8. Students should explain at least three benefits, for example: unions can insist on better working conditions [1], such as improved lighting or proper rest periods [1], and that legislation on these is acted on [1]. Other benefits include: higher pay; protection against unfair employer action; and greater job security. [Give one mark for the benefit, maximum three, and one or two marks for the explanation up to a maximum of six overall.] The final two marks are for saying why they may not always benefit, for example: demands for higher pay may lead employers to look for ways of reducing the number employed [1] such as by substituting capital for labour [1].

9. Extension question: The decline in trade union membership in many Western industrial countries is a result of the change in the types of industries and jobs [1]. The large majority of union members were employed in heavy industries such as coal mining, iron and steel and shipbuilding, that is, manual labour [1]. As these industries declined, they were replaced by more skilled work and in the last twenty years by jobs requiring the use of technology [1]. Many of these jobs are more individual and even isolated so workers do not see the need to band together in unions [1]. The tertiary sector has grown in importance [1], but the tertiary sector has a much lower unionised rate than the secondary sector which is in decline [1]. Other factors include the increase in female workers [1] with women being traditionally less unionised. Lastly, in some countries, such as the UK, legislation was passed to reduce the strength of unions [1] which again led to a fall in collective power and thus workers seeing less need to join [1].

Unit 3.5

1. The primary sector is the direct use of natural resources [1]. It is the extraction of basic materials and goods from the land and sea [1].
2. The tertiary sector consists of all the activities in the economy which involve the idea of a service [2]. [An answer which just says 'work which provides a service' is worth one mark.]
3. One example is a clothing manufacturer. It brings in raw cotton from a primary producer [1] and makes this cotton into clothes [1]. It then sells it to a clothes shop in the tertiary sector [1] which in turn sells the clothes to its customers [1]. [Give two marks for the links with the primary sector and two marks for the links with the tertiary sector.]
4. One advantage is that small firms can be more flexible [1] as they find it easier to adapt to change [1]. Another advantage is that they can focus on niche markets [1] as the small size of the market would not make it profitable for large firms [1]. Other advantages include: personal service; better communication; innovation; lower costs; and community support. [Award one mark for an advantage and one mark for an explanation.]
5. A merger is the process by which two independent firms come together [1] to form a new firm [1].
6. A horizontal merger [1] is when two firms at the same stage of production in the same industry join together [1]. A vertical merger [1] is when two firms at different stages in the same industry join together. Other mergers include: vertical backwards; vertical forwards; and conglomerate. [Award one mark for the type of merger and one mark for the explanation.]
7. Economies of scale are where an increase in the level of production [1] results in a fall in the average costs of production [1].
8. Purchasing economies [1] are where a firm buys in large quantities resulting in a discount leading to a lower cost per unit [1]. Education and training economies of scale [1] are where a local university's research and development facilities can provide help to all the firms in the industry [1]. Other economies include: technical; increased dimensions; division of labour; financial; managerial; marketing; risk bearing (all internal); transport; concentration; location; finance (all external). [If a candidate gives internal and external that is also acceptable. Award one mark for each economy of scale and one mark for the explanation.]
9. Extension question: A forwards vertical merger is when a firm at a previous stage in the production process of an industry takes over a firm at the next stage [1]. One effect would be that as a larger firm they may find it easier and cheaper to borrow money [1] at a lower rate of interest [1] because banks and other lenders see them as having more assets and as less likely to go bankrupt than two smaller firms [1]. Another economy affected would be that the larger firm may be able to employ more specialist staff [1] and thus improve their performance [1]. [Award one mark for a definition of forwards vertical. Award one mark for each economy up to three marks. Award up to five marks for analysis of the effects of a forwards vertical merger on the economies of scale.]

Unit 3.6

1. Production is the total output of the goods and services produced by a firm or industry [1] in a period of time [1].
2. Productivity is the contribution to total output by each factor of production employed [1]. It is measured in terms of output per unit of input [1].
3. Total output = 250 [1] = 10 units per worker [1]; 360 = 12 units per worker [1]

   There has been an increase of 2 [12-10] units per worker [1] or 2 x 100 = 20% [1]
4. Derived demand is when a factor of production is not demanded for itself [1], but is dependent on the demand for the product it helps to produce [1].
5. The first way is if there is an increase in demand for a product [1]. In order to produce more products, more factors of production will be required. Another way is if labour has a higher level of productivity than capital [1] then a firm would want to employ more people [1].

6. One disadvantage of labour-intensive production is that labour with the right skills could be in short supply [1] which would lead to having to pay higher wages, increasing the costs of production [1]. Secondly, if labour relations are poor, then workers can go on strike [1] leading to a loss of production [1]. Other disadvantages include: cost; and less efficient. [Award one mark for an advantage and one mark for an explanation.]
7. One disadvantage of capital-intensive production is that, at present, machinery cannot take responsibility for what happens [1] meaning that if anything goes wrong it cannot be put right without stopping production [1]. Another disadvantage is that machines are inflexible [1] so can only perform the task they have been built for [1]. Other disadvantages include: cost; and need to operate on a large scale. [Award one mark for a disadvantage and one mark for an explanation.]
8. One way would be to increase the use of technology [1] such as tractors and combine harvesters to replace labour as they work faster and can deal with larger areas of land on each day [1]. Another way would be to improve the quality of the raw materials [1] such as the seeds used or the type of sheep which are kept. This would lead, in the case of seeds, to a higher yielding harvest/more output per field [1]. Other ways include: improve the skills of the workers; more effective management; and use of better fertilisers. [Award one mark for a way of improving and one mark for an explanation.]
9. Extension question: Increasing productivity would result in higher output per unit of input [1]. This would enable the firm to gain more output without increasing costs [1]. In turn this would lead to lower average cost [1] and the opportunity to either increase profits and/or reduce prices gaining more sales [1]. Increasing production may be easier than increasing productivity because the latter may require extra cost such as training [1]. Increasing production, however, will mean more cars [1], but the price will remain the same or possibly increase if extra output requires workers to work overtime [1]. As increased production can be very quickly altered this is the short-run answer [1], but increasing productivity is more effective in the long-run [1]. If the main concern, therefore, is to reduce costs, they should increase productivity [1]. On the other hand, if the main concern is to respond to an increase in demand then production should be increased [1]. [Award up to six marks for analysing/explaining the two sides and two marks for comment.]

Unit 3.7

1. Total cost(s) are all [1] the costs of the firm added together [1]. If a student states that TC = FC+VC, one mark can be awarded, but note the maximum of two marks for the question.
2. Average cost is the cost of producing a unit of output [1] and is $\frac{TC}{Q}$ [1].
3. Fixed costs: salaries [1], interest on loans [1], rent [1]. Variable costs: wages [1], raw materials/inputs [1]. Award a maximum of two marks for each type of cost.
4. Average fixed costs continue to fall because the same amount of money (cost) is being divided [1] by an ever larger number [1]. Average variable costs fall and then rise because at first it is easy to get existing variable factors, such as labour, to work more or to get discounts by buying larger quantities of materials [1], but after a while it becomes more and more expensive to obtain extra variable inputs thus forcing AVC to rise [1].
5. Total revenue is the total income [1] of a firm from the sale of its goods or services [1].
6. Average revenue falls because to sell more goods to raise more total revenue [1] the firm has to lower its price [1]. As the price of a good is the same as AR [1] and price is found from the demand line then as demand slopes downwards so does AR [1].
7. Profit maximisation [1] is one objective. This is to gain the most profit possible [1]. Another objective is survival [1]. This is to earn enough money/sell sufficient products to ensure that you remain in business [1]. Other objectives include: sales (revenue) maximisation; and social welfare. Award one mark for the objective and one mark for the explanation.
8.

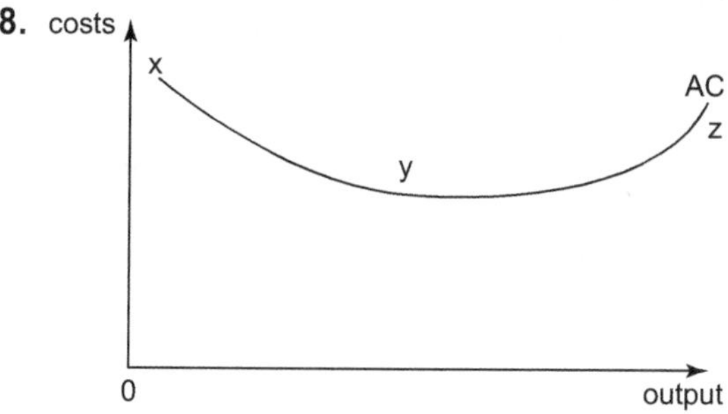

Figure 3.7.2

As a firm grows, both AFC and AVC will at first fall. This leads to the decline in AC as AC = AFC + AVC. [1] This fall in AC (x to y] is a result of the firm benefitting from economies of scale [1] which are advantages gained by increased size. If the firm continues to grow it may encounter diseconomies of scale [1] which are costs caused by the firm becoming too large such as the boredom of the workers or lack of clear control [1]. These will cause AC to rise [y-z] [1]. In addition, AVC rises before AC increases because of the increased costs of the variable factors as they become more difficult to obtain. This rise in AVC pulls up AC [1].

9. Extension question: In theory firms should seek to maximise their profits because in this way they gain the money [1] needed for new investment, for example in new technology, and for growth by building new factories or opening more shops or by taking over other firms [1]. New firms, however, need to concentrate on survival [1] if they are going to continue and have the chance to grow [1]. Other firms may see social welfare [1] in terms of both their workers and the local community as part of their responsibility [1] and devote resources to that objective. Maximising profits may be a long-term objective, but to get there it may in the shorter-term be more important to survive, be seen as a 'good employer' and to focus on market share/sales [1] in order to eventually maximise profits [1]. [Award up to six marks for analysis/explanation of profit maximisation as against other objectives. Award two further marks for comment/discussion.]

Unit 3.8

1. Competition is where different firms [1] are trying to sell a similar product to a customer [1].
2. A competitive market is where a large number of firms compete with each other [1] to satisfy the wants and needs of a large number of consumers [1].
3. Competition leads to lower prices [1], so the consumer can buy more products with the same amount of money [1]. Competition also forces firms to improve the quality of their products [1], so that consumers benefit by buying improved products often at the same price [1]. Other advantages include: greater choice; products meet consumer needs; more innovation. [Award one mark for the advantage and one mark for the explanation.]
4. One effect could be a fall in profits [1] as firms have to lower prices to stay in business without seeing a similar percentage increase in sales [1]. Profits could also rise [1] as firms that are forced to become more efficient and innovative gain market share thus leading to greater profits [1].
5. Monopoly is the sole producer or seller [1] of a good or service [1].
6. Barriers to entry are ways in which new firms are prevented [1] from entering a particular industry [1].
7. One advantage is that a monopoly can gain large economies of scale [1]. By increasing its size, a monopoly can benefit from economies such as bulk buying and increased dimensions so that their average costs fall allowing them to make more profit [1]. Another advantage for a monopoly is that there is no competition [1] which means it can raise prices without losing sales, again leading to higher profits [1]. Other advantages include: growth of research and development; avoidance of wastage; and greater international competitiveness. [Award one mark for an advantage and one mark for the explanation.]
8. The first disadvantage is higher prices [1]. With no competition, the monopoly can raise prices and if the consumer wants the product there is no other choice [1]. Another disadvantage is that there will be fewer new products [1]. Again, with no competition, there is no incentive for the firm to innovate and launch new products to beat their competitors [1]. Other disadvantages include: lower quality; less choice; lack of consumer sovereignty. [Award one mark for a disadvantage and one mark for the explanation.]
9. Extension question: The argument for monopolies always being harmful for consumers rests on the fact that without competition monopolies can raise price, not worry about quality, fail to innovate and not offer the consumer any choice [award two marks for two or more disadvantages]. This means that the consumer is worse off than if there was competition [1]. This, however, is not necessarily the case. Unless the monopoly is owned by the government and protected by laws which prevent any competition [1], a monopoly which ignores the consumer will find that competitors entering the market and eroding its market share [1] force it to, for example, improve the quality of its products [1]. Even a government-owned monopoly may not be entirely harmful as the government may require it to keep prices low [1]. It is unlikely, therefore, that monopolies will always be harmful so long as they are either regulated by the state or are open to potential competition [1]. [Maximum of five marks for a one-sided response.]

Unit 4.1

1. Examples could include: education, vaccinations, health services, street lighting, national defence, city flood defences. [Award one mark for each example] [3]

2. Merit goods are goods and services that have both private benefits for the user and external benefits to third parties. Merit goods tend to be underprovided by the market. Governments therefore seek to produce merit goods in order to make them affordable and accessible for everyone. [1] Examples could include education, vaccinations, health services. [Award one mark for one example.]
3. Street lighting is an example of a public good [1] as it is non-excludable and non-rival as nobody can be excluded from benefiting from street lighting once it is provided [1]. The Police is an example of a public service [1] because the provision of police is considered to be essential for a modern society to function effectively. [1]
4. Extension question: The answer could refer to:

   Health care is a merit good with positive externalities for the economy [1] as it reduces the amount of sick people in the population. [1]

   A National Health Service ensures that all people have access to healthcare and treatment. [1]

   A National Health Service will lead to a healthy workforce. [1]

   Students might refer to arguments that a NHS leads to healthcare being rationed [1] which leads to long waiting lists [1] This is avoided in a private system as there tends to be spare capacity [1] and a private system is more responsive to patients. [1]

   [Award a maximum of five marks for a one-sided response that considers only the government or the private sector'.]

Unit 4.2

1. Full employment (low unemployment), price stability (low stable inflation), sustainable economic growth, redistribution of income, balance of payments stability (value of exports = value of imports). [One mark for each aim identified]
2. Full employment (low unemployment) means that most of those who are willing and able to work have jobs [1]. Full employment is desirable for a country because when people have jobs they have income to spend [1]. More spending generally results in higher standards of living for the population [1]. Consumer spending also results in higher demand in the economy [1] and higher economic growth [1].
3. Inflation is the sustained rise in the general level of prices in an economy over time [1]. When prices rise, consumers' cost of living rises [1]. Goods and services may therefore become less affordable [1]. If inflation is high, consumer confidence may fall [1] as their money buys less [1].
4. In order to lower inflation, the government may seek to reduce consumer spending [1] in the economy. This would have the effect of reducing the overall demand in the economy [1] leading to a fall in production by firms [1] and higher unemployment [1].
5. In order to lower unemployment, the government may seek to increase consumer spending [1] in the economy. Higher consumer spending is likely to lead to higher demand for goods and services [1]. Firms will look to increase production [1] in response to the higher demand which will lead to more jobs for workers [1]. However, consumer spending on imports is also likely to increase [1] leading to a trade deficit on the balance of payments.
6. Extension question: Economic growth is when the production of goods and services in an economy increases over time.

   During times of high economic growth:

   - firms seek to hire more workers in order to expand production which lowers unemployment
   - higher incomes lead to higher consumer spending and a rise in living standards
   - higher consumer spending should lead to an increase in sales for most businesses and higher profits.

   [Award up to four marks for talking about the benefits of economic growth]

   However, economic growth may also result in:

   - rising inflation due to higher consumer spending and higher overall demand in the economy
   - a trade deficit on the balance of payments as consumers spend more on imported goods
   - an increase in pollution and environmental damage
   - depletion of a country's natural resources
   - a widening gap between rich and poor as some benefit from the higher economic growth more than others.

   [Award up to four marks for talking about the drawbacks of economic growth.]

Whether economic growth should be the main aim depends on the state of the economy. If economic growth is low and unemployment is high, then economic growth should probably be the government's main aim. [Maximum of four marks for a one-sided discussion.]

Unit 4.3

1. The annual financial statement showing the government's proposed revenues and spending. [2]
2. One mark for each reason identified with a brief explanation. Provide public services e.g. Police and Fire; Merit goods provided e.g. healthcare provided for all; Improve infrastructure to boost economy e.g. roads and power supply; Pubic goods provided that private sector could not because of the free rider problem e.g. national defence; Redistribution of income e.g. benefits providing a safety net improving equality; Reduce unemployment e.g. using spending to create jobs; Raise growth by use of government economic policy.
3. Direct tax is paid directly by an individual or organisation [1] e.g. income tax, property taxes [1]. Indirect Tax is collected by an intermediary such as a shop from a person (consumer) who pays the burden of tax [1] e.g. sales tax, VAT [1].
4. Progressive tax is a tax that increases as the payer's income increases [1]. Individuals who earn high incomes have a greater proportion of income taken to pay tax [1]. Regressive tax is a tax where the rate increases as a payer's income decreases [1]. For example, a sales tax is assessed as a % of the item bought so a 10% sales tax has a greater burden on lower income earners than on wealthy as ability to pay not taken into account [1].
5. Where a government adjusts its spending and tax rates to influence an economy [2]
6. One mark for each component identified. Consumption-consumer spending in the economy; [1] Investment – capital goods used to expand production [1]; Government spending – building more roads will lead to more jobs, and wages earned will impact on AD [1];Net Exports – difference between the value of exports and imports – more exports than imports then AD could rise [1].
7. Contractionary – reduce government spending and/or raise taxation [1] to check inflation and de-stimulate the economy [1]. Expansionary – increase government spending or lower taxes [1] to stimulate the economy [1].
8. Reduced income tax increases disposable income [1] this leads to increased spending [1] this leads to increased demand for goods and services which causes firms to increase output [1]. In order to increase output, firms hire more labour [1] which results in a fall in cyclical unemployment [1].
9. A government might choose to reduce spending for a variety of reasons. They might want to bring a budget deficit under control [1]. A budget deficit means that a government has to borrow money and is spending more than it is receiving in tax revenues [1]. The government might want to reduce taxation on individuals and business and so by reducing spending they can afford to implement tax cuts [1]. Reducing taxes would boost aggregate demand as consumers spend their tax cuts on goods and services. This would stimulate growth and incentives in the economy. [1]
10. A reduction in government spending is likely to lead to cutbacks in state-funded projects – for example, construction of new roads. This would lead to a rise in unemployment.
11. There is a compelling argument that healthcare should be provided by the government. This is because healthcare is a merit good. This means that it has beneficial positive externalities. Individuals benefit from others being healthy because it reduces the likelihood of catching their illness. People benefit from a positive externality of others receiving healthcare. [2] If private sector provided then the poorer people might not be able to afford. Their real disposable income would fall as larger proportion of income goes on healthcare. [2] Publicly provided healthcare will contribute towards a healthy workforce which will have a positive impact on productivity and costs [2]. However, there is opportunity cost of government providing healthcare in terms of less resources for other areas of government spending; taxes could be lower if the private sector provided, taxes could be lower if private sector provided [2].

Unit 4.4

1. Money supply is the quantity of money in circulation in the economy. [Award two marks for a correct definition.]
2. Monetary policy is control of the money supply to achieve macroeconomic aims. [Award two marks for a correct definition.]
3. Expansionary monetary policy seeks to increase activity, growth and jobs [1]. Contractionary monetary policy seeks to reduce activity to control inflation and/or the balance of payments. [1]
4. Higher interest rates, revaluation or reducing cash for bank lending could lower inflation. [Award one mark for each policy measure identified.] [3]

5. A decrease in interest rates is used as part of an expansionary monetary policy [1]. Expansionary monetary policy is likely to result in lower unemployment and higher economic growth. [1] Consumer spending and total spending in the economy increases [1]. The increase in total spending could lead to the rate of price change (inflation) rising. [1]
6. An increase in interest rates is used as part of a contractionary monetary policy. [1] Higher interest rates will increase the cost of borrowing. [1] The consequent reduction in consumption and investment will reduce the quantity of money in circulation. [1] As a result, total spending in the economy will fall [1] putting downward pressure on the general price level [1]. [Award one mark per point up to the maximum.]
7. Extension question: [Award up to three marks for a discussion of expansionary monetary policy and up to three marks for a discussion of expansionary fiscal policy. Award up to two marks for a discussion of which is more effective and why.]

   Expansionary monetary policy:

   - The increase in the money supply by the government leading to a rise in total spending to achieve macroeconomic goals
   - The central bank lowers interest rates and the cost of borrowing falls
   - Consumer spending and business investment increases
   - Result is lower unemployment and higher economic growth

   However:

   - Prices could rise as a result of higher consumer spending and increased business investment and higher consumer spending on imports worsens the trade balance on the current account of the balance of payments

   Expansionary fiscal policy:

   - An increase in government spending and/or a reduction in income tax rates in order to increase total spending in the economy
   - Government increases spending leading to an increase in total spending in the economy
   - Government lowers income tax rate and consumer spending increases causing total spending in the economy to increase
   - Result is lower unemployment and higher economic growth

   However:

   - Higher spending in the economy puts upward pressure on prices and rising incomes result in increased spending on imports
   - Consumers might choose to save rather than spend after the fall in tax rate.

Unit 4.5

1. A supply-side policy is a measure taken by a government to increase the aggregate supply of an economy [1]. A demand supply policy is a measure to increase total spending in an economy (aggregate demand) [1].
2. Privatisation is the transfer of a business, industry or service [1] from public to private ownership and control. [1]
3. Deregulation is the process of removing [1] or reducing state regulations. [1]
4. Students can choose three of the following: Education and training to improve productivity of labour; Labour market reform such as reducing trade union power; Lowering income tax and business taxes as incentives; Increasing competition through deregulation and privatisation; Encouraging entrepreneurship through subsidies and grants leading to product innovation and process innovation; Improving infrastructure such as transport, communication and power grids.

   [Award one mark for each of the three supply side policies and one mark for its impact.] [6]
5. Government spending on education and training should lead to an improvement in workers' knowledge and skills over time. [2] This may lead to an increase in the productivity of labour (the output per worker) [2]. This leads to an increase in the productive potential of the economy and a fall in unemployment [2].
6. Extension question: This question is an extension question as it tests understanding of concepts that are beyond IGCSE. Extension students need to identify a supply-side measure to reduce inflation. Supply-side policies have the effect of increasing the productive capacity of the economy, shifting the aggregate supply curve outwards to the right.

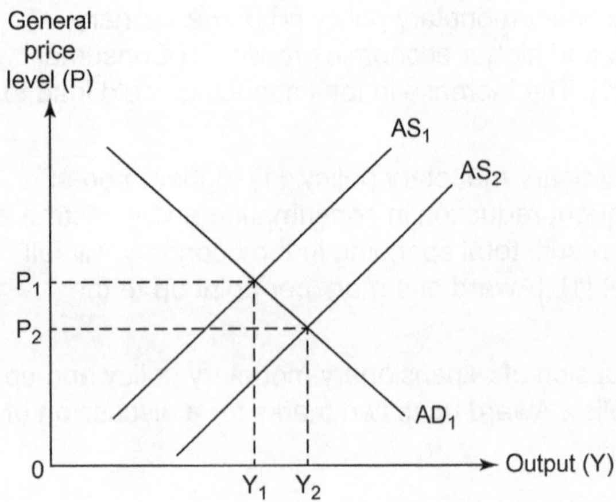

Students need to identify a demand side measure to reduce inflation.

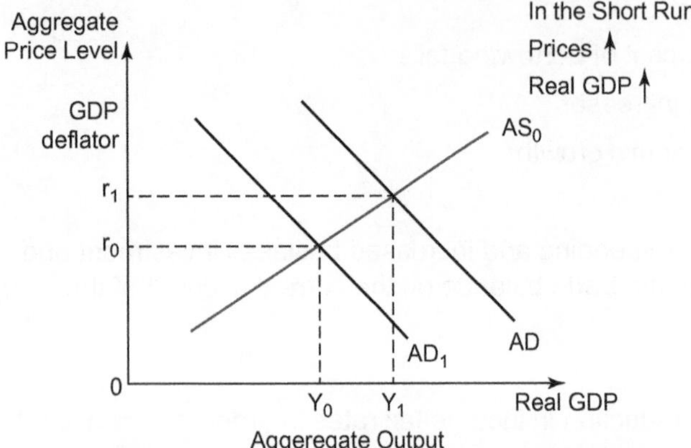

Both these diagrams show that the Price level has fallen as a result of the measures.

The student needs to point out one advantage and one disadvantage of supply-side and demand-side measures before coming to a conclusion.

[Award one mark for identification of supply-side measure; one mark for a supply-side diagram; one mark for identification of a demand-side measure; one mark for a demand-side diagram; one mark for an advantage [1] and disadvantage of a supply-side measure[1]; one mark for an advantage [1] and disadvantage of a demand-side measure [1].] [8]

Unit 4.6

1. The increase in the value of goods and services produced in an economy [1] over time (usually a year). [1]
2. It is measured using gross domestic product (GDP). [1] GDP is the total value of all final goods and services produced within a country over a year; GDP is measured by adding up the total spending on final goods and services produced in a country over a one-year period. [1] This includes household spending on consumer goods, business spending on capital goods, government spending and net spending by foreigners on exports. [Award two marks for all the components and one mark for a partial answer.] [2]
3. Money GDP is the total money value of the goods and services produced in an economy, [1] not accounting for inflation (may also be referred to as GDP or nominal GDP) [1]. Real GDP is the total value for goods and services produced in an economy which has been adjusted to take inflation into account. [1]
4. Real GDP per head (Capita) measures the average income of a population. [1] Real GDP can be calculated as:

   Real GDP per head = Real GDP / Population. [1]
5. A recession is a sustained period of negative GDP in the economy over time. It is also defined as two consecutive quarters (three-monthly periods) of negative economic growth. [2]
6. Extension question: The following PPC diagram shows the impact of a recession on an economy. [4]

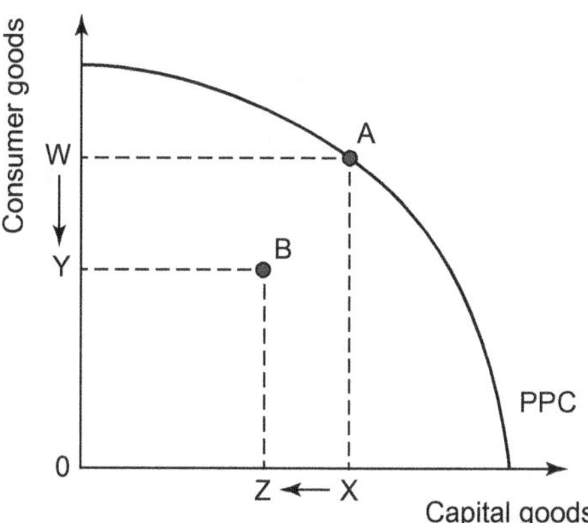

Figure TG 4.5.1

The impact of a recession can be shown in the above diagram. The economy is at point A before the recession. After the recession the economy is at Point B. [1] There are unemployed resources and both consumer goods output and capital goods output have fallen. [1]

[Also award one mark for a correctly labelled PPC and one mark for showing unemployed resources.] [2].

7. Demand-side causes of economic growth include: an increase in consumer spending resulting in higher demand for goods and services, an increase in investment in capital equipment and machinery by firms as they seek to expand production, a rise in government spending, a rise in net exports. [Award one mark for identifying demand-side causes and two marks for an explanation].

   Supply-side factors causing growth include: business investment in capital equipment and machinery leading to an increase in productivity; development of new technology used in the production process, increasing productivity and lowering unit costs; immigration of skilled labour into the country; the discovery of natural resources in a country, such as oil, coal or iron ore. [Award one mark for identifying supply side factor and two marks for an explanation].

   Students can gain full marks from any two developed points.

8. Lower interest reduces the cost of borrowing [1] so firms will increase investment [1] which will increase efficiency [1] increasing exports [1] and so leads to economic growth.

   However, lower interest rates increase borrowing by households [1] increasing spending on goods [1] so firms increase production [1] in order to meet the increased demand [1].

9. Extension question: Economic growth leads to increased employment opportunities for individuals as firms expand production. [1] This results in rising incomes and higher living standards. [1] Rising sales and profits occur as a result and firms expand production by investing in capital equipment and machinery. [1] Government receive higher tax revenue because economic growth generally results in higher incomes for individuals and businesses. [1]

   However:

   The benefits of economic growth are not shared equally throughout the population. [1] Some individuals benefit a lot, while others may not benefit at all or may even become worse off. [1] As the economy grows, resources such as labour and raw materials are likely to become increasingly scarce. Competition for these resources may mean that firms have to pay more for them. [1] Economic growth could lead to depletion of non-renewable natural resources; pollution and environmental damage. [1]

   This question requires a discussion of benefits and costs of growth. [Award a maximum of five marks for a one-sided answer.]

Unit 4.7

1. The state of being without paid work but willing and able to work if a job becomes available. [Award only one mark if the answer does not state willing and able; award two marks for a full definition.]
2. The condition in which virtually all who are able and willing to work are employed. [Award only one mark if the answer does not state willing and able; award two marks for a full definition.]

3. The claimant count method involves counting all individuals who register as unemployed. [1] In most countries, this is done by counting the number of people claiming unemployment benefits. [1]

   The Labour Force Survey (LFS) is a government survey of a sample of households in a country to determine who is employed and who is unemployed. From this information the government is able to calculate the unemployment rate for the country. [1] The LFS is used by countries worldwide under the guidance of the International Labour Organisation (ILO) and provides a standardised measure for unemployment which can be compared between countries. [1]

4. Students could refer to seasonal, frictional, technological, structural or cyclical. [Award two marks for the description of the chosen type of unemployment.]
   - Frictional unemployment: exists when people are between jobs [1] moving from one job to another [1].
   - Seasonal unemployment: when workers are not needed all year round [1] such as those working in the tourism industry [1].
   - Technological unemployment: unemployment that exists because people are replaced by machines [1] such as the use of robotics in the car industry [1].
   - Structural unemployment: exists due to a change in the structure of an economy [1] such as when countries develop and move from being primarily a manufacturing nation to one which is service-industry-focussed. [1]
   - Cyclical unemployment: exists due to falling total spending in the economy [1] which occurs when an economy enters a recessionary period in its economic cycle. [1] [Up to 6 marks in total]

5. Students could refer to:
   - Reduced efficiency as unemployment is an inefficient use of an economy's resources as labour is not being fully utilised. This is wasteful and is likely to result in lost productivity and reduced economic growth.
   - Increased poverty as unemployment is one of the main causes of poverty in many countries and widens the gap between rich and poor.
   - Falling economic growth because when unemployment is high, consumer spending is likely to decrease leading to falling sales for many firms.
   - Lower inflation/deflation as falling aggregate demand from reduced consumer spending and business investment during a period of high unemployment is likely to result in lower inflation.

   [Award one mark for each effect identified [maximum of three marks] plus one mark for each explanatory point made.]

6. Students could refer to:
   - Make improvements in education and training and retraining workers so that they have the skills needed to find jobs in other industries and sectors in response to structural unemployment.
   - Reduce the power of trade unions by making it more difficult for them to take strike action. Lower wages could result which would cut firms' costs.
   - Provide incentives for workers by lowering income tax rates, thereby increasing the disposable income they would receive from working.
   - Provide incentives for firms to encourage them to set up in regions suffering from high unemployment.

   [Award one mark for a supply-side measure and one mark for an explanation up to a maximum of 6.]

7. Extension question: Students could refer to an increase in government spending on the construction of roads, schools or hospitals, which will create jobs helping to lower unemployment. Higher incomes from rising levels of employment are likely to lead to an increase in consumer spending, increasing aggregate demand in the economy. Firms are likely to employ more workers to expand production in response to the increased demand for goods and services.

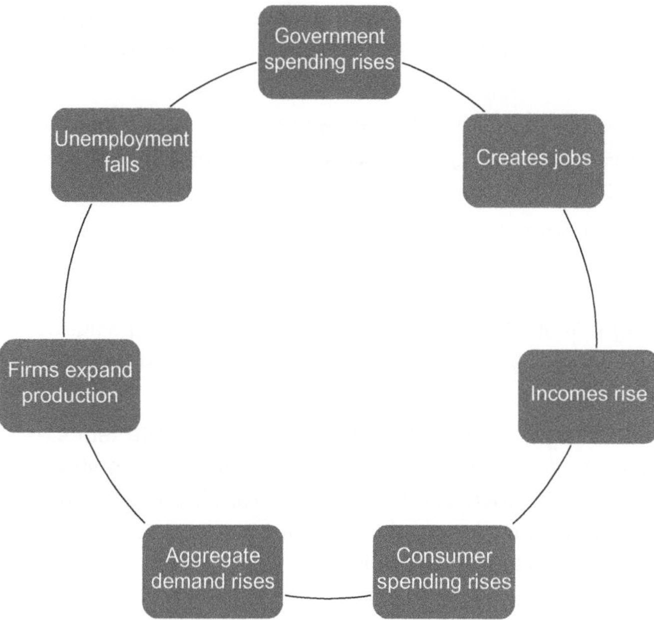

Figure 4.7.2

An increase in government spending will lead to more jobs being created and increased production.

The effectiveness of fiscal policy will depend on the level of spending increase. The larger the increase, the greater the impact on aggregate demand and employment.

However, an increase in government spending could lead to higher total spending in the economy (increase in aggregated demand) and puts upward pressure on prices. This could put up firms costs which they pass on in higher prices and which makes them uncompetitive.

Another consideration is that higher incomes could result in increased spending on imports.

Success will also depend on aggregate supply in the economy. Falling aggregate supply will limit the impact of increasing spending in lowering unemployment. Rising aggregate supply, on the other hand, will increase its effectiveness as it means the economy is able to produce more goods and services over time.

[Award up to four marks for the explanation of how increased spending would reduce unemployment and up to four marks for the consideration of how successful it might be. Maximum of five marks for a one-sided discussion.]

Unit 4.8

1. Inflation is the sustained rise in the general level of prices of goods and services in an economy over time. [Students must use the word sustained to be awarded two marks.]
2. Deflation is the sustained fall in the general level of prices of goods and services in an economy over time. [Students must use the term sustained fall to be awarded two marks.]
3. Changes in the general price level are measured using the weighted Consumer Price Index [1]. Household survey of spending patterns is used to come up with a basket of goods and services and prices for each of the items in the basket are collected [1]. A weighted average is used reflecting the importance in a household's budget. [1] This is multiplied by its respective weighting. The final figure is the average change in the general price level in the economy. [1]
4. The causes are Demand-pull inflation and Cost-push inflation.

   Demand-pull is when an increase in the general price level in an economy is caused by an increase in aggregate demand [1] stimulated by an increase in consumer spending or business investment. [1]

   Cost-push inflation is when the general price level in an economy rises due to an increase in firms' production costs such as an increase in the cost of raw materials. [1] An increase in these costs would make it more expensive for firms to produce their products so firms would decrease the quantity of goods and services they supply leading to a fall in the aggregate supply of the economy. [1]

5. Deflation can occur during a recession when unemployment is high and incomes are falling. [1] Consumer spending and business investment could fall leading to a fall in aggregate demand and a downward pressure on prices. [1]

   On the supply side, a falling general price level can be the result of a decrease in costs of production such as raw materials leading to cheaper prices for a range of goods. [1] This increase in aggregate supply can lead to lower unemployment and higher economic growth in an economy. [1]

6. High inflation may require firms to make frequent adjustments to the prices of the products they sell. [2] During periods of high inflation, businesses try to hold as little cash as possible. Instead they may seek to hold money in other forms such as interest-bearing bank accounts which offer a better store of value. [2] Workers may demand higher wages in periods of high inflation when their living costs are rising. Higher wages increase firms' production costs. Some of this increase in costs may be passed onto consumers in the form of higher prices [2].

7. Extension question: Students could use and explain the aggregate supply diagram from the Student's Book (Figure 4.8.4) where Aggregate supply shifts to the right. An increase in aggregate supply shifts the AS curve from AS1 to AS2 in Figure 4.8.4, resulting in an increase in real GDP from Y1 to Y2 and a fall in the general price level from P1 to P2. Again, this fall in the general price level would result in lower inflation and could lead to deflation if the increase in supply is large enough.

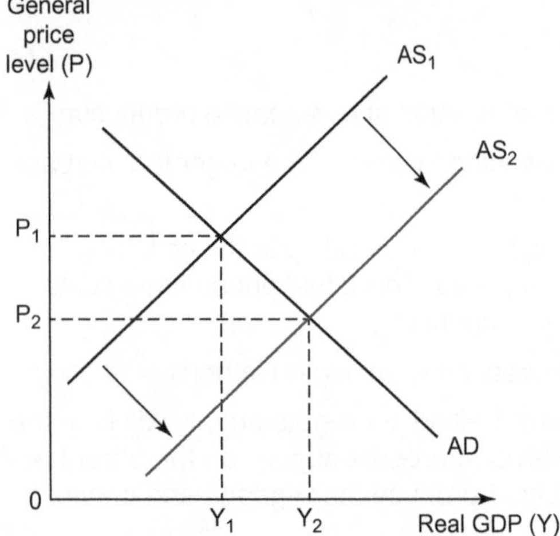

Figure SB 4.8.4

Lower costs help domestic firms to be more competitive. Consumers purchase fewer imports as they can buy local goods at cheaper prices. With higher demand, firms will increase production leading to taking on more workers.

Deflation resulting from a fall in aggregate demand, on the other hand, can be a serious problem for an economy.

[Award three marks for the diagram and three marks for the explanation. Award two further marks for coming to a conclusion.]

Unit 5.1

1. Gross domestic product of a country [1], divided by its population. [1]
2. The data is collected by the United Nations [1] and so can be trusted to be accurate [1]. It is a wider measure of living standards [1] than other measures such as real GDP per head [1].
3. The distribution of income may be uneven [1], so some people may be working in low income occupations [1]. Government policy [1] may favour one group over another, e.g. people with families may receive more benefits [1].
4. Some countries may be less developed than others [1] and therefore have lower incomes [1]. Some countries may have better factor endowments, e.g. oil reserves [1] which allow them to increase government spending on the welfare of the population [1].
5. Education could help the workforce to be become more literate [1] and skilled [1] enabling them to become employed in higher income occupations [1], e.g. IT [1]. The population would become more aware of key issues such as birth control [1] and the environment [1] which could encourage decision making [1] that improves living standards.

6. Extension question: Real GDP is a good measure of living standards as the level of income has a direct impact on living standards [1]. The figure is adjusted to take account of the effect of inflation [1] and the number of people in the population [1]. It is also easy to understand [1] and the data needed is regularly collected by most countries [1]. However real GDP per head does not cover some factors that affect living standards [1], e.g. the availability of health care and education [1], so some countries may prefer to use a broader measure [1], such as HDI [1]. Real GDP per head also does not take into account the distribution of income [1]. On balance, real GDP per head is not the best measure of living standards as other, more sophisticated [1], measures are available [1].

   [Answers exclusively in favour of, or against, real GDP per head would be given a maximum of five marks.]

Unit 5.2

1. Absolute poverty is said to exist when a person cannot afford to meet their basic needs [1], e.g. food and shelter [1]. It is also defined as having an income of less than US$1.90 per day [1]. Earlier figures, e.g. one dollar per day, would be accepted, at present.
2. Relative poverty exists when a person cannot afford to purchase the goods and services normally consumed in their society [1], e.g. in a developed economy a person may not be able to afford a colour television or mobile phone [1].
3. Poverty can be caused by war, particularly civil war [1]. This means that the normal activities of the country, e.g. food production, are likely to be disrupted [1]. People may also lose their homes [1] if they are in the war zone [1]. Unemployment [1] is another cause of poverty, leading to people being unable to purchase goods and services [1]. This problem would be worse in countries with little or no welfare benefits for the unemployed [1].
4. Lower interest rates could encourage higher borrowing [1] by businesses [1] which could allow them to invest in more capital equipment and training [1]. In the long term, this could lead to more successful businesses [1], employing more people [1] and providing cheaper goods and services [1]. Consumers could also borrow at lower cost [1], enabling them to purchase more goods and services [1] in the short term [1].
5. Extension question: In the long term [1] education could be the best way to alleviate poverty. Improvements in basic literacy and numeracy [1] could help to make people more employable [1]. Education could also enable people to make better choices with regard to financial planning [1], health choices [1] and family planning [1]. However, other issues may be more important in the short term, e.g. food supply to solve problems of malnutrition [1] or medical care [1]. Education is of little benefit if you are too ill to make use of it [1]. Also children staying longer in education, when they would otherwise be working [1], would reduce the incomes of some families [1], in the short term [1]. Maximum of five for an answer exclusively in favour of, or against, education.

Unit 5.3

1. The number of live births for every thousand people [1] in the population, per year [1].
2. The number of deaths for every thousand people [1] in the population, per year [1].
3. The population may increase more rapidly in developing countries because these countries may not have good social security arrangements for old people [1], therefore families require children to support them in old age [1]. Also the economy may still have a large amount of subsistence farming [1], so children would be a valuable source of free labour [1]. Both these factors would lead to higher birth rates [1] and increased population [1].
4. Optimum population arises when there is neither a surplus nor shortage of resources available in the country [1]. Efficiency/output per head [1] is maximised.
5. An ageing population may help the economic growth of a country by spending wealth they have accumulated during their lifetimes, e.g. pension funds [1]. This spending will create demand in the economy [1]. Older people may also contribute to economic growth by working beyond retirement age [1] and passing on skills to the younger generation [1]. However, older workers may not be as adaptable [1] or as aware of new technology [1] as young workers, so this may hamper growth [1]. There may also be a general shortage of workers in the labour force [1].
6. Extension question: An increase in population may not cause a rise in unemployment. If the increase is caused by an increase in migrant workers [1] the percentage of people unemployed would fall [1]. If the increase is caused by a rising birth rate then the percentage of unemployed may rise [1], as the total population has increased [1]. However, the number of people unemployed may fall [1], as more health workers are needed to provide social care. In the long term, a rising population may lead to unemployment if the economy cannot generate sufficient demand [1] to allow the inflow of new workers

to be employed [1]. Also, there may be a shortage of other resources, e.g. land, for the new workers to use [1]. To conclude, the impact of an increase in population size on unemployment will depend on how unemployment is measured [1], the cause of the increase in population [1] and underlying condition of the economy [1]. [A maximum of five marks for a one-sided discussion.]

Unit 5.4

1. Economic development refers to the ability of nation to meet the economic and social needs [1] of its people. This includes the ability to meet the basic needs of the population [1] and the extent to which consumer goods and services are available [1].
2. A developed country will meet the basic needs of almost all its population [1] and will have well-developed education [1] and health [1] services available to all people.
3. A developing country is likely to have a high proportion of people employed in the primary sector [1]. It may also have low GDP per head [1] and a low HDI ranking [1].
4. In the long term, investment in education should improve educational standards [1], leading to a labour force that is easier to train [1], more attractive to inward investors [1] and more capable of working in the tertiary sector [1]. The workforce should become more productive [1] and there should be more opportunities to reduce intergenerational poverty [1]. The need to rely on other countries for expertise, for example engineering skills [1], should gradually be reduced [1].
5. Extension question: The benefits of economic development will vary, depending on the state of the country before development takes place [1]. The people of a very poor country will benefit from improved nutrition [1], health care [1] and shelter [1]. Economic development may be the difference between life and death [1]. In more developed countries the benefits will be in terms of improved access to consumer goods and services [1] and more opportunities for leisure [1] and leisure pursuits [1]. However, some economic development may be associated with environmental damage [1], such as pollution [1], unsustainable depletion of natural resources [1] and overcrowding [1]. Changes to the way of life needed to generate development, e.g. moving from subsistence agriculture to being employed, may lead to social problems [1]. [Award a maximum of five marks for a one-sided discussion.]

Unit 6.1

1. Specialisation involves focusing on one particular activity, e.g. a worker who only carries out one part of the production process. [Allow two marks.]
2. One benefit is that specialisation will allow firms to lower costs [1], leading to lower prices for consumers [1]. Also, products may be of higher quality [1] and the consumer may have more choice [1].
3. Specialisation may allow a country to produce more output [1], thereby raising GDP [1]. Output may also be produced at lower unit cost [1], increasing the possibility of export sales [1].
4. Extension question: It is possible that all countries could benefit from specialising. They could produce more [1] high quality [1] products by working more efficiently [1] and benefiting from economies of scale [1]. All countries could then benefit by trading with each other [1] to obtain the goods they have not produced [1]. However, they may not benefit if they cannot obtain the products they are not producing from other countries [1] at fair prices [1]. Countries may also suffer from over-dependency on one or a few products [1] and may face problems if the world demand for that product falls suddenly [1].

   Reference to the terms of trade, comparative advantage or absolute advantage would not be expected at this level but should be credited, if used.

   [Note there are more than 6 marks available above. This is because there is more than one way to achieve maximum marks. A maximum of 4 marks would be given for a one-sided answer, e.g. only in favour of specialisation.]

Unit 6.2

1. Globalisation refers to fact consumers from different parts of the world [1] can purchase goods and services from producers in different parts of the world. [1]
2. A multinational company operates (produces) [1] in more than one country. [1]
3. One drawback to the host country is that local businesses in the same industry may be forced to close [1] due to competition from the MNC [1]. Another drawback is increased pollution [1] reducing the quality of life [1] for the host country population.

4. Domestic producers would gain increased access to overseas markets [1], enabling them to increase sales/profits/revenue [1]. Increased sales would give more scope for economies of scale [1], reducing the unit costs of the producers [1].
5. A tariff is a tax [1], placed on an imported good or service [1] that increases its price [1]
6. A quota is a physical quantity [1]. It is the maximum number of a product [1] that can be imported into a country [1] in a given time period [1].
7. A tariff will help domestic producers [1]. It will increase the price of imports [1], making the prices of domestic producers more competitive [1] and therefore increasing sales/profits [1].
8. Protection may give infant businesses within an industry time to grow [1]. As a business grows it can experience economies of scale [1] which should lower unit costs [1], enabling the business to compete with larger overseas rivals [1].
9. Extension question: There are some benefits to free trade. Consumers may have more choice [1] and pay lower prices. Employment will increase in businesses that can access overseas markets [1] and these businesses should become more profitable due to increased sales [1] and lower costs [1]. However, competition may lead to some workers losing their jobs [1] and, in the long term, consumers may face higher prices [1] if local competition is eliminated [1]. Countries may sell resources in the short term which would have been more usefully conserved [1] to sustain the country in the long run [1], e.g. rainforest timber. The benefits and costs of free trade may not be shared throughout a national community [1]. In theory the 'winners' from free trade should be able to compensate the 'losers' [1] but in many countries the mechanisms to do this are poorly developed [1]. [Maximum of five marks for an answer exclusively in favour of [or against] free trade.]

Unit 6.3

1. The price of one currency [1], expressed in terms of another [1].
2. The demand for a currency is determined by the underlying demand for a nation's products [1]. If more overseas customers want to buy these products they will have to purchase more currency to buy them [1]. If MNCs want to invest in the country [1], e.g. purchase assets, they will have to purchase currency to make such investments [1].
3. Currency is supplied when consumers want to purchase imports [1], therefore the price of such imports [1] will influence the supply of the currency. If MNCs from a country wish to invest overseas [1] they will have to supply currency in order to purchase the assets of overseas countries [1].
4. Standard supply and demand diagram. Correct labelling of axes and curves [1], correct identification of equilibrium point [1] and a short explanation, e.g. where demand meets supply [1].
5. A floating exchange rate can change [1] frequently as it is determined by the forces of supply and demand for the currency [1]. A fixed exchange rate is set by the government or central bank of a country [1]. The central bank intervenes in the market to maintain a fixed exchange rate [1].
6. A floating rate can adjust helping to correct current account surpluses or deficits [1], e.g. when the current account is in deficit the exchange rate should fall [1], making exports more competitive [1]. A floating rate also allows the government to focus on other macro-economic objectives [1] because the government does not need to use policy measures such as interest changes to correct current account deficits or surpluses [1].
7. A fixed exchange rate will help businesses to plan [1] as there will be less uncertainty regarding import and export prices [1]. Currency speculation may be discouraged [1] as the government should act to support the existing exchange rate [1].
8. An appreciation of the exchange rate should lead, other things being equal [1], to a fall in cost of imports [1] for producers. This should enable producers to reduce the price of their output [1] which would lead to a fall in the rate of inflation [1]. However, the strength of this effect would depend on how important imported factor inputs were to the economy [1] and the extent to which producers were prepared to pass on cost savings in the form of reduced prices [1].
9. Extension question: It would be expected that an exchange rate depreciation might lead to more competitive export prices [1] and therefore more exports [1]. Conversely import prices should rise [1] leading to a fall in imports [1]. The extent of any change would be dependent on the elasticity of demand for exports and imports [1] (the more elastic, the more pronounced the changes) [1].

Unit 6.4

1. The four components of the current account are:
   - the trade in goods [1], which records trade in visible (tangible) imports and exports [1]
   - the trade in services [1], which records trade in invisible (intangible) imports and exports [1]
   - primary income [1], which is the return on factors of production, e.g. wages, interest, profits and dividends [1]
   - secondary income [1], which arises from current transfers, e.g. foreign aid [1]
2. A current account deficit arises when a country spends more foreign currency [1] than it earns [1] across the four components of the current account [1]. One or more of the components may be in surplus while others are in deficit [1]. Allow 'more money' as an alternative to 'foreign currency'.
3. A current account deficit may be caused by a rise in the rate of inflation [1] which makes exports less competitive [1] and imports more attractive [1]. Another cause could be a rise in consumer incomes [1] which leads to an increase in demand for imports [1].
4. A current account surplus indicates that there has been rising demand for domestic currency [1]; this demand would increase the price of the domestic currency [1]. Also, low prices of domestic goods may have reduced the demand for imports [1], leading to a fall in supply of the domestic currency [1], therefore increasing the price of the domestic currency.
5. A devaluation would increase the price of imports [1] and reduce the price of exports [1] thus reducing the demand for imports [1] and increasing the demand for exports [1]. Total spending on imports should fall [1] and total spending on exports should rise [1] thus improving a current account deficit. However, the extent of any improvement would depend on the price elasticity of demand for imports/exports [1] and the time period involved [1].
6. Domestic producers could be subsidised [1]. This would lower their costs [1] and allow them to reduce export prices [1], thereby increasing export revenue [1]. Tariffs could be imposed on imports [1], making them less attractive to domestic consumers [1] and causing total spending on imports to fall [1].
7. Extension question: The answer to this question would depend on the size of the deficit in relation to GDP [1] and the direction of travel of the deficit: is it rising or falling [1] and is the change slow or rapid? A negative aspect of a deficit is that a country is spending foreign currency that it is not earning [1] and so the pattern of spending/consumption may not be sustainable [1]. To correct a deficit a government may need to take unpopular measures such as increasing interest rates [1] or increasing taxes on imports [1]. The country may also have to pay interest [1] on any foreign currency borrowing it has undertaken to finance the deficit [1]. A deficit may be seen as being positive if it is caused by increased imports of capital goods [1] which may improve the productive potential of the country [1]. Also, a current account deficit may represent an improvement in living standards [1] as it may be indicative of increased consumption [1]. To conclude, most governments would prefer not to run a deficit on their current account [1] but a small, static deficit [1] that can be readily financed [1] may be seen as acceptable in terms of maintaining living standards. [Maximum five marks for a one-sided answer.]

1 Answers to review questions

MULTIPLE-CHOICE QUESTIONS

1 C

2 B

3 D

4 B

5 D

6 B

7 A

8 A

9 D

10 C

Structured question

1 (a) Labour [1], Capital [1]

(b) If the German government increases spending on new roads then it will forgo increased spending on education. [1] The opportunity cost of new roads being built is additional spending on education that is foregone. [1]

If the German government reduces income tax then it will reduce its spending on services such as health care. [1] The opportunity cost of reducing income tax is the spending on healthcare it could have made. [1]

(c)

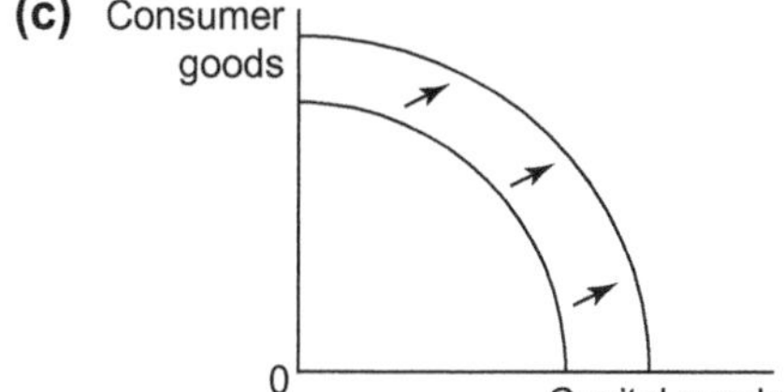

3 marks for a correctly drawn and labeled diagram. Note that the labels on the axes may be different; it is acceptable to just say product A and product B. (1 mark for axes labeled; 1 mark for original PPC and 1 mark for the new PPC at a position further to the right).

3 marks for explanation – increased immigration will lead to higher amounts of the economic resource labour to be available to the economy – this will shift out the PPC to a new position further out from the original curve – leading to the economy being able to produce more producer goods and capital goods.

(d) Yes immigration is beneficial:

- Increases the amount of economic resources available for firms to employ [1]
- Shifts out the PPC [1]
- Higher output can be produced by the economy [1]
- Increases the productive potential of the economic allowing economic growth [1]
- Increased government revenue from income tax [1]
- Increased demand for goods and services produced by firms [1]

No immigration is not beneficial:

- Increased demand for resources such as health care and education [1] – larger class sizes and longer waiting times for treatment [1]
- Increased government spending on public services [1]
- Increased demand for housing from immigrants [1] may lead to higher house prices/rent paid [1]
- Increased supply of labour may lead to downward pressure on wage rates [1] leading to lower incomes for some households [1]

Maximum of 5 marks for a one-sided answer.

2 Answers to review questions

MULTIPLE-CHOICE QUESTIONS

1 C

2 A

3 D

4 A

5 A

6 D

7 A

8 B

9 C

10 A

Structured questions

1 (a)
- Finding new oil supplies
- Improvements in technology means some supplies of oil can now be extracted
- Cost of extracting oil changes
- Tax and/or subsidies are imposed

1 mark for each correct answer – up to 2 marks.

(b)
- Cannot increase supply of oil quickly – as need to find new sources of oil
- When new supplies of oil found it will take time to start the flow of oil – as the wells need to be drilled for the oil to be extracted therefore it cannot be extracted quickly

1 mark for each reason plus 1 mark for each explanation of the reason.

(c)

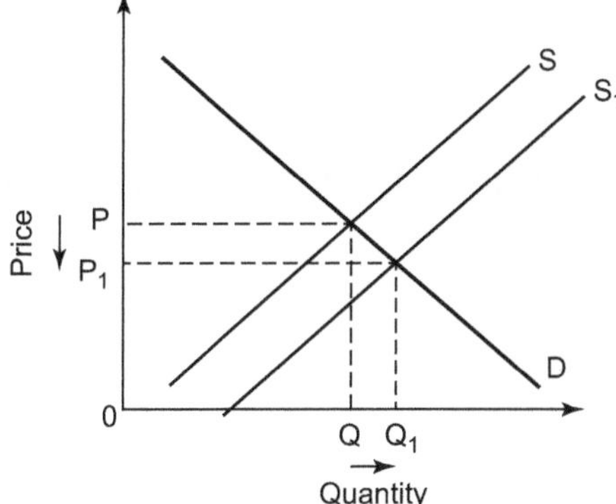

1 mark for correctly labeled axes and original supply and demand lines

1 mark for new supply line shifted to the right

1 mark for change in price showing lower price

1 mark for change in quantity supplied and demanded showing an increase

4 marks for a correctly drawn diagram.

Answer states that supply has increased from S to S_1 leading to a fall in price [1] – Price has fallen from P to P_1 [1] and an increase in sales of oil from Q to Q_1. [1]

(d) Fall in price will benefit the US economy:

- Petrol prices lower [1]
- Less income spent on petrol so more money available for increased purchases [1]
- Lower transport costs for business reducing costs (1) and possibly prices [1]
- Lower inflation rates [1]
- Higher economic growth from increased demand [1]

Fall in price will not benefit the US economy:

- Lower revenue for oil companies [1]
- Lower profit (1) and lower dividends paid to shareholders of oil companies [1]
- Less profit for oil companies so lower company profit tax paid to government [1]
- Lower export earnings from oil exports [1]

Maximum of 5 marks for a one-sided answer

2 **(a)**
- Profit for the oil companies
- Revenue earned by selling the oil
- Benefit the consumer receives by using the oil

1 mark for each correct answer – up to 2 marks.

(b)
- Oil spill – this affects people who live near the oil well as they are harmed by the oil spill but are not involved in the production of oil and are therefore third parties.
- Contamination of water supplies – affects third parties in the local community that are nothing to do with oil extraction but are harmed by not having clean water.

1 mark for each external cost identified (maximum of 2 marks) and 1 mark for each explanation of why it is an external cost (maximum of 2 marks)

(c) Market failure is when supply does not equal demand [1] when the full external costs and external benefits are taken into account [1] the market is not in equilibrium or at the social optimum. [1] As well as private costs fracking has external costs that are not taken into account by the oil companies [1] these external costs spillover onto third parties [1] there are more costs than benefits at the price charged for oil and therefore there is market failure. [1]

1 mark for each point made up to 6 marks maximum.

(d) Indirect taxes on oil producers will reduce the problems:

- Indirect tax will shift supply curve up by the amount of the indirect tax [1]
- This increases the price of oil [1]
- The increased price of oil will lead to decreased quantity demand for oil [1] that is, lower sales of oil [1]
- The equilibrium is at a lower output [1] and nearer to the social optimum. [1]

Indirect taxes on oil producers will not reduce the problems:

- Indirect tax will have little effect if demand is inelastic [1]
- No alternative for consumers to buy instead of oil so demand remains at a similar level to before the tax was imposed [1]
- Oil producers may put down prices and reduce profit to reduce the effects of the tax on prices [1]
- The quantity demanded may not reduce enough to move to the social optimum and remove the market failure [1]
- The indirect tax may not be high enough to reduce quantity demanded to the output at the social optimum. [1]

Maximum of 5 marks for a one-sided answer.

3 Answers to review questions

MULTIPLE-CHOICE QUESTIONS

1 D

2 B

3 A

4 D

5 B

6 C

7 A

8 C

9 C

10 B

Structured questions

1 (a) Brazil [1]

(b) The rise in production could be due to new technology/fall in the value of the Yen/improved quality [1], while the fall could be due to a fall in demand/ rise in value of the Yen/Japanese consumers preferring to save rather than spend [1].

Give 1 mark a point explaining the increase and 1 mark for a point explaining the fall. Allow any valid reasons.

(c) Production is the total output of the goods and services produced by a firm or industry in a period of time [1]. Productivity measures the contribution to production by each factor of production employed [1]. Production is about total output while productivity is about relating input to output [1]

(d) The productivity trend in Canada has been more stable than in Finland [1]; between +3% and +1% compared with +5% to 0% [1]; Canada's productivity has been relatively stable while Finland's has fallen [1]; Canada's productivity has had lower highs than Finland 5% versus 7.4% [1]; Canada's productivity has never fallen as low as Finland's -1% versus -4.8%. Award 1 mark for each valid comparison up to a max of 3 marks.

(e) Some countries have focused efforts on reducing unemployment [1] so that inputs have increased nearly as fast as output [1]. The level of education and training may be insufficient [1] so that there are not enough skilled workers to raise productivity [1]. Management may not be efficient [1] so that resources are not employed effectively to raise productivity [1].

Award 1 mark for each point up to a max of 3 marks and 1 mark for each analytical development up to a max of 5 marks. Overall maximum of 6 marks.

(f) If a worker increases their productivity then they are producing more, for example, each week [1] so an employer can afford to pay them more because they have more output to sell [1] leading to greater profits [1]. If productivity raises only slowly then output, sales, profit only increase by a small amount thus limiting the ability of employers to pay higher wages [1].

(g) Skilled workers are in relatively short supply having an inelastic supply [1] while unskilled workers are plentiful and have an elastic supply [1]. This means that if demand for both increases [1] the rise in wages for the skilled workers will be much more than for the unskilled [1] because to get sufficient extra skilled workers employers have to pay a lot more whereas for unskilled only a small pay rise will result in many more workers [1].

If diagram/s is/are drawn then award up to 3 marks for correctly drawn and labelled diagram/s, with 2 marks for the explanation.

(h) 1 mark can be awarded for a correct statement on specialisation related to producers, for example: the process by which firms concentrate on producing those products in which they have an advantage [1].

Benefits up to a max of 4 marks:

Higher output as there is a greater production [1]

Higher quality as the best and most suitable factors of production can be employed to produce the output [1]

Higher productivity as workers who specialise in one task become skilled [1]

Bigger market as if all producers specialise then for each product there should be more buyers for each producer [1]

Greater economies of scale as larger output will enable the producer to gain economies of scale [1]

Time saving as it takes time to stop producing one product and to start another, so specialisation saves time and money [1]

Costs up to a max of 4 marks:

Rise in costs due to continuing increase in output requires more and more resources which then become ever scarcer and/or leads to diseconomies of scale [1]

Greater dependency as problems such as a technical failure or a strike can lead to the whole process stopping [1]

High labour turnover as workers become bored and leave so that new workers have to be recruited and trained [1]

Maximum of 4 marks for a one-sided response.

2 (a) Medium of exchange [1]; measure of value/unit of account [1]; store of value [1]. Any two of these for 2 marks.

(b) Durable [1] as money needs to last for a reasonable amount of time [1]

Scarce [1] as otherwise it quickly becomes worthless [1]

Recognisable [1] as this increases confidence in it [1]

Stability of value [1] or there will be a loss of confidence in it [1]

Stability of supply [1] as if it increases too fast it will cause inflation/loss of confidence in it [1]

Uniformity [1] so that every coin or note of a particular value used in an economy is the same [1]

Give 1 mark for each characteristic up to 2 marks [not acceptable or divisible] and 1 mark for each explanation up to 2 marks.

(c) In most countries the only issuer of notes and coins is the central bank. [1], while in all countries it is the central bank's role to supervise the supply of money in the economy [1] which means that money retains its characteristic of being scarce [1]. In addition, the central bank sets the base rate [1] from which all other rates of interest, for example, those of the commercial banks, are set [1]. All of this shows that the central bank acts as banker to the commercial banks [1].

Reference can also be made to: managing the foreign exchange reserves; banker to the government, quantitative easing and lender of last resort.

Give 1 mark for each role of the central bank to a max of 3. For each development award 1 mark up to a max of 5.

(d) Advantages of increase in bank lending [up to 5 marks]:

Provides means for consumers and firms to have more money/credit to spend [1] thus enabling them to purchase more goods and services [1]. This in turn allows the economy to grow [1]. Consumers can buy items which are beyond their normal purchasing power such as housing [1].

Disadvantages of increase in bank lending [up to 5 marks]:

Bank lending can lead to inflation [1] which means that people on fixed incomes cannot afford as many products [1]. It can also mean that exports are more expensive and imports cheaper [1] so that home production falls [1] and people become unemployed [1].

Maximum of 5 marks for a one-sided response.

3 (a) Public sector consists of organisations that are owned and controlled by the government [1] and exist to provide services for its citizens [1].

(b) Trade unions protect jobs [1] by representing workers in disputes with employers [1]. They ensure that laws such as health and safety are implemented [1] in order to improve workers' conditions at work [1].

Answers may also refer to: improve the quality of public services and influence governments.

Give 1 mark for the advantage and 1 mark for the explanation up to a max of 2 for both.

(c)

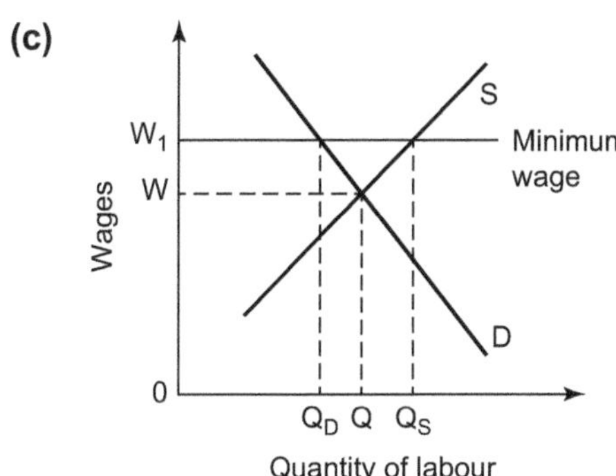

Give 1 mark for correctly drawn and labelled axes.

Give 1 mark for correctly drawn and labelled supply and demand lines

Give 1 mark for showing the minimum wage above the equilibrium

Give 1 mark for correctly drawing and labelling the two new quantities.

Give 2 marks for explanation of the diagram:

By setting the minimum wage at W_1 which is above the equilibrium price and quantity [W/Q] [1] the result is that the quantity of labour supplied increases to Q_S while the quantity demanded falls to Q_D leading to a loss of jobs/excess supply [1].

(d) Advantages [up to a max of 5 marks]:

Higher pay [1] as trade unions can use collective bargaining to achieve higher pay than individual workers could [1]

Better working conditions [1] as trade unions will ensure that legislation is adhered to [1]

Better fringe benefits [1] because as part of collective bargaining the unions may accept benefits in exchange for not pressing for even higher wages [1]

Job security [1] as unions will work to protect both workers as a whole as well as individuals against employers [1]

Disadvantages [up to a max of 5 marks]:

Cost of membership [1] may be very high in relation to any benefit the worker may gain [1]

Reduction in jobs [1] as one way unions can raise wages is to restrict supply so making it difficult for those not in work to find a job [1]

Encourage employers to use capital instead of labour [1] because high wages price workers out of work [1]

Disagree with union policies [1], but may have to go on strike even though they do not want to [1]

Maximum of 5 marks for a one-sided response.

4 (a) A monopoly is the sole producer or seller [1] of a good or service [1].

(b) Conglomerate mergers can provide consumers with a one-stop 'shop' [1] so they do not have to go round to endless suppliers to get what they want [1]. As one part of the firm can support other parts they are less likely to close down if demand for a product declines [1] so consumers can still access these products [1].

Give 1 mark for each advantage, max 2 marks, and 1 mark for each explanation, max 2 marks.

(c)

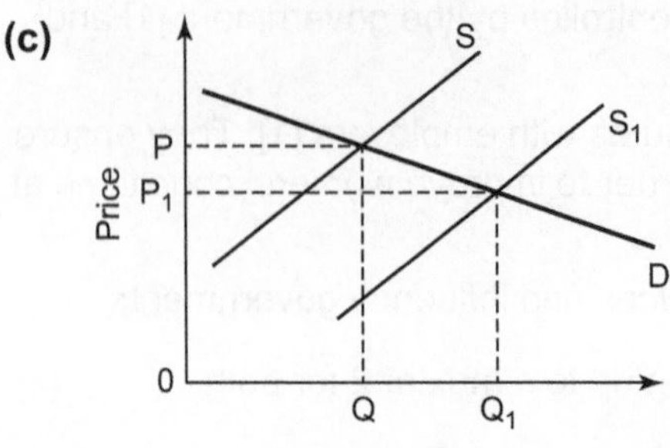

1 mark for correctly drawn and labelled axes.

1 mark for correctly drawn and labelled original supply and demand lines.

1 mark for shifting the supply line to the right and correctly labelling it.

1 mark for correctly drawing and labelling the two prices and quantities.

2 marks for explanation of the diagram:

Increased competition means more firms enter the market increasing supply from S to S_1 [1]. This results in a fall in price for consumers from P to P_1 [1].

(d) Advantages of large firms [up to a max of 5 marks]:

Can gain economies of scale [1] leading to lower average costs and thus lower prices [1].

Larger range of products [1] so consumers can have more variety of choice [1].

Less likely to go out of business [1] so consumers can go back for more products like the ones they have already bought [1]

Spend more on research and development [1] so that consumers can benefit from new and improved products [1].

Disadvantages of large firms [up to a max of 5 marks]:

Lack of personal service [1] so that the customer may not get the best deal or the most suitable product [1].

Lack of flexibility [1] so products cannot be focused on individual customers' needs [1].

Higher prices [1] as large firms may suffer from diseconomies of scale [1].

Lack of variety [1] as large firms, especially monopolies, may not face competition [1].

Allow any valid point.

Maximum of 5 marks for a one-sided response.

4 Answers to review questions

MULTIPLE-CHOICE QUESTIONS

1 B

2 A

3 D

4 C

5 D

6 C

7 C

8 B

9 D

10 A

Structured questions

1 (a) positive economic growth [1], low inflation [1] and low unemployment [1]

(b) A policy which improves the quality and/or quantity of resources [1] in an economy which enables it to increase its production of goods and services [1].

Examples of supply-side policies mentioned in the text: privatisation; the removal of tariffs (taxes on imports); the lowering of income tax rates; deregulation of industries; the lowering of corporate tax rates. [1 for an example from the extract]

(c)
- Increased competition in the economy through privatisation [1] and deregulation [1] have increased productivity [1], increasing aggregate supply and lowering the price level [1];
- lower income tax rates [1] have increased individuals incentive to work [1] increasing aggregate supply and lowering the price level;
- the removal of tariffs [1] increased competition from cheaper imports [1] leading to increased productivity [1] and a lower price level;
- lower corporate tax rates [1] increased the incentive for entrepreneurs to start up new businesses [1] increasing the productive potential of the economy and lowering the price level [1]

Award a maximum of two marks for identifying the correct cause and two marks for further explanation.

(d)
- To raise tax revenue [1] which can be used to increase public spending on areas including infrastructure and public services such as healthcare and education [1].
- To reduce corporate tax rates paid by small businesses [1] in order to encourage small businesses to start up and expand [1].

(e) A direct tax is a tax income [1]. For example, income tax on workers' wages (1) and corporation tax on business' profits (1).

(f) The MRRT taxed profits of mining companies by 30%.

This could have the following effects:

- Lower profit [1] may reduce the incentive [1] mining companies have to increase production [1]. As a result, mining companies many employ fewer workers [1] and invest less in capital equipment and machinery [1].
- With lower profits, fewer new firms may enter the mining industry in Australia. [1]

- Mining companies may increase their prices [1] in order to maintain their profits. However, this may result in falling sales [1] of their product, particularly if demand is price elastic [1].

(g) Strong demand for exports of minerals and energy leads to an increase in their production by firms in Australia [1]. In order to increase production, firms employ more workers, lowering unemployment [1] and raising incomes [1]. The increased production of minerals and energy also increased aggregate demand [1] in the economy thus increasing economic growth [1]. Higher incomes [1] from the increase in the number of jobs in the mining industry leads to higher consumer spending [1] which also increases aggregate demand [1] resulting in economic growth [1].

(h) Regulations are rules and laws passed by the government in order to control the behaviour of private producers [1].

Arguments for regulation [up to 4 marks] may include:

- Helps to protect third parties (for example, the local community, wildlife and environment) from the effects of pollution by firms [1];
- helps to protect consumers from paying excessively high prices [1];
- helps to protect workers from low wages and unfair working conditions [1];
- can help to improve efficiency in the economy (correct for market failure) [1].

Arguments against regulation [up to 4 marks] may include:

- If regulations are too strict, they could lead to inefficiency within the economy [1];
- regulations may increase firms' cost of production making them less competitive with goods produced overseas [1]. As a result of lower production, firms may employ fewer workers raising unemployment [1]. Some forms may be forced to close down [1].

Students must address 'always' in their conclusion.

2 (a) The changing of interest rates [1] in the economy to influence the money supply [1] and aggregate demand [1] by encouraging more or less borrowing by consumers and businesses.

(b)
- Price stability/a low and stable inflation rate [1] – the general level of prices in the economy is low and stable. [1]
- Full employment/low unemployment [1] – most people in the economy who are willing and able to work have paid jobs. [1]
- Economic growth [1] – the production of goods and services in the economy is increasing over time [1]/rising GDP [1].
- Balance of payments stability [1] – the money flowing into the country from abroad and the money flowing out of the country are about equal [1], large deficits/surpluses in the current account balance are avoided [1].
- Redistribution of income [1] – reduction in absolute/relative poverty [1], reducing the gap between rich and poor [1].

(c) Inflation is the sustained rise in the general price level in an economy over time [1]. Raising interest rates [1] will increase the cost of borrowing [1] and encourage saving [1]. As a result, spending is likely to decrease [1] thereby leading to a decrease in aggregate demand [1] in the economy and a fall in the general level of prices [1] resulting in lower inflation.

(d) Reasons for a conflict [up to 4 marks]:

Expansionary demand-side policies would increase aggregate demand in the economy [1] leading to an increase in production and economic growth [1]. However, higher aggregate demand is also likely to result in higher inflation [1]. Furthermore, as the output of the economy gets closer to full employment and labour becomes increasingly scarce, wages may start to rise [1] increasing costs of production for businesses [1]. Some businesses may seek to pass these higher costs onto consumers in the form of higher prices [1] leading to higher inflation.

Reasons why there might not be a conflict [up to 4 marks]:

The government could use supply-side policy [1] to increase the productive capacity of the economy [1], for example, investing in education and training, subsidising research and development etc. [1] Increasing aggregate supply in the economy would help to lower inflation [1] while still increasing achieving positive economic growth [1].

Other points:

Lower inflation could increase the competitiveness of exports [1] which could result in increased aggregate demand and economic growth [1].

Lower inflation could provide greater certainty [1] increasing business confidence and stimulating investment [1] in the economy and resulting in long run economic growth.

Maximum 5 marks for a one-sided answer.

3 (a) An indirect tax is a tax on expenditure [1]. For example, VAT, excise duties, tariffs [1]

(b)

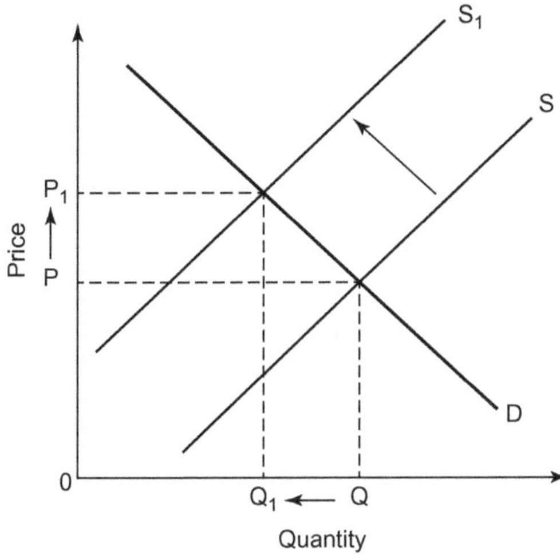

[4 marks for a diagram correctly drawn and correctly labelled]

(c) VAT is an indirect tax (a tax on expenditure) [1] and is regressive in nature [1]. The introduction of the VAT would increase the cost of production to firms [1]. Firms may seek to pass the higher cost onto consumers in the form of higher prices [1]. Cost of living would rise [1]. The tax would be felt more heavily by the poor [1] who spend a higher proportion of their income [1]. As a result of higher production costs, some firms may cut back production [1] resulting in some unemployment [1]. Higher unemployment may result in an increase in poverty [1]. However, the revenue raised from the tax could be used to improve welfare benefits and public services such as education, healthcare for the population or improvement in infrastructure [1] potentially improving the distribution of income in the economy [1].

(d) Reasons why education should be provided by the public sector [up to 4 marks]:

Education is a merit good [1], that is, there are positive externalities [1] that result from having a well-educated population, such as an increase in the productive capacity of the economy [1]. Therefore, the government should provide education so that it is accessible [1] and affordable [1] for all members of the population to increase consumption and production to an efficient level (to correct for market failure) [1].

Reasons why education should be provided by the private sector [up to 4 marks]:

Education is a private good [1] that is, it is excludable and rival [1]. Private firms can therefore profit from providing it [1]. In a competitive market, private producers, motivated by the profit incentive [1], are likely to provide a quality service [1] in order to attract customers. Competition will also help to lower costs [1], thereby improving productivity and efficiency [1]. However, the price is likely to be high and not all consumers would be able to afford an education [1]. Also, consumers in remote locations may not have a school nearby [1]. There is therefore a role for the government, as well as private sector producers, to provide education so that all consumers in the economy can benefit [1].

Maximum 5 marks for a one-sided answer.

4 (a) Deflation is the sustained fall [1] in the general level of prices [1] in an economy over time [1].

(b)
- Survey of household expenditure [1]
- Basket of goods constructed – goods normally consumed by a typical household [1]
- Change in the prices of goods in the basket of goods monitored recorded over time [1]

- Weighted average calculated [1]
- Percentage change in price converted to index form [1] with a base year of 100 [1]

(c) Lower interest rates reduce the cost of borrowing [1]. Consumers reduce saving and increase borrowing [1] leading to an increase in consumer spending [1]. As a result, production increases [1] leading to higher economic growth [1].

Lower interest rates also reduce the cost of borrowing for businesses [1]. Businesses expand production [1] by investing in capital equipment and machinery [1] and increasing demand for factor inputs [1] such as raw materials [1].

As production expands, more jobs are created [1] and workers' incomes rise [1]. This may lead to higher consumer spending [1] and increased demand for goods and services [1] leading to further increased output by firms [1] and higher economic growth [1].

(d) Reasons why deflation may be harmful:

- The fall in the general price level is caused by low aggregate demand in the economy [1].
- Falling aggregate demand reduces economic growth [1] and may lead to higher unemployment [1].
- If consumers expect prices to fall, they may delay future consumption [1] causing aggregate demand to decrease [1] further and worsening deflation [1].
- Rather than invest in expanding production, firms may instead hold onto their cash [1], the real value of which is increasing due to the falling price level [1]. This may result in falling aggregate demand [1] and worsen the problem of deflation [1].
- Borrowing is discouraged [1] as the real value of money increases over time [1]. Reduced borrow may lead to a reduction in consumption and investment [1].

Reasons why deflation may not be harmful:

- Causes a fall in aggregate supply [1] in the economy such as a fall in the price of oil [1]. This lowers firms' cost of production [1] which may lead to an increase in the productive capacity of the economy [1] and higher economic growth [1].

Maximum 5 marks for a one-sided answer.

5 Answers to review questions

MULTIPLE-CHOICE QUESTIONS

1 A

2 C

3 B

4 D

5 D

6 A

7 B

8 D

9 C

10 D

Structured questions

1 (a) Absolute poverty, low HDI value/ranking, low GDP per head, high proportion of employment in primary sector, relatively young population, poor education system, poor healthcare system, lack of infrastructure [water supply, sewage etc.]. One mark for each relevant point identified to a maximum of 3 marks.

(b) Correct figures selected: 2 977 000 and 3 027 000 [1]

Absolute change correctly calculated – 50 000 [1]

Percentage change correctly calculated - 1.68% [1]. Percentage symbol must be given for the mark to be awarded.

(c) Economic growth fell due to a fall in the price of Mongolia's exports [1] leading to a fall in export revenue [1]. Also, slower economic growth in China [1] led to a fall in the demand for exports from Mongolia because China purchases 90% of Mongolia's exports [1].

(d) HDI could be improved by any of the following:

- Improving living standards [1] – Increasing gross national income/real GDP per head [1]
- Improving education [1] – building more schools leading to an increase in expected years in schooling [1]
- Improving healthcare [1] – provision of hospitals and medical services leading to an increase in life expectancy [1]

1 mark for identification of a relevant point and a further mark for development of that point. Maximum of 2 relevant points per response.

(e) GDP per head may be a good indicator of living standards as it takes into account the population of the country [1]. It is calculated using data that is available and relatively easy to access [1] and can be used to compare living standards between countries as all countries record real GDP and population [1]. GDP per head may a good indicator of the income available for consumer spending [1].

However GDP per head only measures average income [1] and ignores other factors which may affect living standards [1]. It does not allow for inflation [1] and gives no indication as to how income is distributed within a country [1]. It does not take into account the types of goods and services that are produced [1] and the existence of a large informal economy may affect the accuracy of the figure for a country's GDP [1].

Maximum of 4 marks for a one-sided discussion

(f) Investment in education, for example, building more schools, will make education more available and accessible to children in poverty [1]. A better education will improve children's skills, for example, literacy [1] which will enable them to get higher paying jobs in the future [1]. Higher income will help to improve living standards and raise them out of poverty in the long run [1].

(g) Benefits to Mongolia from immigration:

- Immigration of skilled workers in the mining industry to help exploit minerals and increase economic growth [1]
- If immigrants are highly skilled the productive capacity of the economy will increase [1]
- Skilled immigrants may be able to pass their knowledge and skills on to local workers [1], increasing productivity [1]
- If immigrants are of working age, there will be a larger working population to support the dependent population [1] for example, the government could use revenue from income tax to pay pensions to the elderly [1]

Drawbacks of immigration

- The increase in population may increase demand for goods and services, such as housing, which may lead to higher prices [1]
- May increase the dependent population if children and old people immigrate into Mongolia [1]
- May increase unemployment if there are not enough jobs for everyone [1]
- Immigrants may send money back to their home countries rather than spending it in Mongolia [1]

Maximum of 4 marks for a one-sided discussion

2 (a) The number of live births for every 1,000 people in a country [1] in a year [1].

(b) A decline in population could be caused by any of the following causes:

- Higher death rate [1] – war and violent conflict, natural disaster, famine, disease, epidemic... [1 mark for any cause of higher death rate]
- Lower birth rate [1] – development, changing social attitudes (for example, women in work), contraception and family planning, higher cost of children...[1 mark for any cause of lower birth rate]
- Net outward migration [1] – people moving abroad for work, education, to escape conflict etc. ... [1 mark for any cause of net outward migration]

1 mark for identifying a cause and one for explaining the cause. Maximum of two causes per response.

(c) A falling population may lead to fewer people of working age [1]. This reduces the productive capacity of the economy [1]. Output of the economy falls [1] and economic growth is reduced (last point not credited because it is 'in the question'). If the fall in population is due to net outward migration then the country is losing the labour [1] and skills [1] needed to develop the resources available in the economy [1].

(d) An ageing population could be a problem for a country because it could lead to high costs to the government [1] for example, healthcare [1] and provision of state pensions [1], which may lead to higher taxes for the working population [1]. With more dependents and fewer people working the productive capacity of the economy will be reduced [1] which may lead to a fall in GDP / economic growth [1].

However, an ageing population may increase the number of people of working age [1] and could increase the productive potential of the economy [1]. Older people may be able to pass their skills and experience on to the younger generation [1], increasing productivity [1]. The existence of an ageing population may be seen as an indicator of rising living standards [1] and industries that serve older people, for example, healthcare, may flourish [1].

Maximum of 5 marks for a one-sided answer, that is, an answer that focuses exclusively on advantages or disadvantages.

3 (a) A situation in which an individual does not have enough income to satisfy their most basic needs [1] of food, clean water, clothing, shelter, education and healthcare [1 mark for any example of basic needs]. 1 mark for 'living on less than $1.25 a day' (or similar amount).

(b) 1 mark for identifying a cause and 1 for explaining the cause. Maximum of two causes per response.

Unemployment [1] could lead to low incomes [1]

Low wages [1] may be enough to purchase basic needs [1]

Old age [1] may lead to low incomes if social security payments are not adequate [1]

Sickness and disability [1] – may lead to low incomes if social security payments are not adequate [1]

Drought, crop failure, natural disasters in rural regions [1] may reduce income/food supplies

War and conflict [1] may prevent people from working/reduce food supplies [1]

(c) In economies with high incomes, households, firms, governments are able to save.

- Households can use savings to invest and build wealth or enjoy higher living standards.
- Firms can use savings to invest in capital equipment and machinery [1] which leads to an increase in productivity [1] and increases the productive potential of the economy. As a result, the output of the economy increases leading to economic growth [1].
- The government is able to use savings to invest in improving education and training [1], public services and infrastructure [1] in the economy. Investment in education is likely to improve the productivity of the labour force [1], leading to increased production and economic growth. Improved infrastructure is also likely to lead to increased efficiency and productivity [1].

(d) An increase in HDI indicates an increase in a country's living standards for the following reasons:

- Indicates an improvement in life expectancy [1] due to improved healthcare/ sanitation/ healthier lifestyle choices of a population [1]
- Indicates an improvement in education [1] due to an increase in expected years in schooling [1]. This leads to a more skilled workforce [1], improved job opportunities [1], reduced poverty/ higher living standards [1].
- Indicates an improvement in incomes [1] due to an increase in real GDP per capita [1]. As a result, households are able to afford more consumer goods [1] leading to higher living standards.

An increase in HDI might not indicate an increase in a country's living standards for the following reasons:

- Ignores some factors impacting people's living standards [1] such as the level of pollution [1], hours worked [1], political freedom [1], income distribution [1], cost of living [1], level of crime [1].

4 (a) A situation where a population is sufficient to ensure that all resources in a country are fully/efficiently utilised [1] and output per head of population is maximised [1]. Output on its own is insufficient for this mark – students must refer to output per head (or equivalent term).

(b) The consequences of gender imbalance:

- Lower economic growth [1] – Some jobs are performed much more productively by women rather than men / with fewer women to do these jobs, the productive capacity of the economy may be reduced [1]
- Future labour shortages [1] caused by reduced reproductive capacity in the population as a whole [1]
- Immediate labour shortages [1] if males emigrate to find partners [1]

(c) Overpopulation is a situation where there are not enough resources to sustain the population of a country.

- Overpopulation may result in shortages of essential goods, such as food and housing [1]. A shortage of resources is likely to drive prices higher [1]. People with fixed incomes such as pensioners will become worse off [1], increasing their relative poverty. [1]
- Increased competition for jobs may also increase unemployment and/or drive down wages [1]. The impact of this competition is likely to be greater for unskilled/lower paid workers [1] thereby increasing income inequality [1].
- Overpopulation is likely to reduce income per head [1]. Falling income is likely to lead to reduced tax revenues [1] so the government will have reduced capacity to undertake measures to redistribute income [1], for example, welfare payments [1].

(d) Economic growth may fall if:

- those who have emigrated abroad are highly skilled members of the country's working age population [1], for example, doctors and engineers [1 for any example of skilled worker]. This is likely to decrease the productive potential of the economy [1] and reduce output/ economic growth [1].
- the country is dependent on labour intensive industries [1], for example, agriculture [1]. Output may fall [1] if workers migrate to improve their living standards [1]

Economic growth may increase if:

- individuals who have emigrated abroad send money home to their relatives [1]. This will increase people's incomes [1], leading to a rise in living standards/ consumer spending [1] and economic growth
- those who have migrated abroad are part of the dependent population [1], for example, the elderly [1]
- those who have emigrated later return to their home country with improved skills/ education [1], thus increasing the productivity /productive potential of the economy [1].

Maximum 5 marks for a one-sided response.

6 Answers to review questions

MULTIPLE-CHOICE QUESTIONS

1 C

2 A

3 C

4 B

5 D

6 D

7 C

8 A

9 B

10 A

Structured questions

1 **(a)** Value of visible exports – value of visible imports = $33.27 billion - $36.4 billion = -$3.13 billion (A deficit of $3.13 billion) [2 marks for a correct answer. 1 mark for an incorrect answer but some correct working, eg 3.13bn (1 mark), $33.27bn - $36.4bn = $2.13bn (1 mark)]

(b) Factor endowments are the land, labour and capital [1] which the country has available [1]. Nigeria's factor endowments include reserves of oil, a large youthful population, the climate and skills needed to grow cocoa and rubber [1].

(c) [1 mark for identifying the disadvantage and 1 mark for the explanation]

- Overdependence [1] – Nigeria was overly dependent on oil for its revenue (petroleum and petroleum products made up 90% of the country's export revenue, 40% of GDP and 80% of government revenue). The fall in the price of oil resulted in a fall in export revenue, negative growth and a fall in government revenue as the country was overly dependent on oil [1].
- Exchange rate fluctuations [1] – By specialising in the production of oil, cocoa and rubber and exporting to other countries, Nigeria is vulnerable to changes in the exchange rates which can affect the price they receive for their exports [1].
- Exploitation and depletion of natural resources [1] – By specialising in oil production, oil reserves are being depleted and will not be available for future generations [1]. Also, the exploitation of oil reserves in Nigeria is causing considerable harm to the environment and the livelihoods of the communities who live in the Niger Delta [1].

(d) The deficit on the current account reduced/improved [1] from -$15.44 billion in 2015 to -$2.856 billion in 2016 [1].

(e) [For each of two reasons: 1 mark for identifying the reason plus one mark for a valid explanation. Maximum 2 marks for a list of reasons with no supporting explanation.]

- To protect jobs in the Nigerian shoe industry [1] – The imposition of protection policies on imported shoes will help to maintain the competitiveness of Nigerian shoe manufacturers. As a result, they will continue to operate and employ workers [1].
- Nigerian shoe manufacturing may be an infant industry [1] in need of protection from large foreign companies who benefit from economies of scale [1] and, as a result, are able to charge low prices [1].
- To protect Nigerian shoe producers from dumping [1] by foreign shoe manufacturers – foreign shoe manufacturers selling imported shoes at prices below cost of production would be unfair for Nigerian shoe manufacturers and justify protection [1].

(f) Trade in goods [1], trade in services [1], primary income [1] and secondary income [1].

(g)
- A fall in oil prices is likely to reduce the export revenue [1] earned by Nigeria resulting in a worsening of the balance of trade (an increasing trade deficit) on the current account [1].
- MNCs are likely to suffer a fall in profits [1] leading to a reduction in the outflow of profits [1] in the primary income component of the current account [1].

(h) Up to 4 marks for discussing why multinationals are bad for a host country:

- Low skilled jobs – only low skilled jobs created
- Closure of local businesses – unable to compete with MNCs
- Depletion of natural resources
- Exploitation of labour
- Outflow of profits to MNC home countries
- Increased pollution

Up to 4 marks for discussing why multinationals might be beneficial for a host country:

- Lower unemployment – creation of jobs
- Increased profits for local businesses – for example, for local suppliers of raw materials and component parts to MNCs
- Transfer of knowledge and skills to local workers and businesses
- Lower prices for consumers – from increased competition in the domestic market
- Inflow of investment capital – to set up operations in the host country
- Increased economic growth – from the production of goods and services by MNCs
- Increase in tax revenue – government can use this to invest in infrastructure and public services
- Improved trade balance – increased exports

2 (a) A tariff is a tax [1] imposed on imports [1].

(b) [For each of two reasons: 1 mark for identifying the reason plus one mark for a valid explanation. Maximum 2 marks for a list of reasons with no supporting explanation.]

To protect jobs [1] – Higher import prices will make domestic produced goods more competitive thereby protecting jobs in the domestic economy [1].

To protect infant industries [1] – Industries which are relatively new may require protection as they may be unable to compete with large foreign rivals who benefit from significant economies of scale [1].

To protect domestic producers from dumping [1] – Foreign companies may dump their products in a country, selling their products at prices below the cost of production [1], in order to destroy local competition or to get rid of surplus stock. This is considered anti-competitive and justifies the use of protection policies. [1]

To protect declining industry [1] – A government may wish to protect an industry which is experiencing declining sales in order to prevent wide-scale structural unemployment [1].

To protect strategic industries [1] – A government may wish to protect industries which are of strategic importance, such as food production, energy or telecommunications [1].

To correct a current account deficit [1 by making imports more expensive [1].

(c)
- The removal of tariffs will reduce the price of imports [1]. More imports will be consumed by domestic consumers [1] worsening the balance of trade [1].
- Cheaper imports will reduce the cost of imported raw materials [1] lowering the cost of production [1].
- Over time, domestic businesses will need to innovate [1] to compete with the cheaper imports. Increasing productivity and lower production costs may lead to a fall in the price of exports [1] in the longer run and an improvement in the balance of trade [1].

(d) Reasons why free trade area may improve living standards [up to 5 marks]

- Increased choice for consumers [1] – Increased choice from import goods and services [1].
- Lower prices for consumers [1] – The prices of imports may be cheaper if they are made by countries which are able to produce them more efficiently [1]. Increased competition from imports may also result in lower prices of domestic goods [1].
- Exporters may expand production creating more jobs and higher incomes for some people [1] – An increase in sales of exports abroad will result create more jobs in export industries [1].

[Award 1 mark for satisfactory explanations]

Reasons why free trade area may reduce living standards [up to 5 marks]

- Unequal distribution of the benefits of free trade [1] – Not all consumers benefit equally from free trade. Those on higher incomes will be able to enjoy the higher living standards [1] that come from the consumption of imports, such as luxury brand name products. Those on low incomes, however, are unlikely to be able to afford these products and may experience little or no change in their standards of living [1].
- Loss of jobs [1] – Increased competition from cheaper imports may result in job losses as domestic firms lay off workers due to falling sales [1].
- Environmental damage [1] – The use of fossil fuels to transport goods, pollution and global warming may reduce living standards [1].
- Exploitation of labour [1] – Workers in some countries may be very paid low wages or be made to work long hours when producing goods for overseas markets [1].
- Depletion of natural resources [1] – A country's natural resources may be depleted reducing the productive potential of the economy for future generations [1].

3 (a) A fall in a value of a currency [1] relative to other currencies [1].

(b) [For each of two factors: 1 mark for identifying the factor plus one mark for a valid explanation. Maximum 2 marks for a list of factors with no supporting explanation.]

A fall in the demand for the currency [1] brought about by a fall in the demand for exports [1], a fall in domestic interest rates [1] or speculation that the value of the domestic currency will fall in the future [1].

A rise in the supply [1] of the currency as a result of an increase in spending on imports [1], a rise in interest rates in other countries [1] or speculation that other currencies will rise in value in the future [1].

(c) A depreciation of an exchange rate will make the price of imports more expensive [1] and the price of exports cheaper [1]. As a result, sales of imports will fall and sales of exports will rise [1]. In the long run, when PED is elastic [1], this will lead to a rise in the value of exports/export revenue [1] and a fall in the value of imports/import expenditure [1] and an improvement in the balance of trade [1].

(d) Reasons why a devaluation lowers unemployment [up to 5 marks]

- Cheaper exports [1] are likely to increase the sales of exports abroad creating more jobs in export industries [1].
- Higher priced imports [1] are likely to result in reduced spending on imports [1] (PED elastic) [1]. As a result, domestic consumers are likely to switch to purchasing locally made goods [1] creating jobs in domestic industries [1].

Reasons why a devaluation may not lower unemployment [up to 5 marks]

- In the short run, when PED of exports is inelastic [1], export revenue may fall [1] which may lead to higher unemployment [1].
- If the country is already at full employment [1], higher demand for exports may put upward pressure on wage rates [1] without affecting the level of unemployment.
- The devaluation will cause the cost of imported raw materials to increase [1]. This may lead to an increase in the price of domestically produced goods [1], making them less competitive at home and abroad [1]. As a result, sales may fall and unemployment may rise [1].
- Trading partners may retaliate [1] by imposing of trade barriers on the country's exports [1].

4 **(a)** Money flowing out of the country from visible and invisible exports and primary and secondary income [1] is greater than money flowing in from spending on visible and invisible imports and primary and secondary income [1].

(b) [For each of two causes: 1 mark for identifying the cause plus one mark for a valid explanation. Maximum 2 marks for a list of causes with no supporting explanation.]

- An increase in the value of the currency (appreciation or revaluation) [1] – The price of imports falls resulting in higher spending on imports. The price of exports rises resulting in a fall in spending on exports (PED elastic). [1]
- Higher inflation relative to other countries [1] – Makes exports less competitive leading to a fall in revenue from exports [1].
- Rising aggregate demand in the economy (economic boom) [1] – Results in higher consumer incomes which may lead to increased spending on imports [1].
- Protection policies [1] – Protection policies which make exports less competitive and/or imports more competitive (for example, the removal of tariffs on imports) [1].
- Changes in productivity [1] – A fall in productivity relative to other countries will reduce the competitiveness of exports [1].
- Operations of multinational companies (MNCs) [1] – Outflow of profits overseas as a result of foreign MNCs setting up in a country [1].

(c) An appreciation of a currency means that the value of the currency increases relative to the value of other currencies [1]. As a result, the price of exports is likely to rise [1] and the price of imports is likely to fall [1]. Reduced demand for exports will result in a fall in aggregate demand [1] in the domestic economy and a fall in demand-pull inflation [1]. Cheaper imports will reduce the cost of imported raw materials [1] for firms resulting in a fall in cost-push inflation [1].

(d) Reasons why a trade deficit might not be a problem [up to 5 marks]:

A deficit on the balance of trade is not a problem if it is small [1] as a proportion of a country's GDP or temporary (short-term) in nature [1]. Nor is it necessarily a problem if the imbalance is due to purchases of capital equipment and machinery [1], as imports of this kind are investment and will increase the future output of the economy [1]. It is also not a problem if it is offset by a surplus in the trade in services component of the current account [1].

Reasons why a trade deficit might be a problem [up to 5 marks]:

A deficit on the balance of trade may be a problem if it is large [1] as a proportion of the country's GDP and persists [1] over a long period of time. In this situation, the trade deficit will have to be financed [1] either using foreign currency reserves [1] or by borrowing from abroad [1]. Large, persistent deficits financed by borrowing can have a destabilising effect on an economy [1], particularly if there is a sudden fall in a country's income, as the country may struggle to repay the overseas debt and make interest payments [1].

